POST-CLASSICAL CINEMA
An International Poetics of Film Narration

Eleftheria Thanouli

WALLFLOWER PRESS
LONDON & NEW YORK

First published in Great Britain in 2009 by
Wallflower Press
6 Market Place, London W1W 8AF
www.wallflowerpress.co.uk

A catalogue record for this book is available from the British Library

ISBN 978-1-906660-09-3 (pbk)
ISBN 978-1-906660-10-9 (hbk)

Book design by Elsa Mathern

Printed in India by Imprint Digital

CONTENTS

This book is dedicated
to Warren Buckland

ACKNOWLEDGEMENTS

This book is the result of a durable struggle with theories and theorists, with films from the past and present and with a persistent insight about the significance of something new in the way movies have been telling us their stories for the last couple of decades. Many people helped me in the process but I will begin by singling out the following three in chronological order: Grigoris Paschalidis, who took me to a screening of *Europa*; Warren Buckland, who jokingly said in our first meeting that I should try to add a chapter to David Bordwell's *Narration in the Fiction Film*; and Thomas Elsaesser, who actually agreed to show me how to do it.

Next, I would like to thank my colleagues at the University of Amsterdam, and particularly the Cinema/Media Europe research group, for their useful comments and observations. After the book was completed, a number of people encouraged me to publish it. Among them, my special thanks go to Steve Neale, Dudley Andrew, Peter Kramer and Yannis Tzioumakis for their long-lasting support. I owe the title of this book to a brainstorming session on a boat trip through the Amsterdam canals with the following participants: Thomas Elsaesser, Warren Buckland, Peter Kramer and Michael Wedel. Their enthusiastic involvement was deeply touching. My deepest gratitude also goes to Yoram Allon who has been extremely supportive of my work and made my first book publication an enjoyable experience.

I am also indebted to the *New Review of Film and Television Studies* for allowing me to reproduce as the first part of my conclusion a revised version of my essay: 'Post-Classical Narration: A New Paradigm in Contemporary Cinema', which appeared in the *New Review of Film and Television Studies*, vol. 4, no.3, December 2006, 183–96.

Finally, I would like to thank my close as well as extended family members: my mom who has dedicated her entire life to me, my friends Stamatis Vala-siadis and Giorgos Konstantinidis who spent endless hours discussing and fantasising about this book and, last but not least, my husband Achilleas and my daughter Anastasia. Even though they were not with me when I wrote the book, they will be by my side when I have the pleasure of finally holding it in my hands.

INTRODUCTION

Studying contemporary cinema is a particularly daunting task, as the film scholar has to overcome three important obstacles: the problem of familiarity, superfluous literature and the 'already said'. To tackle the former, she has to adopt the eye of an alien in order to be able to trace the historicity of forms and images that look so natural and engaging. In many ways it is easier to observe the peculiarities of a German silent film from the 1910s than the novelties of an American blockbuster from the new millennium. An extensive and ascetic reading schedule can gradually transform contemporary films into total strangers, but soon one is confronted with the second difficulty, namely the need to separate the wheat from the chaff and to discern from an ever-expanding universe of texts, writers and theories those that can be carried along in the exploration. Finally, the analyst is obliged to delineate a new territory and formulate a set of questions that will lead to a truly original contribution to academic scholarship. This last challenge becomes exceptionally overwhelming when the research focuses on aspects of contemporary cinema that have been studied exhaustively by other researchers and leave little room for innovation.

When I decided to work with contemporary popular films in order to focus on the worn-out topic of postmodern/post-classical cinema, I found these difficulties not only intimidating but also off-putting. There were times when I even felt embarrassed to talk to my colleagues about this interest of mine, as the entire field of film studies seemed to be moving towards uncharted territories, bringing new concepts and agendas into vogue. Yet, nothing could take my mind off what a friend once told me after a screening of Lars von Trier's *Europa* (1991): 'If *Citizen Kane* summarises what classical cinema is, then *Europa* summarises what postmodern cinema is.' This unsolicited but certainly powerful statement of a cinephile was meant to plant a seed of enquiring doubt that came to haunt me for years. As I voraciously studied everything that was related to postmodernism and cinema, I was able to produce numerous explanations why a film like that could be labelled postmodern: nostalgia about the past, a 'post-histoire' approach to World War Two, fragmentation, blurred boundaries, depthlessness and alienation in a post-industrial consumer society. And, indeed, this is probably what my friend had in mind at the time. But for some reason, these terms could not capture what *I* saw in *Europa* and could not explain why I felt that his words had inadvertently captured something much more significant; that, in fact, this film was the epitome of something new in contemporary cinema in the same ingenious way that *Citizen Kane* (1941) could be regarded as the epitome in classical Hollywood cinema.

In my effort to understand the puzzle I had in hand, I started to notice that the vast majority of articles or books on postmodern cinema would put under the same umbrella films as disparate as *Hitler – ein Film aus Deutschland* (*Hitler, A Film from Germany*, 1977), *Blade Runner* (1982), *Blue Velvet* (1986), *Terrorizer* (1986) and *When Harry Met Sally* (1989). What made this type of classification possible was merely the fact that film scholars paid very little attention to the actual films and their narrative or stylistic traits. This particular limitation, combined with *Europa*'s rich visual language, led me to believe that there must also be a way to theorise the postmodern in formal terms. Unfortunately, when I turned to one of the most prominent figures in formalist analysis, David Bordwell, and his meticulous works on narrative theory, I was confronted with his fierce opposition to the concept of postmodernism and his strong arguments about the persistence of the classical narrative formulas to this date. Although one could be easily discouraged by his stance and abandon the idea of approaching postmodern cinema at a strictly formal level, I gradually became convinced that, paradoxically enough, it was Bordwell who could help me in this admittedly venturesome exploration. The solution to this paradox came when I was able to differentiate the broad theoretical approach called 'historical poetics', which encompasses a wide range of research areas and questions, from the way Bordwell has employed it so far to defend his specific position about the stability of the classical narration. Once this distinction was clear in my mind, I was determined to explore the idea that sprung from *Europa* by launching a highly challenging enterprise: to use historical poetics – Bordwell's own tools, in other words – in order to contradict his firm defence of classicism in contemporary cinema and, consequently, to succeed in revealing the important formal transformation that I suspected had taken place in the cinematic language in the last couple of decades.

This book is the fruit of this enterprise, which turned out to be extremely rich and rewarding in terms of results and findings. With a careful and systematic poetic analysis of a sample of contemporary films I was able to formulate a new coherent narrative paradigm, which I decided to call post-classical. The impatient reader who cannot wait to see the characteristics of this new narrative model is advised to go directly to chapter one where the exposition begins. However, as it is customary – and absolutely essential in this case – I would like to anchor my own study to the significant theoretical and historical research that preceded it and to lay out the foundations of post-classical narration. First, I would like to describe the theoretical framework of 'historical poetics' and introduce the terms and concepts that I will be employing throughout the book. Then, I will present a critical overview of Bordwell's recent writings on contemporary cinema in order to show how he has insisted on reading contemporary films from within the old and well-established paradigms. In addition, I will juxtapose this position with other theorists' swift eagerness to conceptualise and interpret the developments in American and international cinema from the 1970s onwards through the prism of postmodernism. Finally, I will explain the precise goals and methodology of this book in order to demonstrate how it will manage to pass between the Symplegades without clashing and will try to demarcate its own territory in film scholarship.

Historical poetics and the study of narration

> Historical poetics becomes not one method but a model of basic research into cinema. It offers the best current hope for setting high intellectual standards for film study. (Bordwell 1989b: 392)

Over the last three decades, Bordwell has been consistently trying to develop the concept of 'historical poetics' in cinema studies and to establish it as one of the most promising research traditions in the field. Borrowing the term from literary theory and drawing heavily on the work of the Russian and Slavic formalists in the first half of the twentieth century, Bordwell created a wide and elaborate theoretical and methodological framework, which, as the quote suggests, does not simply consist of one method but of a research model with several branches and research subjects. In broad terms, historical poetics aims at producing knowledge by exploring two basic questions:

1. What are the principles according to which films are constructed and by means of which they achieve particular effects?
2. How and why have these principles arisen and changed in particular empirical circumstances? (see 1989b: 371)

These two dense and multifaceted questions put under the microscope several issues, ranging from the institutional background of a film to the analysis of its stylistic features and its public reception. Yet, what characterises historical poetics, whether it focuses on narrative, style or production values, is that it constitutes a data-driven approach, which studies facts and concrete elements, in order to formulate arguments and inferences that are corrigible and falsifiable. It poses concise and theoretically defined questions, it forms open hypotheses that are not committed to *a priori* conclusions, and it originates answers and concepts that can be constantly re-defined through an encounter with the films and their surrounding evidence (see 1989b: 381).

The positivist nature of historical poetics and Bordwell's emphasis on a bottom-up type of research spurred a significant opposition to the grand theories in the humanities, such as Saussurean semiotics, Lacanian psychoanalysis, Althusserian Marxism and Barthesian textual analysis – what Bordwell likes to acronymically call SLAB theories (see 1989b: 385). Instead of applying a general social or cultural theory to a film and looking for the manifestations of certain concepts like 'Oedipal trajectory' or 'mirror stage' on the screen, Bordwell prefers to ask specific low-scale questions about the construction of films that will potentially lead to more general and broad theoretical or historical observations. As he clearly puts it:

> Poetics is thus not another critical 'approach', like myth criticism or deconstruction. Nor is it a 'theory' like psychoanalysis or Marxism. In its broadest compass, it is a conceptual framework within which particular questions about films' composition and effects can be posed. (1989a: 273)

Bordwell's own research in a thirty-year career has produced several historical poetics projects, culminating in two highly influential books that came out the same year and soon became a staple of the curricula in every film department in the world.[1] I am referring to *The Classical Hollywood Cinema* (1985), which he co-authored with Janet Staiger and Kristin Thompson, and *Narration in the Fiction Film* (1985). The former is a monumental piece of work that examines the film style and mode of production in Hollywood until 1960, the year that is considered to signal the end of a great era in Hollywood filmmaking. Here, I would like to briefly introduce some of Bordwell's chief arguments about classical Hollywood because it is alongside these arguments that my own research will try to articulate the presence of post-classical narration in contemporary cinema.

First of all, I think that the heart of Bordwell's account can be summarised in the following statement: 'Hollywood films constitute a fairly coherent aesthetic tradition which sustains individual creation' (Bordwell *et al.* 1985: 4).

As the analysis of a representative and extensive body of works indicates,[2] Hollywood films seem to adhere to integral and consistent stylistic and narrational conventions that are not reducible to the initiative of isolated filmmakers. However, instead of comparing the Hollywood formulas with other industrial commodities that are produced in a serial and mechanical manner, Bordwell encourages us to think of these conventions as an over-arching 'aesthetic norm', in Jan Mukařovský's terms. According to the latter, a norm should not be considered as a stringent rule, but as 'a regulating energetic principle', something that permits the artwork to come into being (Mukařovský 1978: 49).

By applying Mukařovský's notion of the 'aesthetic norm' to the study of Hollywood films, Bordwell makes an invaluable observation; that, in fact, multiple norms work upon the same film and, therefore, it is not possible to trace all the classical norms of Hollywood filmmaking in a single film nor should that be desirable. As he succinctly notes, 'no Hollywood film *is* the classical system; each is an 'unstable equilibrium' of classical norms' (Bordwell *et al.* 1985: 5). The idea of an unstable equilibrium leads us to the concept of the 'paradigm' as a 'set of elements which can, according to rules, substitute for one another' (ibid.). By considering Hollywood filmmaking as a paradigm with several alternatives, we can make an inventory of the options that were or still are available to the filmmakers who work within this tradition. The paradigm, on the one hand, gives them the freedom to make use of the 'bounded alternatives' and the 'functional equivalents' that it contains but, on the other hand, it provides them with limitations. Bordwell illustrates this principle with the following example:

> If you are a classical filmmaker, you cannot light a scene in such a way as to obscure the locale entirely (cf. Godard in *Le gai savoir*); you cannot pan or track without some narrative or generic motivation; you cannot make every shot one second long (cf. avant-garde works). Both the alternatives and the limitations of the style remain clear if we think of the paradigm as creating *functional equivalents*: a cut-in may replace a track-in, or colour may replace lighting as a way to demarcate volumes, because each device fulfils the same role. (Ibid.; emphasis in original)

The paradigm of classical Hollywood cinema was developed by organising the numerous individual film analyses along the following three levels of generality:

1. *Devices*: technical elements like centred framings, continuity editing and so forth.

2. *Systems*: the system of narrative logic, cinematic time and cinematic space are the three systems present in any film and result from the various functions and combinations of the devices.

3. *Relations of systems*: the three systems can work in various ways within a film. For instance, in a classical film the narrative logic subordinates the temporal and spatial system whereas in other paradigms the three systems could function independently of each other.

With the help of this schematic distinction, Bordwell was able to classify his findings and to gradually mould a very clear and detailed account of what classical Hollywood narration consists of, what kind of norms regulate the construction of the films and what bounds of difference exist within this cinematic tradition. The momentum that historical poetics gained with *The Classical Hollywood Cinema* continued some months later with *Narration in the Fiction Film*, where the significance of a cinematic paradigm is further developed and, more importantly, is given a historical perspective.[3] Here the concept of the paradigm is supplemented by the term 'mode of narration' which signifies 'a historically distinct set of norms of narrational construction and comprehension' (Bordwell 1985: 150). A mode of narration transcends genres, schools, movements and even national cinemas because it is wider in scope and relatively stable and consistent over time. After having analysed a very extensive body of films from a wide range of cinematic traditions on a global scale, Bordwell formulated four historical modes of narration that each presents the filmmakers with specific constructional patterns and options.

Firstly, there is the *classical* mode that is epitomised in Hollywood cinema from the years 1917–60 and has prevailed as the dominant narrative model in the history of cinema.[4] Its main features include the emphasis on character-centred causality, the use of classical Bazinian realism, the clear presentation of the characters and the plot as well as the unobtrusiveness of its style. Secondly, there is the *art cinema* mode exemplified in the works of European filmmakers, such as Alain Resnais, Michelangelo Antonioni and Ingmar Bergman, from the late 1950s to the early 1970s. The films that belong to this category are permeated by a strong sense of objective and subjective realism, while their textual elements often carry the personal signature of their auteurs. Thirdly, there is the *historical-materialist* mode, which was fully developed in the works of the Soviet filmmakers of the period 1925–33 and is characterised by an openly didactic and political style that supports the Marxist-Leninist doctrine. Lastly, the fourth mode is called *parametric* and applies only to 'isolated filmmakers and fugitive films' (1985: 274). The best examples of this mode come from works by Robert Bresson and Yasujiro Ozu, as their films' stylistic system is based on a distinct pattern of 'parameters' (film techniques) that function autonomously from the development of the plot. The rather slippery nature of this category prevented it from gaining wider recognition in film studies circles.

Yet, the overall scheme of the four distinct modes of narration that Bordwell put forward in this book has had a considerable impact on how film scholars conceptualise the various cinematic traditions, especially the opposition between Hollywood and Europe. With the identification of the specific rules and conventions that prevailed in diverse types of filmmaking at different historical junctures and geographical junctions, he demonstrated plainly not only the inexhaustible powers of cinematic language but also the value of historical poetics for the study of cinema.

Before concluding my reference to these two books, however, I would like to make a final observation about his choice of terms and their wider implications. It is noteworthy that he evades touching openly upon the distinction between classicism and modernism and their historical or ideological underpinnings. Nonetheless, it seems possible to schematise broadly this dichotomy by drawing on some of his piecemeal remarks on the issue. More specifically, he employs the term 'classical' for Hollywood cinema[5] due to its formal harmony, proportion, respect for tradition and self-effacing craftsmanship (see Bordwell *et al.* 1985: 4), while on the other hand, he claims that the other three paradigms could all qualify as modernist, depending on which aspect of modernism we want to emphasise (see Bordwell 1985: 310). His conscious refusal to classify in an explicit and systematic manner the various cinematic traditions along the classical/modernist axis is also indicative of his objection to the concept of postmodernism, a word that inevitably appears when we turn to contemporary cinema and the choices that are available to filmmakers today.

Avoiding the postmodern: historical poetics on contemporary cinema

As we move towards the present and the film production of the last twenty years, the established works of historical poetics are faced with new questions and fresh challenges. Bordwell's accounts of the different kinds of narration and the evolution of visual style are extremely enlightening but also open to critical evaluation and constant re-working. As he admits,

> A great deal of theorising about norms remains to be done ... These are not definite analyses; they are attempts to chart the range of constructional options open to filmmakers at various historical conjunctures, and the results are always open to revision. (1989b: 381)

Unfortunately, no matter how flexible and conciliatory this statement may sound, Bordwell has proved to be particularly adamant about his theoretical formulations and historical observations, especially regarding the classical mode of narration. In this section, I would like to present some examples of his resistance to the possibility of revision and his tenacious defence of his own traditional paradigms. Given that, in recent years, Bordwell has become almost legendary for his firm belief that there is no such thing as postmodern/post-classical cinema at a formal level, I think it would be interesting to go over the rhetorical strategies with which he sustained this premise.

The first important declaration was already incorporated in *The Classical Hollywood Cinema*; in the thirtieth chapter of the book he claims that this mode of narration persists even after the demise of the studio system and continues to apply to the films of the 'New Hollywood' in the 1970s. Although the works of the major European auteurs undoubtedly influenced the new generation of American filmmakers, such as Robert Altman, Woody Allen, Martin Scorsese and Francis Ford Coppola, Bordwell feels that the latter have not managed to develop styles and visions personal or idiosyncratic enough to dissociate them from the dominant paradigm of Hollywood cinema. On a similar note, he emphasises the fact that the intricate relations with and influences from European art cinema is a regular phenomenon that has not succeeded so far in producing a new model that is distinctly diverse from the classical. As he repeatedly notes:

> ...these new films do not constitute a sharply distinct style, but can better be explained by that process of stylistic assimilation we have seen at work throughout Hollywood's history. As the 'old' Hollywood had incorporated and refunctionalised devices from German Expressionism and Soviet montage, the 'New' Hollywood has selectively borrowed from the international art cinema. (Bordwell *et al.* 1985: 373)

'Stylistic assimilation' becomes the key phrase for explaining any kind of deviation from the well-established norms and patterns of Hollywood cinema and for describing all the changes in the style and narrative of the contemporary American films. It is remarkable how far Bordwell can go to sustain his argument and the analysis of *The Conversation* (1974), which appears in the same chapter, is an illustrative example of his fixed position. In a nutshell, Coppola's film is described as a detective film with classical narrational strategies, which occasionally borrows various art cinema elements. What is astounding, however, is that he has to use equal writing space in order to account, on the one hand, for the film's adherence to the classical rules and to indicate, on the other, its deviances from them. One cannot help wondering then how his

conclusion that 'the New Hollywood can explore ambiguous narrational possibilities but those explorations remain within classical boundaries' can be
justified (Bordwell *et al.* 1985: 377). It is one thing to 'read' Alfred Hitchcock's
Suspicion (1941) or Fritz Lang's *The Woman in the Window* (1944) as classical
films within the bounds of difference and another to insist that a film like *The
Conversation* can be comfortably accommodated in the classical paradigm.[6]
Even though I would not dare to call this film post-classical either, I think it is
essential to be able to draw a line where the classical ends and something else
begins, even if that 'something else' is not yet easily identifiable or classifiable.
Besides, if we agree that the classical mode had a powerful and solid presence for more than five decades, it would be highly unlikely that a radically
new and full-blown mode of narration would surface within a decade of its
demise. It would be more reasonable to consider the films of the American
auteurs of the 1970s as preparing the ground for the emergence of something
new that would require more time to develop into something concrete. Of
course, this may sound a safe assumption from our current standpoint but,
nonetheless, Bordwell's argument on 'stylistic assimilation' put forward already in 1985 was a precursor of his resistance to new terms and concepts
that follows him to this date.

For instance, one cannot help noticing that his persistence on the solidity
of the classical paradigm is always coupled with a blazing objection to the
concept of the postmodern. He usually feels obliged to address this issue but
only to express his doubts about the existence of postmodern films or the
usefulness of this term in theorising about cinema. For instance, in the book
On the History of Film Style (1997), he launches his attack on the framework
of postmodernism with regard to its rejection of the 'grand narratives'. As he
observes:

> The postmodernist will add that to try to write a history of film style is to
> indulge in the fantasy of a 'grand narrative' that will give meaning to what
> are, in our current circumstances, only fragments of experience, a flotsam of
> isolated artefacts and indefinitely indeterminate documents ... An enquiry
> into film style must stand or fall by its plausibility compared to that of its
> rivals, and if a 'grand narrative' addresses a problem more convincingly than
> a 'microhistory' does, we cannot dismiss it out of hand for theoretical incor-
> rectness. (1997: 5–6)

It is indeed quite striking how Bordwell sides with the 'grand narratives' in
this case, while in fact it is these 'grand narratives' that historical poetics is
trying to replace in the study of cinema. His long-standing critique of the so-
called SLAB theories has always been part and parcel of his wider antithesis

towards totalising theories that refuse to pose open-ended questions and pay very little attention to the details that only close textual analysis is able to unearth.

The second objection that he raises in this book regards the fact that post-modernity is thought by many scholars to have created a new way of perceiving, which manifests itself in contemporary film style. As he begins to refute the various accounts on the history of vision that argue for a new perceptual mode, he makes a significant concession:

> This view needs to be distinguished from the view that the contemporary art world has created a distinct style, Postmodernism, with its own conventions. Thus, *Blade Runner*, *True Stories*, and *Wings of Desire* can be seen as Postmodernist films. Postmodernist style is purportedly distinguished by fragmentation, nostalgia, pastiche, a dwelling on 'surfaces', a 'technological sublime', and other strategies. In my view, these qualities are so loosely characterised that, guided by intuition, association of ideas, and urgent rhetoric, the critic may fit many features of many artworks to them. In any event, the existence of a Postmodernist style would not establish the major point: that social life within postmodernity creates a distinct mode of perception that leaves its traces in artworks. (1997: 146)

This is one of the very few times that Bordwell leaves open the possibility for the existence of a 'postmodern style', even if he does not consider it to result from a shift in the mode of perception in contemporary social life. The poor theorisation of postmodern style and the superficial recycling of a number of stereotypical tropes should not diminish the significance of the new stylistic trend nor should they avert us from facing it head-on. On the contrary, the profusion of oversimplistic or ambiguous labels should function as a challenge for the poetician to look beyond all that unnecessary jargon and make an effort to conceptualise the evident changes in contemporary cinema with the help of historical poetics' clear and reliable methodology.

Instead of moving towards this direction, however, Bordwell tries to account for the various stylistic developments both in American and international films by searching for a replacement for the name 'postmodern'. For example, in his article 'Toto le moderne: la narration dans le cinéma européen d' après 1970' (1994), he focuses on a Belgian film called *Toto le héros* (*Toto the Hero*, 1991) by Jaco van Dormael in order to examine the status of narration in European cinema after the 1970s. According to his close analysis, the film seems to adhere to some of the standard norms of art cinema, like subjective/objective realism and authorial commentary, but at the same time it presents some striking similarities with the Hollywood tradition, such as the redundant narration, three-act structure, rapid rhythm and happy ending. In addition, it contains several allusions to art films such as *Jules et Jim* (*Jules and Jim*, 1962) and *Mon oncle d'Amérique* (1980), as well as to Hollywood action movies or classics like *Sunset Blvd.* (1950). In his conclusion, Bordwell again poses the question: 'Postmodernism'? I would rather suggest *light modernism*, somewhere between Hollywood and Europe (1994b: 39; emphasis in original; author's translation). In my view, the recourse to a term like 'light modernism' results in an oxymoron that certainly creates more problems than it solves. Modernism in art is almost intrinsically oppositional to the idea of 'lightness' or 'in-betweenness', establishing principles that defy the idea of negotiation. I believe that the conceptualisation of European cinema after the 1970s as 'lightly modernist' is a virtual dead-end and that probably explains why Bordwell himself did not pursue this concept further.

On another occasion, in his book on contemporary Hong Kong cinema, he uses the term 'avant-pop' to describe a cinematic tradition that, despite being mass-produced and popular, demonstrates many significant artistic elements. With Hollywood as a strong reference point, Hong Kong films embrace various popular genres and exhibit strong elements of intertextuality, parody and pastiche. A highly expressive and mannerist style combined with an episodic structure and tonal ruptures signifies the heavy influence of television and music video aesthetics and the drive for new opportunities and innovations. This mixture of popular and experimental techniques is succinctly articulated in the following passage about the film *First Love* (1997):

> ...the style is a frantic collection of fish-eye distortions, anti-phonal voice-overs, variable-speed movement, splashes of colour, and parodic inserts. Whenever a scene seems to be building, it falls to bits, interrupted by foggy frames, or a new bit of action elsewhere. *First Love* is indeed litter on the breeze, but it does dramatise the avant-pop potential of Hong Kong cinema: in few nations would such an offhand exercise employ big stars and wind up screened in multiplexes. (Bordwell 2000a: 267)

The predilection for the term 'avant-pop' again seems to be a façade for the need to circumvent the pertinence of the postmodern in the discussion about Hong Kong cinema. Besides, all the 'loosely characterised qualities' such as fragmentation, technological sublime and parody, which were so condescendingly rejected in the previous quote for their association with the postmodernist style, are now deployed to describe the style of contemporary Hong Kong films.

I would now like to refer to the book *Visual Style in the Cinema* (2000), which was published only in German and was based on a series of lectures that Bordwell gave on the history of style. In the last chapter we find an analysis of Tom Tykwer's *Lola Rennt* (*Run Lola Run*, 1998) as a typical example of filmmaking in the 1990s, characterised by a stylistic eclecticism. In this case, Bordwell is careful not to reiterate his old terms, such as classical, art cinema or parametric narration, and steers clear from all-encompassing categorisations. Instead, he makes the following insightful remark:

> While European filmmakers start to explore the devices of discontinuity-montage more and more thoroughly, there are some that adopt a style that one might call Baukasten (construction kit) or bricolage aesthetics. That means that they are conscious of the history of cinema, they are conscious of the craft and formal possibilities of their métier. They line up all these possibilities that are given to them in one film, as in an anthology. There is one sequence that is divided into different shots according to the best technique of montage; next to it is one with very long shots and camera movements, and then there is one after another pattern. In other words: a kind of style pluralism or eclecticism is being practised from film to film. (2000b: 179; author's translation)

In this specific film analysis, one gets the impression that Bordwell can no longer withstand the latest developments with the argument that 'it is all still classical one way or another', and that he is grappling with something new. And, indeed, the observation on 'bricolage aesthetics', along with most of the preceding ones, would be most valuable if they were followed by a broader reflection on the revision of the four historical modes and if they initiated an endeavour to create either an updated version or possibly a fifth new mode.

And yet, six years later he would decide not to go up that road. In his latest book entitled *The Way Hollywood Tells It: Story and Style in Modern Movies* (2006), where he focuses on films from the period 1960–2004, the verdict is sealed: contemporary cinema, both American and international, is still employing the classical model, despite various noteworthy variations such as 'network narratives' or 'intensified continuity'.[7] The following excerpt leaves no doubt:

> Despite all the historical changes and local variants we find in contemporary film style, we are still dealing with a version of classical filmmaking. An analysis of virtually any film from the period under consideration will confirm the simple truth with which I started: nearly all scenes in nearly all contemporary mass-market movies (and in most 'independent' films) are staged, shot, and cut according to principles that crystallised in the 1910s and 1920s. (2006: 180)

This powerful statement is, in a way, the tombstone of historical poetics. Even if a number of contemporary films like *Jerry Maguire* (1996) or *Two Weeks Notice* (2002) – two key case studies in the book – are still fairly classical, this does not justify the authoritarian tone that emanates from the choice of words such as 'virtually any', 'nearly all' and 'the simple truth'. What this paragraph betrays is an underlying refusal to reconsider the classical mode of narration and to allow other poetic reconfigurations to come into being. And this is where Bordwell's work on classical cinema begins to limit or even work against the potential of the overall framework of historical poetics that he himself fought so hard and for so long to establish in film studies. If we go back to the fundamental principles of historical poetics, which advocate a flexible and open-ended model of research that produces corrigible and falsifiable evidence, then we realise that on no account should poetic analysis be incompatible with the concept of postmodernism, post-classicism or any other new concept for that matter. Similarly, if the descriptions of the four narrational modes set out to be historical and not ontological, they should inevitably be subject to change and revision. In fact, it was Boris Eichenbaum who issued a dire warning:

> We are too well trained by history itself to think that it can be avoided. When we feel that we have a theory that explains everything, a ready-made theory explaining all past and future events and therefore needing neither evolution nor anything like it – then we must recognise that the formal method has come to an end, that the spirit of scientific investigation has departed from it. (1965: 139)

Although I am confident that Bordwell knows Eichenbaum all too well in theory, his practice remained too attached to his well-established constructions that turned into ready-made applications for any new formal element. In a way, he reversed the method of enquiry and transformed his historical poetics into a top-down approach that uses as a starting point the conviction that one way or another we can still fit everything into the existing paradigms. By insisting on the notion of 'assimilation' and emphasising the stability of the classical mode of narration, he downplayed several significant innovations that were introduced in American and international filmmaking and transformed the way movies – or at least *some* movies – look today.

The purpose of this book is partly to restore the function of historical poetics and to endeavour to start afresh in the examination of contemporary cinema. The task to investigate the poetics of current films and to study the evolution of cinematic language is now more intriguing than ever, as the increasing fluidity of formal elements across different media and art forms challenges all sorts of established norms and boundaries. The results of my attempt will unfold in detail in the subsequent chapters but, before that, it is still important to look at the way other theorists approached these changes in contemporary cinema. In sharp contrast to Bordwell, the majority of film scholars were more than eager to theorise the break of current filmmaking practices with the traditions of the past, mainly in connection with the broader ideological horizon of our epoch and the highly contested phenomenon of postmodernism.

Entering the hot debate: postmodernism, post-classicism and other 'posts'

The fervent discussions around the cultural phenomenon of postmodernity that have dominated most of the academic disciplines for the last forty years have inevitably penetrated the field of film studies with very contradictory results. The introduction of the terms 'postmodernism' and 'post-classicism', along with other 'posts', in the various critical debates was justified by a growing concern for conceptualising the historical changes in American cinema and for identifying and explaining epochal shifts. Peter Kramer's article 'Post-classical Cinema' (1998) provides a concise overview of the developments in film criticism both in the United States and in Europe that founded some of the distinctions between Old and New Hollywood, Classicism and Post-classicism. He rightly states that the transitional period from the 1940s to the mid-1960s welcomed the first critical responses to the postwar changes in Hollywood aesthetics and the gradual decline of the studio system. At the same time, the emergence of the new wave cinemas on the other side of the Atlantic and the long list of European auteurs who experimented with new means of expression created a mounting anticipation in critics' circles for 'something new' in America too. And then came Arthur Penn's *Bonnie and Clyde* (1967). As Kramer notes:

> For [Pauline] Kael and other critics, Hollywood's long-awaited renaissance finally occurred when the traditional qualities of American filmmaking were combined with the intellectual sophistication and stylistic innovations of the new directors and new waves of European cinema in films addressing contemporary and specifically American subject-matter. It is clear, both from critical responses at the time and from later retrospective accounts, that the film which most clearly marked the beginning of this renaissance was *Bonnie and Clyde*. (1998: 297)

This 'long-awaited renaissance' was promptly designated by the writers of *Monogram*, and especially Thomas Elsaesser, who inventoried some of the key distinctive features of the New Hollywood in his two highly influential articles, 'The American Cinema: Why Hollywood?' (1971) and 'The Pathos of Failure. American Films in the 1970s: Notes on the Unmotivated Hero' (1975). However, while Elsaesser aimed at discerning the innovations in the works of the new generation of American filmmakers, such as 'the baroque and ornate elaboration of basically simple plots' and 'the increasingly dislocated emotional identity of the central protagonist' (quoted in Kramer 1998: 299), other critics took the opposite turn. For example, in an article called 'New Hollywood Cinema', published in *Screen* in 1976, Steve Neale insisted that, despite the changes in the production and narrative construction of the films, the New Hollywood continued to function as a capitalist enterprise that reinforces the hegemonic project of classical cinema (see 1976: 120–1). These two epigrammatic extracts from the theoretical deliberations about American cinema in the 1970s offer a sketchy sample of debates that are still ongoing. The conundrum would be further complicated by the thrust of another term, namely the 'postmodern'. Again, Kramer says:

> Since the mid-70s, then, critical debates about the New Hollywood have been characterised by a confusing proliferation of contradictory and shifting definitions of the term, and by different attempts to conceptualise the development of mainstream American cinema in the postwar era with reference to modernism and postmodernism. (1998: 305)

These different and contradictory attempts to map contemporary cinema in the continuum between modernism and postmodernism is something I would like to dwell upon in order to elaborate some of the concepts that became prominent in this debate. My account is certainly not meant to be exhaustive, as there are several readers in postmodernism that cover this ground thoroughly. My goal is to go over some of the key arguments on postmodern cinema in order to underline their theoretical underpinnings and their methodological tools. This analytical engagement will enable me to position my own work later on and to emphasise the importance of methodology in film research.

One suitable starting point would be to look at Fredric Jameson's famous writings on postmodernism and postmodern cinema. As a literary theorist and a cultural historian, Jameson identified 'postmodernism' as a cultural phenomenon with multiple nuances that bears two principle characteristics; firstly, it functions as a reaction to all the styles of high modernism that became established in the universities, museums and art institutions – from Abstract Expressionism in painting to the International Style in architecture and to the works of T. S. Eliot, Thomas Mann and Ezra Pound in literature.

Secondly, it effectuates this reaction through the effacement of the traditional boundaries between High Culture and popular/mass culture and through
the questioning of long-standing hierarchies and values (see Jameson 1983:
112–13). Postmodernism in Jameson's framework, however, is not merely a
passing style or fad, but rather

> a periodising concept whose function is to correlate the emergence of new
> formal features in culture with the emergence of a new type of social life and
> a new economic order – what is often euphemistically called modernisation,
> post-industrial or consumer society, the society of the media or the spectacle,
> or multinational capitalism. (1983: 112)

The postmodern style is thus a formal manifestation of the deeper social
changes that took place in the phase of late capitalism after World War Two
in the United States and Western Europe. One of the key practices of postmodernism that aptly encapsulates the spirit of the post-industrial consumer
societies is pastiche. According to Jameson's definition,

> Pastiche is, like parody, the imitation of a peculiar or unique style, the wearing
> of a stylistic mask, speech in a dead language: but it is a neutral practice of
> such mimicry, without parody's ulterior motive, without the satirical impulse,
> without laughter, without that still latent feeling that there exists something
> normal compared to which what is being imitated is rather comic. Pastiche is
> blank parody, parody that has lost its sense of humour. (1983: 114)

The blank parody, the imitation of dead styles and the recycling of dead signifiers is the only expressive strategy available to postmodern artists who live
in a world where the possibility for stylistic innovations and, generally, for
creating something 'new' does not exist. In cinema, this tendency is translated into the 'nostalgia film', which consists, in narrow terms, of 'films about
the past and about specific generational moments of the past' (1983: 116). In
order to broaden his scope and include more films under this umbrella term,
Jameson discusses various films as representative of four different strands in
the nostalgia mode. These are the following:

> 1. Films that portray the life in the periods of the past and try to recapture the
> atmosphere of older eras. Examples would include Bernardo Bertolucci's *Il
> Conformista* (*The Conformist*, 1970), George Lucas's *American Graffiti* (1973)
> and Roman Polanski's *Chinatown* (1974).
> 2. Films that evoke the past metonymically by trying to reinvent 'the feel and
> shape of characteristic art objects of an older period' and by reawakening 'a

sense of the past associated with those objects' (ibid.). The example here is Lucas's *Star Wars* (1977), a film that makes older generations return with nostalgia to the Saturday afternoon popular serials from the 1930s to the 1950s.

3. Films that combine the previous two strategies and evoke the past both literally and metonymically, with Steven Spielberg's *Raiders of the Lost Ark* (1981) as a main example.

4. Films that, despite their contemporary settings, try to conceal discreetly their contemporary references and their connections to the contemporary social reality. They create an archaic feeling and invite a nostalgic viewing experience, as if they took place in an eternal past, 'beyond history'. The classic example of this apparently broad category is Lawrence Kasdan's *Body Heat* (1981).

As Jameson argues, the main indictment of postmodern cinema and the nostalgia films is their inability to deal with time and history. Although they appear to be treating historical subjects and referring to things of the past, the extensive employment of pastiche and the infinite recycling of stereotypes and glossy images prevent them from accessing the past in 'real' terms. The postmodern pastiche and nostalgia signal the eclipse of reality and historicity, which is evidently symptomatic of the wider late-capitalist social and economic order.

Jameson's positions and terminology have had tremendous impact on the works of other film scholars who adopted his critical framework in order to explore further the characteristics of postmodern cinema (Corrigan 1991; Denzin 1991; Landy & Fischer 1994). The only one I would like to discuss at length for the purposes of this introduction is Christopher Sharrett's article 'No More Going Back and Forth as in the Past: Notes on the Fate of History in Recent European film' (1990) because it adds to the whole debate about postmodern cinema an often-overlooked European perspective. According to Sharrett, who brings together Jameson's nostalgia and Jean-François Lyotard's 'death of grand narratives', the European cinema of the 1980s presents a postmodern 'sensibility' that expresses a disruption in the relationship between art and history. More specifically he observes:

A typological strategy is needed to describe the features of this cinema, but a few controlling ideas are immediately available: the failure of history anymore to convey symbolic values; the disappearance of history as 'grand narrative'; the isolation of the subject from the historical context; the panic over history's exposure and collision with myth; the impossibility of 'knowing' history. (1990: 29)

However, without any apparent 'typological strategy', Sharrett analyses a series of contemporary films in order to identify specific manifestations of these 'controlling ideas' and to prove that, along with American cinema, a large portion of contemporary European filmmaking is also postmodern. First and foremost, according to Sharrett, it is New German Cinema that illustrates an inability to deal in real terms with the recent historical past and the signal moment of the Holocaust (see 1990: 29–30). For example, he argues that Wim Wenders' *Wings of Desire* (1987) presents a disjointed narrative, featuring fragmented urban experiences in contemporary Berlin where the humans are too weak to even try to know their history and the angels reminisce nostalgically about an innocent past. The pastiche and recycling of cultural signifiers that Jameson ascribed to postmodern cinema is also revealed in the characters' language. As Sharrett notes:

> His [Peter Falk's] knowledge of Berlin is a free-form 'cultural literacy' exercise drawn from scattered, dissociated fragments of knowledge: 'Berlin ... Emil Jannings, Kennedy, Von Stauffenberg'. The Weimar cinema, JFK's speech at the Berlin Wall, and the July Plot against Hitler constitute the shards of memory as history disappears and as specific moments are synthesised into contemporary media tableaux. (1990: 31)

The depiction of postmodern Europe and the disintegrated concept of history are also identified in a number of other German films, such as Hans-Jürgen Syberberg's trilogy *Hitler, A Film from Germany, Parsifal* (1983) and *Die Nacht* (1985); Volker Schlöndorff's *Die Fälschung* (*Circle of Deceit*, 1981); and Rainer Werner Fassbinder's *Querelle* (1982). From the list of the Spanish, British and French works that Sharrett discusses, I would like to single out a film by Jean-Jacques Beineix, a filmmaker regularly classified as postmodern. In *La lune dans le caniveau* (*The Moon in the Gutter*, 1983) Beineix exemplifies the fascination of French cinema with American popular culture and cinephilia. With a film noir atmosphere and a pastiche of cinematic images from both the Hollywood and the European tradition, the film nostalgically commemorates numerous cinematic signifiers but, according to Sharrett, it remains oblivious to their politics and the politics of cinema in general (see 1990: 36).

Nonetheless, the negative attitude towards nostalgia and the grievances against the loss of historicity in the postmodern world represent only one side of the critics' stance. With an entirely different perspective on postmodern cinema and the place of history in postmodern representations, Linda Hutcheon criticises Jameson's rhetoric as follows:

Jameson laments the loss of a sense of his particular kind of history, then, while dismissing as nostalgia the only kind of history we may (honestly, in good faith) be able to acknowledge; a contingent and inescapably intertextual history. To write this off as pastiche and nostalgia and then to lament that our contemporary social system has 'begun to lose its capacity to retain each own past, has begun to live in a perpetual present' seems of questionable value. Postmodernist film and fiction are, if anything, obsessed with history *and* with how we can *know* the past today. (1990: 129; emphasis in original)

What this quote makes plain is that beneath the surface opposition between Jameson and Hutcheon on postmodern cinema lies a more fundamental discrepancy between their respective notions of 'history'; where the former defends a Marxist model of history with a firm belief in the 'real referent' of the historical discourse, the latter endorses the postmodern realisation that 'there is no directly and unproblematically *accessible past* "real" for us today: we can only know the past through its traces, its texts' (Hutcheon 1990: 128; emphasis in original). Postmodern films, like all postmodern art, epitomise the postmodern approach to history through two different expressive strategies: parody and self-reflexivity. Where Jameson sees blank irony and pastiche, Hutcheon discovers the workings of a Bakhtinian parody that can be 'constructively and deconstructively critical, challenging the monologic dominant discourse with a second voice, a second level of meaning that destabilises prior authority and unexamined power' (1990: 129). At the same time, parody as a self-conscious technique succeeds in foregrounding the process of production and reception of the films and discloses the constructed nature of narrativity. But what differentiates it from modernist reflexivity and what happens, for instance, when the self-reflexive Woody Allen parodies the already self-reflexive Federico Fellini of *8½* (1963) in *Stardust Memories* (1980)? This is a question that Hutcheon poses herself and answers as follows:

What happens, I think, is something we could label 'postmodernist', something that has the same relation to its modernist cinematic past as can be seen in postmodern architecture today – both a respectful awareness of cultural continuity and a need to adapt to changing formal demands and social conditions through an ironic challenging of authority of that same continuity. (1990: 125)

All these ideas about postmodern cinema become more specific when Hutcheon examines an array of contemporary American and European films. For example, Allen's *Zelig* (1983) is a film made entirely of parodic intertexts that play with the conventions of documentary and fiction in order to depict the story of Leonard Zelig, a chameleon personality that ironically symbolises the history and politics of the 1920s. The historical developments of that period are embedded in Zelig's adventurous life to such degree that life and art can no longer be easily separated. The testimonies of real personalities like Susan Sontag and Saul Bellow, combined with the manipulation of historical footage such as Leni Riefenstahl's *Triumph des willens* (*Triumph of the Will*, 1935), result in a blending of fact and fiction that ultimately 'questions the nature of the "real" and its relation to the "reel"' (1990: 126).

A similar meta-cinematic play along with other postmodern qualities are identified in various works: Carlos Saura's *Carmen* (1983) 'transcodes' French high art into the conventions of Spanish flamenco, Wim Wenders' *Der Stand der Dinge* (*The State of Things*, 1982) parodies Hollywood cinema thus inviting a double-decoding of their ideological inscriptions, Donna Deitch's *Desert Hearts* (1985) depicts the love of two women through the reworking of the heterosexual romance conventions, while Brian De Palma's *Phantom of the Paradise* (1974) and Coppola's *The Cotton Club* (1984) engage in overt parody and challenge genre boundaries in order to deal with the politics of art. Overall, Hutcheon concludes with the following observation:

> Postmodern film is much more resolutely dialogic or paradoxical. Its tensions are deliberately left unresolved; its contradictions deliberately left manifest. Its constant double encoding – inscribing and subverting prevailing conventions – is what causes some critics to reject utterly, while others acclaim enthusiastically. (1990: 132)

Another theorist who would be found among the ones that 'acclaim enthusiastically' is Jim Collins in his book *Uncommon Cultures: Popular Culture and Post-Modernism* (1989). The book deals with various strands of popular culture and, when it comes to cinema, Collins feels the need to respond directly to Jameson's wholesale rejection of nostalgia. Although he agrees that the retro style of *Body Heat* or *Raiders of the Lost Ark* is merely a gratuitous revivalism aimed at promoting certain tendencies in fashion and interior design, there are other films that entail a more complex 'layering' of past styles (Collins 1989: 133). One typical example of this category is Ridley Scott's *Blade Runner* (1982), a film that envisions a world of the future, founded on the simultaneous presence of different time frames. These time frames are visualised in the urban architecture, which revisits various stages of history and juxtaposes images from assorted artists and architects such as William Hogarth, Edward Hopper, Frank Lloyd Wright and Möbius. The result of this archeological delving into the representations of the past is not simple escapism but a deeper attempt to understand our culture through previous codes and conventions. And there is rooted, according to Collins, the distinction between modernism and postmodernism:

> Modernist and Postmodernist texts differ fundamentally, then, in their respective attitudes toward the 'already said'. The former constructs a dialogic relationship with previous representations only to reject them as outmoded, resulting in an asemiotic zero-sum game. The latter constructs an entirely different relationship with the accumulated representational activity, recognising that this activity cannot be conjured away by a sudden rupture because it forms the very fabric of our 'structures of feeling'. (1989: 134)

This postmodern principle is also found in Syberberg's *Parsifal*, a film that was characterised as postmodern by Sharrett as well, albeit in a more pessimistic tone. Here, Collins celebrates the film's diversity of expressive modes – photos, puppet shows, found footage, contrasting sets, symbolic props and of course music – and borrows some of Elsaesser's ideas to argue that Syberberg creates discursive juxtapositions and deconstructs not only our perception of history but also the cinematic space of representation (see 1989: 140). This mixture of cultural signifiers does not lead to 'pastiche' and 'blank parody', however; it endorses a 'productive engagement with antecedent and contemporary modes of organising experience as a way of making sense of life in decentred cultures' (ibid.).

This small sample of conflicting views on postmodern cinema clearly shows the importance of the underlying assumptions and the personal predisposition of each theorist in the way they approach and evaluate this phenomenon. Apart from the issue of history, however, these lengthy debates focus on other concepts as well, such as identity, ideology or gender, and emphasised elements such as 'decentredness', 'incoherence', 'fragmentation', 'surface' and so on. Yet, in all these discussions the overall framework of postmodernism appears to be too inconclusive, too evasive or too fragmented itself to provide a solid and consistent explanation for the entire spectrum of contemporary cinema. This conceptual problem has been boldly indicated by Yvonne Tasker, who notes:

> Using postmodernism as a framework within which to position the contemporary popular cinema, rather than particular examples of it, has proved problematic ... Yet if the framework of postmodernism does have a value for an analysis of contemporary cinema, it must also be involved in thinking beyond individual films as 'postmodern' or as symptoms of postmodernity. (1996: 225)

The common strategy used to search for postmodern symptoms in contemporary films is particularly illustrative in the case of *Blade Runner*, which
has been treated as the epitome of postmodern cinema for the following five
reasons:

1. The setting, the *mise-en-scène* and the mixture of architectural styles in the
representation of urban space.
2. The references and the borrowings from the cinematic past, especially film
noir vocabulary.
3. The questioning of categories of identity and particularly the boundaries
between humans and non-humans.
4. The exploration of the different time/space experiences.
5. The exploration of the relation between images and the construction of
identity and personal history. (Ibid.)

This checklist is exemplary of the attempt to define postmodern cinema by
borrowing terms and arguments from the postmodern debate in other disciplines – especially from architecture and literature – and then trying to
detect them in specific films. In most cases, as I tried to show, each scholar
chooses a small number of films that manifest some of these traits and uses
them as proof of the existence of postmodern cinema, resulting inevitably in
a tautological exercise.

Indicative of this tendency is also a book called *Postmodernism in
the Cinema* (1998), edited by Christina Degli-Esposti. By giving the title
'Postmodernism(s)' to her introduction, Degli-Esposti argues that images
can be postmodern in many different ways and deploys in interchangeable
fashion the terms of key postmodern thinkers, while she lists an assortment
of postmodern manifestations in filmic discourse. The following quote is illustrative:

The contamination of genres in postmodern cinema and the utilisation of
new media such as computer graphics and animation allow diverse fields to
coexist together in hypertexts ... Intertextual and hypertextual travels and
their citational aesthetics are typical features of any postmodern text. They
base their very existence on repetition with a difference, on recycling the past
via the rereading of every story and every meaning. (1998: 6–7)

In this case, Jameson and Hutcheon's rhetoric on the issue of representing
the past come together rather indistinctly to set up the profile of postmodern cinema. Furthermore, Degli-Esposti emphasises the role of computer
technology in creating a 'neo-baroque' visual style and in introducing new

spectatorial regimes. In postmodern films, the baroque fascination with excessive reflexivity, multi-layering and fragmentation entails a displacement of the spectator's attention and invites several levels of perception. The examples that she discusses to account for the numerous postmodernisms – from postmodern aesthetics to postmodern cognitive competence – include some of the 'usual suspects' in this debate like *Zelig*, *Blade Runner*, Quentin Tarantino's *Pulp Fiction* (1994) and David Lynch's *Lost Highway* (1996), but also Peter Greenaway's *Prospero's Books* (1991), Milcho Manchevski's *Before the Rain* (1994), Wenders' *Lisbon Story* (1995) and Gabriele Salvatores' *Nirvana* (1997). Finally, the small sample of the diverse postmodernisms that Degli-Esposti offers in the introduction is further elaborated on in the selection of articles, which presents a remarkably wide range of postmodern concerns in relation to parody, intertextuality, ideology, cross-cultural identity, national cinemas, tourism, (post)history, colonisation and authorial presences. This anthology is clearly representative of the tendency in film studies to relate or identify contemporary cinema – and increasingly international cinema and not just Hollywood[8] – with postmodernism, a blanket term that can account for nearly everything that happens in the cinema today.

A noteworthy attempt to move away from the recycling of postmodern tropes and a clear predilection for the term 'post-classical' are found in *Studying Contemporary American Film* (2002), co-authored by Thomas Elsaesser and Warren Buckland. Both authors had previously tackled the issue of post-modern/post-classical cinema in their respective articles on *Bram Stoker's Dracula* (1992) and *Raiders of the Lost Ark* (Elsaesser 1998b; Buckland 1998), but they come together here with an attempt to develop a *method* for the analysis of post-classical films. Using the blockbuster *Die Hard* (1988) as a case study, they try to demonstrate how a film can be both classical and post-classical depending on the analyst's theoretical and conceptual agenda. Firstly, they try to analyse the film according to two dominant approaches to the classical Hollywood narrative: Bordwell's neo-formalist poetics and a combination of the Proppian and Levi-Straussian structuralist methodology. In both cases, *Die Hard* seems to comply consistently with the rules of classical filmmaking, such as the classical three-act structure, the goal-oriented hero, the continuity editing, the enigmas and the functions, the repetitions and the resolutions, to name just a few. As the writers conclude at the end of the classical reading:

> Thus, the difference between classical and post-classical cannot be established on the basis of a binary opposition such as spectacle vs narrative, nor, we suspect, any other 'either/or' construction of difference. One suggestion was that we may have to look for a definition of the post-classical more along

the lines of an excessive classicism, rather than as a rejection or absence of classicism. (2002: 61)

Having established that the various features of classicism are still an integral part of post-classical Hollywood, the authors go through the different theories about the post-classical/postmodern/New Hollywood cinema – most of which have been laid out here in more detail – in order to distill from them a consistent method of analysis. The connection to the wider framework of postmodernism and postmodernity, however inevitable, is made only briefly through the writings of Fred Pfeil, as the real issue at stake here is to create a specific scheme for conducting a post-classical reading of contemporary American films. This reading depends on the following five lines of thought:

1. Post-classical narratives do not reject the canonical story format, but entail a multiple layering of the plotlines and the characters in order to easily accommodate video game logic.
2. They express a kind of 'knowingness' about the heuristic distinction between surface and deep structure and they play literally with these conceptual categories.
3. They address more openly and explicitly issues of race, gender and the male body, although not necessarily in a more progressive way.
4. They acknowledge their presence in a transnational/post-colonial/globalised world and provide a commentary on the situation at the same time, adopting thus an inside-outside position.
5. They are replete with sliding signifiers, i.e. verbal and visual puns that denote the sophistication and professionalism of the New Hollywood. (See Elsaesser & Buckland 2002: 66)

All these aspects constitute different facets of the essential quality of the post-classical, notably its 'knowingness' described as 'a special sort of awareness of the codes that govern classical representation and its genre conventions, along with a willingness to display this knowingness and make the audience share it, by letting it in on the game' (2002: 78). All things considered, Elsaesser and Buckland conclude that the post-classical cinema has not made a radical break with the classical nor has it created something entirely new; instead, it is distinguished by an excessive classicism, which exults at its mastery of the classical rules and invites a wide range of viewers in a reflexive play with 'sliding signifiers' and multiple access points (ibid.).

With this last approach, I would like to close my overview of the current debate on the status of contemporary American and international cinema and the different characterisations that various theorists have ascribed to it.

The contradictory and shifting definitions of the New Hollywood, 'postmodern' cinema and 'post-classicism' that I have presented here seem to confirm Elsaesser and Buckland's argument that different assumptions and different methods can bring to the surface different facets of the object of analysis and can privilege different labels for it. Along the same lines, one cannot emphasise enough that different selections of films can result in entirely different conclusions, given the enormous worldwide film production available nowadays. In the next section, I will try to position my own research in the midst of these ongoing discussions and I will explain how a particular film sample on the one hand, and the method of historical poetics on the other, can shed new light on an aspect of contemporary cinema that has evaded the attention of film scholars so far.

My project:
historical poetics towards a new paradigm of narration

> In this situation, the conceptual debate about Old Hollywood and New Hollywood, modernism and post-modernism, classicism and post-classicism is perhaps less urgent and productive than the kind of careful, systematic, and complex stylistic analysis which historical poetics demands. (Kramer 1998: 307)

I decided to take Kramer's suggestion rather literally and dedicate this book to the 'complex stylistic analysis' of contemporary films, leaving all the other issues and preoccupations aside. As I have already hinted, I would like to investigate the suspected break of contemporary cinema from the previous cinematic traditions through the lenses of historical poetics, an elaborate research model with very precise methodological and theoretical tools. The ultimate goal is to reconstruct the options that are available to *certain* filmmakers today and to produce knowledge about the rules and norms that shape the dynamics of a *segment* of the current filmmaking practice. By stressing the limitations of this goal, I am trying to avoid any general overstatements or undue exclamations about the 'end of cinema as we know it' (see Lewis 2001) that have blinding effects and undermine the complex and multifaceted nature of cinema.

My preference for the historical poetics approach is not meant to underestimate the validity or usefulness of other research methodologies. There is no doubt that there are various ways to approach the evolution of cinema and to discern a possible distinction between a classical and a post-classical/postmodern cinema; from talking about economics to examining the social representations or the spectatorial identification schemes. Without intending to create a hierarchy between these different areas of interest, my personal research interests will emphasise the importance of the developments in the act of narration because in the current debate, film form and style should occupy a substantial part and not end up – to use Bordwell's metaphor – like music in nineteenth century melodrama: 'always subordinate, vaguely there, of interest only when it underscores a point deemed important on other grounds' (1989a: 261). Therefore, with specific questions about the films' constructive principles, narration and style, I will search for equally specific and convincing answers that can elucidate the whole issue about the existence of a new type of cinema at the level of narration that distinguishes itself from the other established narrative models.

This study will capitalise heavily on Bordwell's contribution to film studies not only because he has demarcated the principles of historical poetics but also because he has produced invaluable knowledge for classical Hollywood and other modes of narration until the 1970s. Any attempt to construct a new paradigm of narration has to be anchored in the poetic history of cinema and to take into consideration the various forms and conventions that have appeared since the inception of the cinematic medium. Evidently, the daunting challenge here is to be able to use Bordwell's very own weapons to fight his objection to the existence of a new paradigm and to discover a new angle about narration in contemporary cinema that, I believe, has been overlooked until now.

On the other hand, the second challenge is to manage to keep the entire framework of postmodernism in the background of this poetic research. Going against the grain, I do not plan to apply the theories and concepts of the postmodern to certain films nor do I want to use the latter as proof of the postmodern manifestations in cinema. Instead, I will follow the bottom-up manner that historical poetics endorses and, more specifically, I will concentrate on a seemingly simple question: 'What are the principles according to which films are constructed today?' My working hypothesis is that there is a new 'post-classical' paradigm of narration that has surfaced in contemporary world cinema[9] in the last twenty years and encompasses a limited range of constructional rules. In order to investigate this premise I will engage in a close textual analysis of a body of contemporary films, trying to verify the extent to which they adhere to integral and limited stylistic conventions. It is unlikely that any of these films will perfectly embody all the post-classical norms – in other words, no film under examination will be this 'new' system – but they will certainly be archetypical of the new mode to a considerable degree.

Choosing a name for this paradigm is certainly very troublesome since it is bound to be loaded with hidden assumptions and all sorts of connotations that are potential points of contention. My predilection for the term 'post-classical' in this case testifies a need to avoid the notoriety of the 'postmodern' but also hints at the strong affiliation of this new paradigm with the classical cinema and the sense of historical continuity that binds them. Choosing films, on the other hand, is even more challenging, as it requires a break into the so-called 'hermeneutic circle' (Bordwell 1980: 136). This means that in order to delineate a post-classical mode of narration, I first have to delimit a field of data – particular films – that I believe to epitomise the post-classical elements. Yet, the criteria for selecting these films are shaped by a rather pre-constituted idea of what post-classical cinema is. Given that, as an analyst, I have to begin my research by breaking this circle as legitimately as possible, I have chosen the following criteria for my selection.

1. Historical chronology. As we have seen, most film theorists and critics agree that the 1970s signalled the emergence of something new in American cinema and have argued at length that this represents a break from the classical Hollywood tradition. Given that a paradigm shift is a gradual process that allows the new paradigm to develop slowly and steadily, I decided to choose films from the period 1991–2003, assuming that whatever 'began to change' in the 1970s could have reached a full growth from the 1990s onwards.

2. Authorship. Although the notion of the auteur has been repeatedly problematised and re-negotiated in the history of film theory, it seems to be a concept that we cannot ignore altogether. As the gravity and scope of the previous modes of narration were always contingent upon the works of some prominent filmmakers, the post-classical mode could not be an exception. Therefore, I tried to select a sample that would include some prominent contemporary international directors, whose authority would also corroborate the status of this mode in world film production.

3. Literature and criticism. Numerous articles, critiques and film analyses tirelessly reiterate the precepts that indicate the emergence of a distinct approach to film form. All the previous research on the innovations of film style and narration in contemporary cinema provides a strong motivation for my selection but also a challenge, as in some cases I will be able to supplement and refine it, while in others to contradict and refute it.

4. International baseline. In a globalised and conglomerated cinematic universe, the old borders separating American and European cinema no longer seem pertinent. For that reason, I included filmmakers from both sides of the Atlantic in order to emphasise the breakdown of the long-standing Hollywood-Europe opposition. At the same time, I wanted to open up, albeit tentatively, the discussion about post-classical narration as a characteristic of a segment of world cinema. Thus, I chose one film from Hong Kong, one

from Brazil and one from South Korea in order to grant my selection a global scope. Even though the Western perspective is still privileged, I believe that these films coming from different parts of the planet can help us begin to realise how formal changes in a globalised world can emerge and develop on a global terrain in a simultaneous manner that makes it difficult for us to determine their origins offhandedly.

5. My personal intuition. Without diminishing the importance of all the previous criteria, the very first impulse for selecting the films or even for launching this research was my personal sense that some contemporary films not only exhibit a set of 'unclassical' elements but also form a very distinct and coherent ensemble of narrational strategies. During the first viewing of these films I did not possess the theoretical knowledge for grasping their pattern but as soon as I began to ask the basic questions of historical poetics, this inner intuition was fully vindicated.

With the help of all these academic and personal criteria I decided to work with the following 14 films: *Europa, Arizona Dream* (1993), *Chongking Senlin* (*Chungking Express*, 1994), *Natural Born Killers* (1994), *Trainspotting* (1996), *Lola Rennt, Fight Club* (1999), *Magnolia* (1999), *The Million Dollar Hotel* (2000), *Requiem for a Dream* (2000), *Moulin Rouge!* (2001), *Le Fabuleux Destin d' Amélie Poulain* (*Amélie*, 2001), *Cidade de Deus* (*City of God*, 2002) and *Oldboy* (2003).[10] By ignoring their diverse national origins and their differences in production values and critical or public reception, I concentrated on the analysis of these films in their entirety, adhering faithfully to the historical poetics agenda and, particularly, Bordwell's strategy for constituting the classical Hollywood paradigm. Therefore, in chapter one I start by focusing on the system of narrative logic and, specifically, on the type of causality that is at work in the sample films. My aim is to carefully draw a distinguishing line between the classical and post-classical narrative motivations. In chapter two, I turn to the system of narrative space and the changes that are detected in the spatial articulations of the post-classical films. While the classical space was constructed with the help of devices such as depth of field and continuity editing, the post-classical reworks these elements by introducing the concept of spatial montage and intensified continuity. In chapter three, I look at the system of narrative time in order to identify the parameters of temporal construction in the new mode and to reveal how post-classical time gains significant prominence by problematising the linear progression of the story and by multiplying the options of temporal duration and frequency. In chapter four, I evaluate the overall shape of the narration in the sample and analyse it along the three spectra that Bordwell borrows from Meir Sternberg: self-consciousness, knowledgeability and communicativeness (Bordwell *et al.*

1985: 25). In contrast to the classical narration that maintains a low degree of self-consciousness in order to create the feeling of invisibility and transparency, I discuss how the post-classical mode celebrates a high self-reflexivity accomplished through a variety of narrative devices and through the relentless shifting of the narrative levels. Finally, in the conclusion I present the post-classical narrative mode as a coherent narrative model with specific systems of causality, space and time and I delineate its boundaries with the other cinematic paradigms that are also in force in other strands of contemporary world cinema. The final note of this book will be dedicated to the factors that generated this paradigm shift, trying to open a new chapter for further research into the post-classical mode of film production.

I would like to conclude this introduction with a clarification on the method of analysis of the sample and its presentation in the book. All 14 films have been analysed thoroughly, frame by frame, according to the general lines I presented briefly above. However, in order to give this volume a reasonable and readable format and to avoid burdening the text with too many details, I will try to distribute the textual evidence from the films in an economical manner according to the weight of the argument that they support. For instance, in chapters one and three I use the film analyses intermittently around the issue of motivations or the types of temporal construction. On the other hand, in chapters two and four I lay out the theoretical and conceptual agenda around the question of spatial construction and self-consciousness respectively and then I present ten case studies that exemplify the relevant traits of the post-classical paradigm.[11] Hopefully, this type of organisation will be able to prevent any redundancies and will be able to flaunt the new post-classical narrative paradigm in all its grandeur.

STORY CAUSALITY AND
NARRATIVE MOTIVATIONS

The notion of motivation is an indispensable characteristic of all human behaviour that has occupied philosophers and thinkers since the time of Aristo-
tle. A person's behaviour and action is shaped by various intrinsic or extrinsic
motivations that aim at certain goals. Similarly, every narrative film is a human construction that is purposefully created on the basis of several motivations in order to fulfil an overarching function, namely the act of storytelling.
However, just as there are numerous behavioural patterns for humans, there
are even more ways for a film to tell a story. The rich history of cinema has
clearly shown that different filmmakers at various historical junctures have
served this purpose using a wide variety of narrational tools and devices that
are constantly updated and transformed. This chapter will focus on contemporary narrative motivations with the 14 sample films as a guide that will explore the following broad questions: how does a post-classical narration tell a
story? How is its system of narrative logic constructed? What are the principles of causality that connect the events of the story and ensure a seemingly
natural progression? What are the motivations that determine what appears
on the screen? Already these questions introduce some concepts such as narration, system of narrative logic, story, screen and motivation that require
further explanation before starting to look for the actual answers.[1]

    First and foremost, I would like to start with the formal definition of nar-
ration in the fiction film as 'the process whereby the film's syuzhet and style
interact in the course of cueing and channeling the spectator's construction
of the fabula' (Bordwell 1985: 53). The main distinction that this definition
establishes is between the 'fabula' and the 'syuzhet', or the 'story' and the 'plot',
if we translate the words of Russian Formalist critics of the 1920s, such as
Viktor Shklovsky and Yuri Tynianov, who initially identified this distinction

in literary theory. By separating a film into these two constituent parts, we are able to understand better how the narrative act functions. On the one hand, the story consists of the events of the narrative in an *inferred* cause-and-effect chain, while, on the other, the plot consists of the *actual* presentation and arrangement of these events in the film. The former is a mental construction that a viewer builds through assumptions and inferences, whereas the latter is the concrete onscreen manifestation of the story in various causal, spatial and temporal configurations. Furthermore, if we want to be precise about the 'onscreen manifestation', we need to take into consideration the finer distinction between the syuzhet and the style and their interactions during the transmission of the story information. The syuzhet is concerned with the dramaturgical process of presenting the story, while the style determines all the technical choices that shape the filmic texture. Their collaboration in the filmic narration can take different forms, from complete unity in classical films to frustrating dissonance in obscure art films.

The overall narration of a film and the intricate relations between plot, story and style can be analysed along three axes: the narrative logic that regulates the events of the story according to specific principles of causality and motivation, the cinematic space that contains these events and the cinematic time during which these events unfold. Each of these axes will be investigated in separate chapters in order to lay out the characteristics of the post-classical narration. Here, the weight will fall on the first axis, the narrative logic, and for that purpose I would like to flesh out the specific parameters that it contains and the concepts that will occupy a central space in this chapter.

The narrative logic of a film is contingent upon a number of motivations that determine the way that both the story and the plot will evolve. According to Bordwell, 'motivation is the process by which a narrative justifies its story material and the plot's presentation of that story material' (Bordwell *et al.* 1985: 19). Thus, every element that appears on the screen, from a line of dialogue to a lighting scheme, requires a specific justification in order to serve a function or fulfil a role within the story world and to make sense to the viewer. The four main types of motivation in any given narration are the compositional, the realistic, the intertextual/generic and the artistic (ibid.). The most ordinary type of motivation is the compositional, as it refers to the basic cause-and-effect chain of events and it includes principles of causality such as character traits, the goals that are pursued and the romantic twists that create a basic coherence in the development of the story. Moreover, the realistic motivation justifies the representation of the story in terms of verisimilitude and plausibility applying a set of rules that are considered to be 'realistic' in their depiction of the private and public worlds. The third type is the intertextual/generic motivation, which justifies certain aspects of the plot according to particular generic conventions. In a musical, for instance, the actors are allowed to burst into song because it is an established trait of that genre or, in a melodrama, the story can be built on chance encounters and co-incidences because these are traditionally melodramatic devices. Lastly, the artistic motivation invites the use of filmic features that often contradict the other motivations and aim at exposing the artificiality of the narrating act and calling attention to its means of construction.

It is important to note that these four types of motivation potentially form different dynamics among themselves, either by co-operating or working against each other, resulting in unity and coherence or tension and discontinuity respectively. In classical narratives, for example, they usually operate together to justify the parts of the narrative in more than one way. In art films, on the other hand, the artistic motivation might work against the compositional by blocking the causal links between the events and by preventing the creation of a clear cause-and-effect logic in the story. In the case of the post-classical, the shape of the four motivations poses intriguing challenges to our established paradigms and asks us to reconsider some of our long-standing assumptions about causality in narrative cinema.

In the following pages, I will meticulously investigate the four types of motivation and their interactions in the narration of the sample films and I will try to produce helpful observations about their current status and function in the post-classical mode. Above all, the detailed analyses of the system of narrative logic in these films will illustrate the intricate continuities and discontinuities that both relate and separate the post-classical cinema from the classical tradition, thus shunning any theoretical overstatements and aiming at a sober evaluation of the latest narrative evolution.

Compositional motivation

This first type of motivation allows us to make an initial, if hesitant, step towards discerning the changes that the new paradigm has introduced in the way the narration handles the characters and the story events. Before entering the post-classical realm though, let us briefly remember the role of compositional motivation in the classical Hollywood model. The construction of a classical narrative is based on the notion of the characters as primal agents whose actions and reactions propel the chain of events in the story. The personal motivations of psychologically defined individuals regulate the flow of events and determine the outcome of the action. The impersonal causes, such as natural phenomena or historical facts, always play a secondary role by initiating or altering a certain plotline or by simply providing a backdrop against which the human actions occur. Moreover, unmotivated coincidences or chance encounters may influence the progression of the narrative on limited occasions but they are mostly motivated generically, given that certain genres like melodrama and comedy have to use coincidences to generate drama or laughter respectively. As a result, the reliance of the classical film on individual initiatives requires a lucid and consistent delineation of the characters in the story in order to anticipate and justify their deeds. The acquaintance with the characters' personalities is achieved through their speech and physical behaviour while their consistency is often reinforced by means of recurring motifs, i.e. certain characteristics or tags that are attributed to them and are repeated throughout the film (see Bordwell *et al.* 1985: 13–18).

If we begin to look at the sample, we soon realise that all of these conventions of compositional motivation are also quite evident to a similar degree in all the films in question. The character-centred causality remains the main unifying principle of the story and the presentation of the characters' personality becomes a key priority, even more than was usual in Hollywood. For that purpose, the transmission of information about the protagonists is not restricted to their verbal interactions, the tags and recurrent motifs, but is also reinforced by powerful non-diegetic sources – voice-overs, intertitles and inserts[2] – that introduce in explicit and self-conscious fashion their qualities, habits and goals.

I would like to start my analysis with Jean-Pierre Jeunet's *Amélie*, a film that stormed the French box office and triggered hot debates about the politics of representation of the French nation. The story portrays the life of a young woman called Amélie Poulain (Audrey Tautou) who devises elaborate schemes to change other people's lives and finds true romance with a young man, Nino (Mathieu Kassovitz). The opening scene starts with a voice-over narration that specifies the exact moment of Amélie's conception – 3 September 1978, 6.28 pm and 32 seconds – and then, for ten minutes, continues the description of her family, providing us with copious details about their habits, their likes and dislikes, while at the same time indicating some key events that shaped Amélie's personality. When she comes of age, she moves to Paris and starts working as a waitress at a café called Les Deux Moulins. The voice-over introduces us to the people who work there by selecting their typical character traits, which will justify their behaviour in the course of the story. Every time a new person enters the story world, the narration informs us explicitly about their qualities, usually by means of a flashback composed of salient moments from their lives. This clear and overt presentation of the main protagonists delays considerably the initiation of the diegesis and overshadows the development of the plot.

A similar strategy is found in *Fight Club*, David Fincher's anti-New Age satire on the dehumanising impact of consumer society. The film depicts the story of an unnamed protagonist (Edward Norton) who suffers from insomnia and begins to attend various self-help group meetings in search of an emotional outlet. One day he meets an enigmatic character, Tyler Durden (Brad Pitt), who is the founder of Fight Club, an underground group of people who meet regularly to engage in violent physical confrontations. Throughout the film, the protagonist – despite not having a name himself – controls the narration of the story with an authoritative voice-over and describes visually and aurally his life, his house, his work routine and his inner thoughts and desires. When he meets Tyler, he literally freezes the story in order to outline the latter's personality and to provide information about his activities as a waiter and film projectionist, such as the habit of urinating in the soup at fancy restaurants or splicing a couple of frames of a penis into children's films. Moreover, both characters are defined through certain recurring lines of speech that affirm their beliefs and attitudes. For instance, Tyler expresses repeatedly his condemnation of consumer capitalist culture with various Marxist slogans, whereas the narrator asserts his introversion with expressions like 'I am Jack's broken heart' or 'I am Jack's cold sweat'.

Along the same lines, Wim Wenders' *The Million Dollar Hotel* emphasises from the beginning the characterisation of its protagonists. The story is set in Los Angeles in 2001 when a young man called Tom Tom (Jeremy Davies) plunges to his death from the roof of the Million Dollar Hotel. As he falls, he initiates a flashback to the events that took place in the hotel during the previous 14 days and with a voice-over commentary he acquaints us with its residents, describing their odd personalities and their lonely secluded lives. When Special Agent Skinner (Mel Gibson) enters the story world for the first time, Tom Tom tells us 'You could see he was *special* even before he told you', preparing us with a pun for Skinner's peculiar presence in the film. Furthermore, each character is associated with a specific habit or trait; Geronimo with his tar paintings, Dixie with his guitar, Eloise with her books, Izzy's father with a limousine, Tom Tom with running errands for the others and, finally, Skinner with his regular phone calls from his girlfriend Maya.

Recurrent motifs are also Wong Kar-wai's favourite device in *Chungking Express*, a film that has been celebrated by theorists and critics alike as a successful blend of artistry and entertainment. In this case, the motifs are used to delineate the characters' personalities and to signal changes in their behaviour. For example, all the characters are associated with the fast food place Midnight Express which functions as a regular meeting point. Officer 223 (Takeshi Kaneshiro) is obsessed with making or expecting phone calls and collecting canned pineapple with an expiry date on 1 May, the day of his birthday. Officer 663 (Tony Leung) shares his grief at losing his girlfriend with his household objects by having comforting conversations with a 'weeping' towel and a bar of soap that is wasting away. Faye (Faye Wong) incessantly listens to the Mamas and Papas' 'California Dreaming' and pays secret visits to Officer 663's apartment to rearrange things and to lighten up his life. This particular song becomes a trademark for their relationship and their fluctuating dynamics. For example, when he discovers her interventions, she stops listening to the song to show that it does not suit her anymore, while in the end he welcomes her back with 'California Dreaming' affirming his longing expectations.

Next, I would like to refer to Emir Kusturica's *Arizona Dream*, a film about a group of peculiar and incompatible characters that become involved in a very intense and intricate web of relations somewhere in Arizona. The main protagonist is Axel Blackmar (Johnny Depp), who takes charge of the voice-over to introduce himself and share with us intimate information about his occupation, his life in New York as well as the memories of his parents' words like 'Good morning Columbus', a phrase which is going to be reiterated several times during moments of introspection. Apart from the initial exposition, the film attributes very clear-cut characteristics to each character and relates them to certain objects: Axel with fish, his uncle Leo (Jerry Lewis) with Cadillacs, his cousin Paul (Vincent Gallo) with Hollywood films, Elaine (Faye Dunaway) with flying machines and finally Grace (Lili Taylor) with turtles. All these motifs take up a significant part of their characterisation and often foreshadow some of the action. For example, when Grace sets her beloved turtles free into the wild we are indirectly prepared for her imminent suicide.

Lastly, character delineation is also a crucial concern in *City of God*, the Brazilian film co-directed by Fernando Meirelles and Kátia Lund, which depicts life in the slums of Rio de Janeiro in the most exhilarating manner. The story is populated by hundreds of people with a very short life span, but the narration organises the otherwise chaotic and out-of-control happenings in the *favela* by focusing on three main characters: Buscapé (Alexandre Rodriguez), Lil' Ze (Leandro Firmino da Hora) and Bené (Phellipe Haagensen). Buscapé is the central narrator who introduces himself to the audience in the voice-over and assumes the responsibility of guiding us through an endless string of violent killings in the City of God that extend over three decades. From the start he declares his pacifist intentions that distance him from the crime scene and confesses his love for photography. His interest in taking photographs that starts out as a hobby and then becomes a full-time profession is not only Buscapé's key character trait but also becomes a crucial plot element as the film progresses. On the other hand, Lil' Ze is characterised by compulsive killing from the time he was a little boy and it is his total lack of respect for human life that enables him to become the most feared drug dealer in the ghetto. Lil' Ze's personality traits become even more distinct as they are repeatedly compared and contrasted to Bené's qualities and values. Bené is Lil' Ze's right hand in the gang but, unlike him, he is extremely sociable, friendly and popular with everyone around. In a way, he functions as Buscapé's alter ego, as an intermediary between the forces of good and evil, trying to maintain a delicate balance amidst chaos. These three protagonists become the pillars of a particularly convoluted plot and the recurring motifs and tags that are attributed to them play an essential role in keeping the film together.

Overall, the post-classical narration undoubtedly shares with the classical the use of character-centred causality and the portrayal of individuals with the help of recurring motifs. However, the post-classical in-depth presentation of the characters' personalities often reaches such an extreme level of emphasis that it results in a loosening of the goal-oriented progression of the narrative. When a film like *Amélie* or *Arizona Dream* dedicates a large portion of its duration to the extensive presentation of the characters' preferences, habits, thoughts and desires by means of non-diegetic sources, it inevitably reduces the length of the diegesis, it slackens the development of the action and privileges a more episodic exposition of the story events. This effect is even further intensified by the fact that post-classical films have significantly increased the number of protagonists and the plotlines that they are involved in. Whereas the classical Hollywood hero was a causal agent with clear goals and objectives that advanced the story and narrowed the range of alternative outcomes for the action, the post-classical hero is merely one source of agency among numerous others. The post-classical narration uses a plurality of characters and multiplies their interactions in order to create a diversification and fragmentation of their goals and their consequent fulfilment. The two classical plotlines – the formation of the heterosexual couple and the undertaking of a mission – remain persistently present in post-classical story construction but they acquire other dimensions, as they extend and bifurcate into various parallel or intertwined subplots.

The plot patterns of the sample films exhibit a far wider variety than the typical Hollywood formula of Exposition, Conflict, Complication, Crisis and Denouement. Although these dramaturgical stages are not abolished, they are reconfigured and embedded in episodic structures, spliced plots and 'forking-path narratives' (Bordwell 2002a: 101). The variety and multiplicity of plotlines that develop at different paces within the same film work against Hollywood's classical tight causality, yet without eliminating it altogether. The continuity of the story slackens up considerably but it maintains a basic level of coherence with the aid of various narrative devices. Firstly, the clear and concise depiction of the characters and their mental states, performed by the overwhelming and enlightening voice-overs, navigates the viewer through the narrative and gradually fills most of the basic causal gaps. Secondly, all the branches and diversions of the plots are signposted with clear formal tactics such as freeze-frames, intertitles and crosscutting so as to keep the viewer constantly updated about the manner in which the story progresses. Lastly, the central ideas that run through the films establish a sense of closure in the end, however provisional or fragile it might appear when it is contrasted with the finality of the classical Hollywood ending.

An indicative case of episodic and fragmented structure is found in *Amélie*, where the central character triggers several plotlines concerning her father, her colleagues at the bar and the people in her neighbourhood, while she is pursuing Nino, the object of her affection. After the long introduction of most of the principal characters, we see Amélie living in Paris alone after experiencing various disappointing affairs. The following stories are initiated one by one and are subsequently intertwined:

1. Amélie accidentally discovers a box in the bathroom that belonged to a previous tenant and she decides to return it.
2. She runs into Nino at the subway station and falls in love.
3. She meets an old painter with glass-bone disease who lives secluded in his apartment opposite hers.
4. She has a chat with the concierge who is a widow and still mourns her husband who died in World War Two.
5. She tries to match one of her colleagues at work with a regular customer.
6. She wants to punish the nasty grocer across the street for treating his assistant badly.
7. She wants to convince her father to start travelling by devising a trick with exotic photos.
8. She wants to discover the identity of a mystery man in Nino's photo album.

All these stories intermingle and their paths converge in several instances; for example, the old painter tries to convince Amélie to have a date with Nino and her colleague tests Nino to check if he is suitable for Amélie. However, the clear delineation of the characters, the informative voice-over and the familiarity of the settings established early on do not leave any chance for misunderstandings or ambiguities. All the subplots progress in a linear fashion towards their final resolution, which is laboriously revealed by the parallel editing of the last sequence, where we can marvel at the positive changes that Amélie brought to all those people's lives, including her own.

Boasting a similar episodic structure but with a much darker atmosphere,

Requiem for a Dream, Darren Aronofsky's second feature, depicts the trials and tribulations of four people addicted to drugs. The trajectories of these individuals converge and diverge several times before finally reaching separate but equally horrific destinations. A lonely old woman called Sara Goldfarb (Ellen Burstyn) becomes addicted to a television show and – with the hope of participating in it – she struggles to fit into her beautiful red dress and so starts taking diet pills. Her son Harry (Jared Leto) with his girlfriend Marion (Jennifer Connelly) and their friend Tyrone (Marlon Wayans) are heroin addicts who decide to try a series of get-rich-quick schemes involving selling drugs. The depiction of their lives and conflicts is organised chronologically by the change of seasons, with intertitles signalling the passage from spring to winter, leading to a complete breakdown. The dispersion of their trajectories and the fragmentary exposition maintain a significant level of coherence not only thanks to the overarching feeling of despair but also to specific stylistic devices, such as split-screens and parallel editing.

An even more episodic narration is featured in Paul Thomas Anderson's *Magnolia*, a film hailed for its epic dimensions and stylistic audacity. The story contains a long list of main characters that are linked in various close or loose relationships and are united in their desperate efforts to communicate with each other and resolve their personal conflicts. Each of the following individuals constitutes the focus of a distinct plotline that intersects with the others in many ways:

1. Earl Partridge (Jason Robards) is a wealthy TV station owner who is dying from cancer.
2. Linda Partridge (Julianne Moore) is Earl's young trophy wife, who initially married him for his money but has grown to love him and wants to be removed from his will.
3. Earl's long lost son, Frank T. J. Mackey (Tom Cruise), is a motivational speaker who promises to show men how to empower themselves and tame women.
4. The nurse, Phil Parma (Philip Seymour Hoffman), tends lovingly to Earl on the last day of his life and helps him reconcile with his son.
5. The boy genius, Stanley Spector (Jeremy Blackman), is a pre-pubescent boy who wants to break the record on a game show and make his father proud.
6. The game show host, Jimmy Gator (Philip Baker Hall), is an elderly man who has been estranged from his daughter because of his sexual advances to her and now finds out that he is going to die.
7. His daughter, Claudia Gator (Melora Walters), suffers from depression and is addicted to cocaine.

8. Her mother, Rose Gator (Melinda Dillon), stands by her husband and does not understand why Claudia no longer speaks to them.
9. The ex-boy genius, Donnie Smith (William H. Macy), suffers from loneliness and cannot come to terms with the end of his glory days.
10. The police officer, Jim Kurring (John C. Reilly), is a lonely religious person who falls in love with Claudia Gator.

The different stories of this long list of characters all interweave and coalesce through a feeling of hopelessness that slowly builds to a climax with the storm of frogs in San Fernando Valley. When the storm abates, the characters need to come out strong and rebuild their lives from the ruins.

Apart from the episodic structure found in *Amélie* or *Magnolia*, the post-classical paradigm of narration favours the pattern of the spliced plot. This is a model we find in *Natural Born Killers*, Oliver Stone's highly controversial film about violence and mass media corruption. The story features the adventures of a murderous couple, told in two parts; the first one depicts the turbulent lives of Mickey (Woody Harrelson) and Mallory (Juliette Lewis) from the day they met until the day they were arrested by the police for a long series of vicious murders. It is a rather self-contained episode that portrays the trajectory of the two protagonists, from their explosive passion at first to their 'successful' and celebrated record of killing sprees until, finally, the crisis that led to their arrest. The second part picks up their story one year after the arrest when they are inmates in a high security prison. Wayne Gale (Robert Downey Jr.), the host of a show called *American Maniacs*, gets permission for a live in-depth interview with Mickey, during which the latter triggers a riot among his fellow prisoners. Taking advantage of the turmoil and the panic of the guards, Mickey seizes a shotgun and heads for Mallory's cell with a number of hostages and Gale's camera crew. After liberating her, the couple force their way out of the prison and decide to start a new life from scratch. The closing sequence shows them united and happy, driving a trailer with their small children. It is evident that both parts consist of separate climactic moments and resolutions that are merged in an innovative way before confirming, in the end, the classical formula of the formation of the heterosexual couple.

In *Chungking Express* the spliced plot is even more accentuated, as it contains two entirely separate stories that are presented successively and joined with a freeze-frame. The first one portrays three days in the life of Officer 223, a 25-year-old cop, who is struggling to come to terms with the fact that his girlfriend May has left him for good. As he desperately wanders around the city, he meets a mysterious blonde woman, a drug smuggler having trouble with one of her drug deals. The second story features the life of another cop,

Officer 663, who is also abandoned by his air hostess girlfriend and becomes the object of affection of another girl called Faye. The two plotlines converge at the Midnight Express, a fast-food counter that both cops frequent, while the passage from the first to the second part is made when Officer 223 bumps accidentally into Faye. Despite the loose structure, these two stories share a large number of common motifs that unify their tone and create a sense of coherence. As Bordwell observes about the narrative structure of film:

> *Chungking Express* focuses on boys meeting, losing, and getting, or not quite getting, girls. But Wong revivifies the formula. Instead of tightening up the plot, he slackens it beyond even Hong Kong's episodic norm, letting a fine network of parallels and recurring motifs come forward. (2000a: 289)

Moreover, an intriguing case of an 'intrinsically' spliced/double plot is found in *Oldboy*, Park Chan-wook's hyperviolent tale of revenge. The story is about an ordinary man called Oh Dae-Su (Choi Min-Sik), who is kidnapped by a stranger and wakes up to find himself in a private makeshift prison. He remains in captivity for 15 years and then one day he is suddenly set free. From then on, Oh Dae-Su is determined not only to avenge his suffering but also to answer the question of why he was imprisoned for 15 years. What follows is a rather classical trajectory, with Oh Dae-Su investigating the situation with the help of various leads and recollections, not to mention the help of a young female called Mido (Kang Hye-Jeong) who becomes his companion and lover. Yet, the film's conventional narrative trajectory becomes radically subverted in the film's revelation scene. The key change regards the question that the hero was supposed to answer; instead of figuring out why he was imprisoned for 15 years, he should have thought about why he was *liberated* after 15 years. The narrative twist hidden in what seems a subtle shift of emphasis generates a complete breakdown of the classical plotline, leading us to a different reading of the events that preceded. The film is not about Oh Dae-Su seeking revenge on his imprisonment, but rather the entire story *is* an act of revenge on the part of the anti-hero, a young man called Lee Woo-Jin (Yu Ji-Tae), who was in love with his sister and lost her because of Oh Dae-Su's gossiping. From start to finish, all the depicted events were carefully orchestrated by Lee Woo-Jin with one single goal – to get even with Oh Dae-Su by mischievously pushing him into an incestuous relationship with his daughter Mido. A significant length of time – 15 years – had to pass before she came of age and during that time the former had to remain secluded. The meeting with the young woman and their instant attraction were guided by the powers of hypnosis and the sinister planning by Lee Woo-Jin.

With these shocking disclosures, the film's plot takes not only an unexpected turn but invites us to re-evaluate the characters' actions in this new light. *Oldboy* acquires thus a Möbius strip structure that assigns its protagonists doubly-coded roles with shifting qualities and dimensions.[3] Who is the perpetrator, who is the victim, which is the revenge, which is the punishment, who is in charge of the story and who is finally vindicated are all questions that become ambiguous, as the positions of the hero and the anti-hero turn out to be doubly occupied by the two male protagonists. The classical character-centred causality that appeared in the first instance to be the only foundation of this narrative becomes daringly challenged, as other powerful compositional elements enter the story, namely the double incest and the existential crisis that the two characters find themselves in. These two elements become catalysts in the film, complicating the narrative structure beyond any classical norms and, above all, preventing it from reaching a stable and clear closure.

On a final note, I would like to discuss Tom Tykwer's *Lola Rennt*, a film that caused a sensation in film circles. One of its most celebrated aspects regards its use of a parallel plot structure, which Bordwell has described as a 'forking-path' plot or a multiple-draft narrative (see 2002a: 101). In the beginning of the film we are introduced to a crisis situation: Lola (Franka Potente) receives a phone call from her boyfriend Manni (Moritz Bleibtreu) asking her to come up with 100,000 marks within twenty minutes or otherwise a murderous gangster will kill him. The narration then presents us with three consecutive drafts of the story that follows this phone call, each presenting a different outcome of Lola's effort to solve this crisis. All three possible paths contain a series of core incidents and encounters, such as Lola going to the bank or bumping into a woman with a trolley, but the changes in their timing considerably influence the flow of events. For instance, when Lola leaves her apartment she meets a punk kid with an unfriendly dog on her way down the stairs. The first time the dog barks but Lola continues to run down. The second time the kid trips her down and Lola arrives at the bank a little later. In the last section the dog barks at Lola but she growls back at him, as she is determined to pursue her goal more decisively. As in all the other films, the coherence of the story is maintained with the repetition of certain formal techniques, such as the animation sequence, while the passages from one path to the next are clearly indicated by replaying the scene of the fall of Lola's red phone receiver. Finally, despite the three possible progressions of the story that the film presents, the one with the happy ending that comes in the end appears to be the least hypothetical (see Bordwell 2002a: 100). In other words, regardless of the parallel structure, the narration creates a feeling that the first two unsuccessful attempts were a sort of trial that Lola had to go through to finally get it right. As Tykwer confirms:

At the end, the viewer must have the impression that Lola has done every-thing that we've just seen (and not just one part, a third of it). She has lived it all – she has died for this man, he has died, and everything that was destined to happen has happened. She has all that behind her, and at the end, she's rewarded. (Quoted in Bordwell 2002a: 100)

Thus the film establishes a sense of closure and a happy ending which, how-ever conditional, manages to offer the story an overall unity.

On the whole, an overview of the compositional motivation of the films in the sample reveals the persistence of some key classical devices, such as the character-centred causality, the use of recurring motifs and the classi-cal double plot structure that interweaves the formation of the heterosexual couple with the undertaking of a mission. At the same time this new para-digm has brought in some noteworthy innovations that include the emphasis on long expository descriptions of the characters that reduce the diegesis, the multiplication of the number of the protagonists and the employment of more episodic structures, such as spliced plots and forking paths, which loosen the tight causality and the goal-oriented progression of the story. The compositional motivation remains a determining aspect of the post-classical system but it is also imbued with additional elements that slacken the tight cause-and-effect chain of events and allow a more free-ranging development of the plot.

Realistic motivation

Realistic motivation is the second type of motivation that regulates the choices of the filmic narration. In the case of Hollywood cinema, realistic representation is subordinate to compositional motivation and functions as 'a supplementary justification for material already motivated composition-ally' (Bordwell *et al.* 1985: 19). However, to understand the role of realistic motivation in the new paradigm, we have to give the issue of realism serious consideration. Realism is a concept with a highly volatile meaning that has been employed as a descriptive or explanatory device for different works at various historical junctures. The following observation could serve as a start-ing point:

Amidst this plurality of uses [of realism], one consistent implication does ap-pear to survive: that the distinctive characteristic of realism resides in the ambition to, in some way or other, approximate reality, to show 'things as they really are'. (Hill 1986: 55)

The attempt to approach reality and to 'show things as they really are' can be carried out through a set of rules and conventions that are accepted as 'realistic' and constitute what we call 'a realistic mode of representation'. At the same time, the conventional nature of such a mode is exactly what makes it inevitably prone to change, as conventions are modified over time as is our perception of what constitutes both reality and realism. This becomes particularly evident when one examines the various cinematic traditions that have been labelled 'realistic' in film history and the different forms, contents and strategies that made an attempt to capture things 'as they are'.

The type of realism that motivates the classical Hollywood narration has been theorised by André Bazin (1967), who considered the works of Orson Welles and William Wyler to have reached a high level of maturity and to have fulfilled the quintessential goal of the cinematic medium, namely to satisfy our obsession with realism. From a close reading of Bazin's teleological account of realism, Thomas Allen Nelson has identified the following principles of realistic representation:

1. *The principle of perceptual correspondence.* This means that the relationship between the private worlds and the outer world, the personal and the public and, ultimately, the objective and the subjective is characterised by stability, continuity, unity and balance.

2. *The principle of narrative continuity.* The narration in a realist film tries to copy our sense of continuity and order in the real world by following the laws of plausibility and by handling the material in front of the camera in an unobtrusive way.

3. *The principle of human centrality.* The human dilemmas and the individual actions and preoccupations are the central concerns of the realist tradition inherited from literature.

4. *The principle of moral/aesthetic balance.* With this principle Bazin underlines the moral aspect of a filmmaker's art, which should be of equal importance as its aesthetic value. In order to achieve that, the artist has to remain faithful to reality's physical unity and its complexity without giving it away for an unbridled fantasy (see 1987: 136).

According to Bazin, all these characteristics of the classical realistic mode of representation have materialised within the Hollywood filmmaking tradition, which should be regarded as 'an art that has attained perfect balance, an ideal form of expression' (1967: 29). The cinematic codes and conventions that fulfil the above principles at the stylistic level and allow the classical film to approach reality could be distinguished into two domains: the *mise-en-scène* and the editing of the film.

Firstly, the realist *mise-en-scène* aims at creating a materially recognisable world and signifying a certain degree of referentiality. As Julia Hallam and Margaret Marshment observe, 'any departure from this recognisability is perceived as a significant departure from verisimilitude, inviting an immediate questioning of its cause and effect' (2000: 80). More specifically, the composition of a classically realistic image depends on the balanced organisation of the actors and the setting within the frame. The characters' faces and movements are privileged over the scenery and other objects because the camera serves the character-centred causality of the narrative. For the same reasons, the lighting and the soundtrack seek to contribute to the impression of a real situation and offer the viewer the ideal visual and aural position. Secondly, the classical film relies on continuity editing devices, such as the shot/reverse-shot, eyeline match or point-of-view cutting, which are able to construct an invisible and seamless representation of the story world, in contrast, for instance, to Sergei Eisenstein's 'montage of attraction', which aimed at destroying the 'illusion' of reality through the collision and discontinuity between the shots.

But what happens to classical Bazinian realism in the post-classical paradigm of narration? The films in my sample appear to prove once again the fundamental quality of 'realism': that it is 'purely conventional and therefore infinitely "corruptible" through repetition' (Elsaesser quoted in Hill 1986: 56). The post-classical films are indeed characterised by a strong realistic motivation but the type of realism that they pursue is entirely different from the classical. Instead of trying to represent reality by means of transparent and seamless images, their search for the real follows the opposite path, the one of hypermediacy. The term 'hypermediacy' is introduced in Jay David Bolter and Robert Grusin's book *Remediation: Understanding New Media* (1999) as a representational logic that opposes the logic of transparent immediacy by privileging fragmentation and heterogeneity and by foregrounding the materiality of representation. As Bolter and Grusin argue:

> If the logic of immediacy leads one either to erase or to render automatic the act of representation, the logic of hypermediacy acknowledges multiple acts of representation and makes them visible. Where immediacy suggests a unified visual space, contemporary hypermediacy offers a heterogeneous space, in which representation is conceived of not as a window on to the world, but as a rather 'windowed' self – with windows that open on to other representations or other media. The logic of hypermediacy multiplies the signs of representation and in this way tries to reproduce the rich sensorium of human experience. (1999: 33–4).

A historical perspective on the concept of hypermediacy would help us understand the lineage of this crucial shift in realistic motivation in the post-classical cinema. According to the authors of *Remediation*, the history of Western art has always been characterised by the tension between the two opposing representational strategies, immediacy and hypermediacy. As they note:

> The logic of immediacy has perhaps been dominant in Western representation, at least from the Renaissance until the coming of modernism, while hypermediacy has often had to content itself with a secondary, if nonetheless important, status ... At the end of the twentieth century, we are in a position to understand hypermediacy as immediacy's opposite number, an alter ego that has never been suppressed fully or for long periods of time. (Ibid.)

From oil painting to computer graphics, the forces of immediacy and hypermediacy have constantly rejuvenated their ongoing battle and created contrasting artistic traditions: from Italian versus Dutch painting to Virtual Reality versus the World Wide Web.[4] It is noteworthy that the logic of hypermediacy acquired a highly elevated status in modernist art around the turn of the twentieth century as a political tool against the classical realist tradition. In the cinematic realm, the modernist agenda was exemplified both in the Soviet filmmaking of the 1920s and the European art cinema of the 1950s and 1960s with works that deliberately broke the transparency of the filmic image and flaunted a high degree of reflexivity.

However, unlike the modernist traditions, the post-classical cinema does not reject the need to capture the real. In fact, it abandons the notion of 'transparent realism' found in classical films for the sake of a 'heightened realism' or what Raymond Durgnat has dubbed 'energy realism': 'what matters, above all, is the headlong, tense, unbroken, "*you are there*" movement of cameras and cast, the confused imbroglio of bodies, gestures, shouted accusations, the sense of mounting spectacle' (quoted in Martin 1992: 2; emphasis added). The pursuit of the real is thus transposed from the unmediated representation to a highly excessive mediation which seeks to 'create a feeling of fullness, a satiety of experience, which can be taken as reality' (Bolter & Grusin 1999: 53).[5]

The hypermediated realism that dominates the narration of the films in this selection is served through various techniques and conventions that defy all the aforementioned principles of the classical realistic motivation in order to reveal the mediated nature of cinematic time and space. If classical filmmaking followed the logic of immediacy by erasing the acts of representation, the post-classical cinema follows the logic of hypermediacy by foregrounding multiple acts of representation in a visible and self-conscious way. The notion of hypermediated realism thus justifies the use of a wide variety of filming techniques, both analogue and digital, to create a multilayered cinematic space and a mediated cinematic time.[6] The technological interventions no longer need to be transparent, as technology is gradually becoming second nature in our current culture and is not considered to be in contradiction with the authenticity of the experience (see Huhtamo 1995: 171). Nowadays, the workings of hypermediacy can serve the need for realistic representation as adequately as immediacy by introducing a new set of conventions and by updating once more the definition of realism.

To illustrate these points, I would like to proceed with the film analyses, starting with Baz Luhrmann's *Moulin Rouge!*, a film that opened at the Cannes Film Festival in 2002 and soon dazzled audiences around the world with its excessive visual style and innovative musical formula. Set in Paris in 1900, it tells the story of Christian (Ewan McGregor), a young British poet who arrives at the Moulin Rouge, the famous French cabaret housed in a windmill in the hilltop Montmartre district. Christian meets Toulouse-Lautrec (John Leguizamo) and his company of bohemian artists and is persuaded to write a play for the Moulin Rouge. As they try to pitch it to the club's owner Harold Zidler (Jim Broadbent), Christian falls in love with the famous courtesan Satine (Nicole Kidman) and a dramatic love affair begins.

The stereotypical story of *Moulin Rouge!*, of a love that only death can tear apart, is told in the most extravagant and hypermediated manner. The visual language of the film is established from the first sequence and remains consistent until the end, creating a view of Paris at the turn of the last century that never existed. As the film's gaffer observes, 'nobody's going to think that we're in Paris, but it looks theatrically real' (quoted in Bosley 2001: 40). The artificiality of the settings, the luscious *mise-en-scène*, the painterly costumes and the excessive colour schemes build up to a lush spectacle that, instead of being historically faithful to the time and place that it describes, aims at constructing a mythical vision of Parisian bohemian life with a very contemporary hypermediated aesthetics.

A careful look at the opening sequence is very enlightening. The film opens with the view of an old theatrical stage with an orchestra. The curtain slowly opens and the 20th Century Fox logo appears as a back projection, followed by a black-and-white early cinema-style intertitle, saying 'Paris, 1900'. The intertitle dissolves in an image composed of nearly visible matte shots that establish the iconography of the story: in the foreground we see Toulouse-Lautrec as the singing narrator of the film, in the middle plane there is the windmill of the Moulin Rouge and in the background there is the Eiffel Tower. When the narrator introduces Christian as the main character, his image appears momentarily in a superimposition on the right side of the frame. This composite image then dissolves into a bird's-eye view of Paris and the camera 'slams-in' to the area of Montmartre, wanders through the streets with frenzied moves, cranes up to Christian's room and finally stops with a close-up on his sad face. Within a few seconds, Luhrmann has thus taken us through the whole history of cinema, from its theatrical origins and early cinema live musical accompaniment to video game-style space navigation and the digitally-generated imagery typical of the latest computer technology. The film thus openly remediates old and new media and it multiplies the visual modalities in an attempt to recreate the energy and the intensity of the story. As the cinematographer, Don McAlpine, testifies about his filming strategies: 'the challenge of shooting a film like *Moulin Rouge!* is the indefinable thing of trying to capture the energy … an attempt to "really" be in there with the energy' (in Bosley 2001: 51).

Equally strong is the hypermediated realism that motivates the choices that Lars von Trier made in *Europa*, which won the Prix de Supérieur Technique and the Prix du Jury at the Cannes Film Festival in 1991. The story portrays the adventures of a young American, Leopold (Jean-Marc Barr), in postwar Germany but the majority of its stylistic features go beyond its compositional needs. The very basic story information is frequently shot in an amazingly complex and unconventional way, employing a large number of technical means in order to create an excessively mediated cinematic reality. In this case, Lars von Trier resorts to some old-fashioned filming methods, as if he were trying to inventory the cinematic techniques available to filmmakers since the emergence of cinema. As the reviewer from *Film Comment* notes:

> Its lexicon of visual artifices – front and back projection, colour and monochrome mixes, surrealist sets, Wellesian shots in which the camera threads the unthreadable – suggests that Von Trier has studied every breakthrough-baroque film from *Citizen Kane* to *Blue Velvet* via *Vertigo*, and refused to tuck their ornate influences tidily away. (Kennedy 1991: 68)

And, indeed, the film skilfully combines front and back projections, superimpositions, miniatures and graphics to build several non-perspectival figurative images. All these traditional cinematic techniques, which were once prevalent in classical filmmaking and were deployed to create a window to the world, are now forming opaque and discontinuous windows that pile up on top of each other. The style no longer pursues a seamless depiction of reality but a cinematic world made up of different planes of representation and modalities.

For instance, one recurring strategy is to place shots in colour in front of a black-and-white back projection. The classicism of the black-and-white creates a feeling of 'pastness' and invokes the cinematic representations of an older era, while the careful mixture with colour veneers it with a fresh dimension. The selective use of coloured planes usually highlights important objects, creates certain contrasts between the characters or suggests moments of passion and tension. More importantly, however, it renders the back projection extremely artificial and emphasises the constructed and layered nature of the moving images.

A similar play regards the classical device of 'staging in depth', which requires the placing of significant objects and figures at distinctly different distances from the camera whether they are in sharp focus or not (see Bordwell 1997: 56). A classical filmmaker like Welles would use deep focus photography and a careful arrangement of characters and objects to create a dense image with sharp differences between foreground/background. This rule of classical realist *mise-en-scène* takes on another shape in the hands of a post-classical director like Von Trier who chooses to generate these distinctions in an entirely hypermediated manner. For instance, there is a shot on the train where the foreground shows the red handle of the emergency brake, the middle plane contains Leopold in black-and-white and the background includes his uncle in the frame. This composite shot is, on the one hand, motivated compositionally, indicating the causal relationship between the characters and the objects, as Leopold will pull the handle despite his uncle's disapproval, while, on the other, it accommodates a strong presence of hypermediated realism. In this case, as in many others, the two types of motivation collaborate and reinforce each other.[7]

Another illustration of hypermediacy is found in *Lola Rennt*, where a rich mixture of technical choices undertakes the depiction of Lola's quest. This film uses animation, video and 35mm film, combined with different rates of fast- and slow-motion, shifting camera angles, split-screens and jump-cuts that seek to visualise the frantic situation. The animation, for instance, is employed right from the credit sequence where we see a redheaded girl running fast against time, smashing the clocks and confronting all the obstacles in her way. Then, once we are in the diegesis, the animation makes a regular appearance in all three episodes in the section that shows Lola's exit from her mother's apartment. When she runs out the door, the camera enters the room where we find the mother talking on the phone. After a masterful 360° Steadicam movement around her, the frame gradually begins to integrate the television screen that is playing nearby in order to show us in a cartoon form Lola's encounter with a punk kid on the staircase. The animated sequence here replaces the live-action without, however, halting the narration. In fact, this particular scene, albeit in a different format, features a key moment in the story that affects the final outcome of the action.

Furthermore, in *Natural Born Killers*, a film about serial crime and violence, psychopaths and media mayhem, hypermediated realism becomes the cornerstone of the entire narration. Oliver Stone rejects classical realism in favour of a heightened reality dictated by the very subject of the film, as he admitted in an interview with Gavin Smith (see 1994: 10). For this purpose, he violently remediates and juxtaposes several television formats, such as sitcoms or news programmes, with various cinematic styles, different film and video stocks, found footage and animation. Like *Moulin Rouge!*, the film introduces us to its hypermediated logic right from the opening sequence, which is shot on a combination of 35mm and high-speed 16mm black-and-white stock, with constantly shifting camera angles and point-of-view shots of spinning bullets and flying knives. As the cinematographer Robert Richardson observes: 'with the first shooting, where the bullet is revolving in front of the camera, you're really jumping off stylistically, and it clearly sets the tone for what will follow. The language has been stated: what you're about to see is not realism' (quoted in Pizello 1994: 41).

The defiance of traditional realism in search of a 'new realism' was also the objective behind the planning and shooting of *City of God*. The cinematographer César Charlone confesses his enthusiasm nearly a year after the completion of the project:

> I'm so in love with this project. I have shot eight other films, and this is the first one in which the main concern was being real, being believable. It goes back to the roots of neorealism, but it's a new realism. We wanted to show this reality as faithfully as we could. (In Oppenheimer 2003: 84)

This avowed concern with realism in this case is satisfied not through the path of immediacy, as was the case with neorealism, but through the creative freedom of hypermediacy that allowed the cinematographer and the two directors to make ample use of fast editing, split-screens, hand-held camera and colour correction in order to emit in each scene what they thought was the 'real' feeling and mood of the action. For instance, the first part, which takes place in the 1960s, is shot with a warm yellow tint that glows with nostalgia about the past. In contrast, the mid-1970s are flooded with colour to indicate the beginning of a hedonistic era when the young teenagers fool around with drugs and enjoy the pleasures of life, such as swimming, partying and racing with bikes. But colour is merely one small fraction of the formal manipulation in this film. The depiction of violence, which is the key theme, takes all possible shapes and forms, from static compositions to frantic tracking shots and from unsteady hand-held camera movements to frenzied cutting. It is through these stylistic devices that the creators strive to fulfil the purpose of 'being real'.

The break from classical realism and the embracing of the logic of hypermediacy in the post-classical narration has had a crucial corollary: an emphasis on 'subjective realism'. Although subjective realism was rather limited in classical Hollywood cinema, it was quite prominent in European art films in the 1950s and 1960s. Bordwell has defined this type of realism as follows:

> This is a fully expressive realism in that the syuzhet can employ film techniques to dramatise private mental processes ... Dreams, memories, hallucinations, daydreams, fantasies and other mental activities can find embodiment in the image or on the soundtrack. (Bordwell 1985: 208)

The extended creative capacities of the new technological tools and the advances in filming practices have considerably reinforced the tendency towards dramatising mental processes and have provided the means to recreate highly subjective and emotional experiences in the most expressive and mannerist way. However, in contrast with the logic and spirit of art cinema, the subjective realism of post-classical films does not aim at ambiguity or introversion; it expresses the need for a heightening of reality and for duplicating the energy and the intensity of real-life experiences. The representation of the psychological states and feelings of the characters is thus significantly hypermediated and excessive, while it remains accessible and coherent for the viewers.

An extreme example of subjective realism is undoubtedly evidenced in *Fight Club*, where the deranged personality of the leading protagonist provides a thematic pretext for the visualisation of the brain processes. When asked about his filming strategy, David Fincher confessed that he wanted to discover a way, in which the camera could illustrate things at the speed of thought (see Smith 1999: 61). The success of his goal is demonstrated right from the opening sequence, which starts from the fear centre of the character's brain showing graphically all the thought processes, the synapses and the transmission of impulses and then moves rapidly to the outer world through his mouth which is blocked by a gun barrel. In the course of the story the image track competes with the character's voice-over commentary, capturing his mental images at the speed of his speech and shifting the shots at a frenzied pace. With the deployment of manifest digital imagery Fincher stretches the boundaries of what can be visualised and broadens the palette of cinematic representation. For instance, after the explosion in his condo the protagonist imagines how the fire could have started according to the police investigations. The image in his mind is visualised digitally showing us how the pilot light of the stove went out, allowing gas to slowly fill the condo over a period of days. When the refrigerator's compressor clicked on, the gas leak caused the enormous explosion and tore everything to pieces. On other occasions, we are shown his fantasies, such as the mid-air collision on the plane, his meditation images, such as the frozen cave with the penguin, or his nightmares. In general, the narration of the film follows the character's stream of consciousness and numerous subjective scenes portray onscreen his fluctuating mental and emotional state.

Requiem for a Dream also contains numerous examples of subjective realism that derives primarily from the theme of human addiction, both to chemical substances and television. The combination of compositional motivation with hypermediated realism causes the narration to display on the screen the subjective experiences of the four main characters through the use of expressionistic camerawork and other flashy techniques. For example, the first sequence features an argument between Harry and his mother Sara in her apartment over the television set. Darren Aronofsky shot the scene with the two protagonists in two different split-screens in order to indicate that they 'were having two completely different subjective experiences of the same event', as he notes in an interview in *American Cinematographer* (see Pizzello 2000: 57). The emphasis on subjective perspective is even more evident in the moments of drug use, when an accelerated series of extreme close-ups of white powder, a lighter, a mixture of substances boiling, the syringe, their arms, the injection, their blood reaction and pupil dilation flash on the screen to signify the excitement and the energy that the drugs fuel into their bodies. Then the pace slows down and their euphoric state is indicated with a white dissolve. In another case, we see the three young characters take their dose and then throw a party, which is shown in a fish-eye distortion in fast-motion signalling again the intensity of their feelings under the influence of drugs. On the other hand, Sara is suffering from loneliness and old age and becomes slowly addicted not only to her favourite television show but also to diet pills which throw her nervous system into complete disarray. Her hallucinations become pervasive in the second half of the film but the most indicative one is when she sees the TV people come to life in her apartment. As she is watching television, she first imagines her idealised self appearing in the show with her red dress and her radiant red hair and being applauded by the audience. However, both she and the host suddenly come out of the screen as electronically distorted phantasms and start to ridicule her. The apartment is gradually transformed into the TV stage where audience and crew revolve frantically around her yelling 'feed me Sara', while she is sitting in her armchair looking horrified. This five-minute-long hallucination ends when the refrigerator bursts open wanting to devour her and she flees from the apartment in a state of shock. The whole scene is staged and filmed in a disturbing way with excessive visuals in order to convey as realistically as possible Sara's state of insanity.

But the emphasis of post-classical cinema on subjective realism goes beyond the case of mentally or psychologically deranged characters. In *Amélie*, for instance, the narration dramatises – with the help of digital imagery – the characters' intense emotional moments and fantasies. When Amélie takes a blind man across the street and gives him a unique tour of the area by spontaneously describing the hustle and bustle of the street, he experiences a feeling of elation indicated by a yellow light glowing around him, as he gazes up at the sky. Moreover, when Amélie meets Nino at the station the first time, the camera penetrates her body and shows us her heart beating quickly. In another scene, when Nino leaves the bar without talking to her, the digital effects transform her into water that drops on the floor, emulating very realistically, albeit metaphorically, her disappointment and despair. The film also depicts a long series of the characters' tricks of their imagination, daydreams and mental images in a hypermediated space. Amélie tends to have fantasies in the form of a black-and-white television programme, as when she watches a documentary of herself as a tragic heroine, in a *Zelig*-like manner.

All things considered, the careful analysis of the 14 films brings to the surface the significant innovation of the post-classical narration in comparison with the classical model. The realistic representation that motivated the Hollywood films belonged to the Bazinian tradition of classical realism, which regarded the screen as a 'window to the world' and required a seamless representation of the story with the use of linear perspective, deep focus cinematography and continuity editing. However, the realistic motivation that motivates the post-classical films is imbued with the logic of hypermediacy that approaches the real by multiplying the planes of representation and intensifying the use of subjective perspectives. This kind of realism tries to recreate the authenticity of the story by using a variety of modalities and 'windows' onto the action and by manipulating the spatial and temporal qualities of the image for a heightening effect. In other words, the post-classical narration does not renounce the importance of the 'real'; what it renounces is the unproblematic and seamless manner that classical Hollywood had used to approach it. In the post-classical mode the real is still an important point of reference but we are asked to access it in a more fragmented and complicated way, through moments of heightened reality, excess and spectacle, through subjective images and experiences that enrich and amplify the representation of reality and our experience of it.

Generic motivation

The third motivation in question concerns the role of genres in the construction of the narration. The generic motivation consists of all those elements that appear on the screen as part of a film's generic identity. Classical Hollywood was undoubtedly a cinema of genres, where generic formulas and conventions regulated the flow of production, in contrast with art cinema where genres were considered as an impediment to artistic creation. Despite the pervasiveness of the generic functions in Hollywood films from the very beginning, the theory of genre made its first steps in the 1960s and remains to date a highly contested theoretical area. A brief mention of the diverse arguments that have been articulated on this topic is an essential prerequisite for evaluating the role of genericity in the post-classical paradigm.

Defining a genre is particularly problematic and many attempts have proven to be unsuccessful. As Boris Tomashevsky observes:

> No firm logical classification of genres is possible. Their demarcation is always historical, that is to say, it is correct only for a specific moment of history; apart from this, they are demarcated by many features at once, and the markers of one genre may be quite different in kind from the markers of another genre and logically they may not exclude one another. (Quoted in Ryall 1998: 328)

The different approaches in genre theory deployed a wide array of strategies in the effort to specify the rules of each genre and to identify the body of conventions that makes, for instance, one film a western and another a musical. One of the starting points was to consider the iconography of the genre as a key differentiating factor for the reason that it builds a consistent generic environment with a stock of conventionalised images. This approach could easily accommodate westerns and gangster films because they both had fairly customary settings, costumes, props and above all familiar stars that built their careers as staple characters in those films (see Ryall 1998: 331). Later on, a more sophisticated account came from Rick Altman with his semantic/ syntactic approach, which aims at a better understanding of genericity by combining the existing theories of genres. More specifically, Altman argued that:

> We can as a whole distinguish between generic definitions that depend on a list of common traits, attitudes, characters, shots, locations and the like ... and definitions that play up instead certain constitutive relationships be-

tween undesignated and variable placeholders ... The semantic approach thus stresses the genre's building blocks, while the syntactic view privileges the structures into which they are arranged ... I maintain that these two categories of generic analysis are complementary, that they can be combined, and in fact that some of the most important questions of genre study can be asked only when they *are* combined. (1999: 634, 636; emphasis in original)

Although Altman attempted to overcome some of the deficiencies of genre theory by pasting together these two broad lines of generic analysis, his approach remains strictly synchronic and, hence, unable to capture the fluid nature of genericity. In a more diachronic method of enquiry, Steve Neale defined genres as 'processes' of systematisation that at once provide regulation and variety, repetition and difference. As he explains:

Each new genre film constitutes an addition to an existing generic corpus and involves a selection from the repertoire of generic elements available at any one point in time ... In this way the elements and conventions of a genre are always *in* play rather than being simply replayed; and any generic corpus is always being expanded. (1995: 170; emphasis in original)

Neale's argument about the process-like nature of genres and the fluidity of generic boundaries is vital for understanding the evolution of genericity throughout film history and for evaluating the role it plays in contemporary filmmaking. By discarding the notion of genres as stable and concrete systems of signification and by bringing in the importance of change and variation, Neale's observations can help us formulate questions about the status of genres today that are theoretically acute and historically aware. For example, the fluid character of the generic qualities and the open-ended development of diverse genres have always had as a corollary the hybidity of many Hollywood films which could be related in various ways to more than one genre. According to Neale:

Hybrids are by no means the rarity in Hollywood many books and articles on genre in the cinema would have us believe ... Moreover, it is at least arguable that many of the most apparently 'pure' and stable genres, both inside and outside the cinema, initially evolved by combining elements from previously discrete and separate genres either within or across specific generic regimes. (1995: 171)

With these important thoughts in mind, the exploration of the qualities of generic motivation in the post-classical narration can overcome some of the common and oversimplifying assumptions about postmodern hybridity that exaggerates the novelties of contemporary filmmaking and implies a radical break with the classical cinema.[8]

Thus, the first overriding observation about the post-classical model is that generic motivation remains a crucial causal factor in its narrative 'infrastructure' and that the variety of generic rules, forms and conventions of the classical Hollywood tradition continue to appear in different configurations in the post-classical films. It seems that all the generic elements that gained prominence and were established in the course of cinematic history are now functioning as a resource pool from which the post-classical filmmakers can choose, depending on their preferences as well as their expressive purposes. In particular, according to the sample analysis, this act of reconfiguring or rearticulating the classical generic aspects seems to follow two separate tendencies in the post-classical narration. Firstly, there are films that employ one or two genres and attempt to revive their most celebrated conventions *across time*. In this case, the filmmakers make an archaeological investigation into the cinematic past of a certain genre, such as film noir or the musical, and then bring together their most distinctive elements, as if desiring to create a generic archetype. On the other hand, there are films that consciously privilege hybridity and build their generic identity with formulas and plots *across genres*. As a result, these films transform the hybridity into a norm of post-classical narration in distinction with the occasional hybrid film that could appear in the classical model.

These qualities of generic motivation in the post-classical narration will be sufficiently illustrated in the film analyses that follow, which I have separated into two sections. The first one contains a more detailed examination of *Europa* and *Moulin Rouge!*, which shows how these two films exemplify the tendency to revive archetypical traits of one or two classical genres, while the second one discusses some of the films that favour selectivity and eclecticism by juxtaposing different and contrasting genres.[9]

The archaeological approach

I would like to begin the investigation of this generic tendency in the post-classical paradigm by focusing on *Europa*, a film that ostensibly flaunts its generic identity. The main genre that dominates its iconography and structure is film noir, the highly stylised genre that developed in Hollywood from the mid-1940s to the early 1950s. If we go through the recurring film techniques that Paul Schrader attributes to this genre, it seems as if Lars von Trier was trying to metamorphose *Europa* into the archetype of film noir. Schrader's list contains the following seven elements:

1. *The majority of scenes are lit for night. One always has the suspicion that if the lights were all suddenly flipped on, the characters would shriek and shrink from the scene like Count Dracula.* In *Europa* all the scenes with no exception are lit for night and there is even one occasion when Leo tries to pull up the curtains to see the daylight but is immediately rebuked by his uncle who pulls them down again, as if he were afraid that they would shrink from the scene.

2. *As in German Expressionism, oblique and vertical lines are preferred to horizontal.* This element is ubiquitous in the *mise-en-scène*, which uses lighting schemes that create odd shapes and oblique lines all across the screen.

3. *The actors and the settings are given equal lighting emphasis.* The *mise-en-scène* demonstrates this principle very emphatically at the dinner party scenes at the Hartmann's house and the train sequences where the lighting often foregrounds objects, lamps and other parts of the décor.

4. *Compositional tension is preferred to physical action.* In *Europa* physical action is very limited and even in violent scenes, like Ravenstein's murder or Hartmann's suicide, the tension results from the choreography of the montage and the complex composition of the images and not from the violent acts themselves.

5. *There seems to be an almost Freudian attachment to water.* Water is a distinctive element in the film as well, not only due to the rain that appears in certain scenes but also on account of the film's two key moments: the suicide scene where the water in the tub very slowly and dramatically floods the bathroom floor and the final scene where the train sinks to the bottom of the sea and Leo slowly drowns.

6. *There is a love of romantic narration. The narration creates a mood of temps perdu: an irretrievable past, a pre-determined fate, and an all-enveloping hopelessness.* Leo's pre-determined fate is increasingly felt as we witness the all-powerful voice-over narrator anticipate every step he makes. Moreover, his passionate relationship with Kate is constantly overshadowed by the tragedy in the Hartmann family and is finally torn apart due to Kate's dark past.

7. *A complex chronological order is frequently used to reinforce the feelings of hopelessness and lost time.* Although the chronological order in *Europa* is rather clear and linear as soon as we enter the diegesis, the feeling of hopelessness becomes pervasive in hindsight, when we realise at the end that the omniscient and omnipotent narrator had taken Leo on a sort of time-travel with a pre-determined fatal ending. (see 1995: 219–21)

Apart from these stylistic elements, however, *Europa* also expresses some of the central themes of classical film noirs, such as disillusionment and fear of the future, while it portrays very faithfully one of the most familiar figures of film noir: the femme fatale. Katharina (Barbara Sukowa) personifies immaculately the 'femme noire, that sultry seductress who preys upon the hero and whose motives and allegiance are in doubt until the film's closing moments' (Schatz 1981: 114). From the beginning of the film Katharina is presented as an enigma and right until the end she remains the unknowable (see Doane 1991: 102).

On the whole, the film blatantly employs most of the characteristics or even the clichés related to film noir, as if trying to build a historical inventory of its traits and then invite them all to a dialogical play. This accumulative strategy towards the generic forms and conventions of the past contrives an additional dimension in the film's generic motivation, which was never part of the film noirs of the classical era or of any other classical genre for that matter.

Along the same lines, *Moulin Rouge!* is a very ambitious attempt to revive the musical and to adapt its long series of plots and conventions to the standards of contemporary experience. As Luhrmann admits, 'we did an archaeological dig through the history of the musical. What we found is that the stories don't change but the way you tell them does' (quoted in Fuller 2001: 16). This 'archaeological dig' materialised on the screen as a film that revels in the rich musical tradition and highlights some of the most celebrated traits of the genre. First and foremost, it adopts the backstage setting that was the most typical feature of the so-called 'backstage musicals' in the 1930s. Like its predecessors, *Moulin Rouge!* fabricates its story around the staging of a show and intertwines it with the 'offstage' conflicts of the performers, which involve courtship, love and rivalry. Moreover, the film casts a group of staple characters, such as the obsessive theatre director (Zidler), the ambitious, talented courtesan (Satine), the inspired writer (Christian) and the villainous, wealthy patron (Duke, played by Richard Roxburgh), whose conflicting attitudes and lifestyles create tension and confusion in the realisation of the show and the fulfilment of the couple's love. The extravagant theatrical space, the rehearsals, the lush musical numbers and the ubiquitous presence of contemporary music infuse the narrative with spectacular energy recreating the atmosphere of a Broadway show or a Busby Berkeley musical. The unravelling of the plotline also follows very familiar steps; the ideal couple in musicals are not usually together in the opening of the film but gradually work their way out of a complex romantic tangle and celebrate their union in the final show (see Schatz 1981: 197). In the end of *Moulin Rouge!* the love of the two protagonists celebrates its victory over all human obstacles and temptations, despite the fact that death remains the final victor.

Aside from the backstage rhetoric, Luhrmann reworks the Orphean myth in a fairy-tale manner and borrows the romantic duets from the operetta tradition, a musical style that was mostly typical of the Ernst Lubitsch and Rouben Mamoulian musicals of the 1930s. Moving up the path of the musical history, the film joins the backstage musicals and operettas together with some of the conventions of the integrated musical from the 1940s. Apart from the musical numbers that are strictly related to the preparation of the show, *Moulin Rouge!* contains songs and dances that are integrated in the narrative in order to convey the characters' motives as well as feelings. For this purpose, many of them are actually medleys composed of carefully edited and modified lyrics that fit to the situation and encapsulate the central concerns of the action. These musical scenes, such as the one with Satine and Christian singing and dancing on top of the elephant, not only continue the flow of the narrative but also humanise the story and its characters (see Kinder 2002: 54).

However, it is important to note that all these musical elements are constantly accompanied and reinforced by the generic conventions of melodrama, another highly popular genre in Hollywood in the late 1940s and 1950s. By extolling the love of its star-crossed lovers, *Moulin Rouge!* employs one of the principal themes of the famous melodramas of that time (see Schatz 1991: 152–5). The stereotypical portrayal of the characters and their relationships results in a melodramatic universe occupied by Manichean conflicts between good and evil, light and darkness (see Williams 1998: 77). The moral dilemmas of Satine, who has to choose between real love and success, and Christian, who must fight against the power of money and fame, are dramatically accentuated and resolved at the last minute with the utter triumph of innocent love. This dramatisation of the emotional and psychological predicaments of the main characters is enhanced by one of melodrama's most memorable aspects – its excessive and baroque style, which sublimates 'dramatic conflict into décor, gesture and composition of frame' (Elsaesser 1991: 76). Additionally, in line with the representations of women in melodramas, Satine tries to prove her strength and heroism by sacrificing herself to save Christian from the Duke's murderous hands and, eventually, atones for her 'sinful' and 'profligate' life by succumbing to her fatal illness (see Creed 1977: 28). Moreover, the role of coincidence and the uneven distribution of knowledge among the characters are the two narrational strategies that regulate the development of the story and contribute to the poignant nature of melodrama (see Neale 1986: 6–7). For example, in the beginning of the film Christian meets Lautrec and his bohemian company of artists by chance, when one of them falls through the ceiling of his hotel room, while, later on, he falls in love with Satine when she mistakes him for the rich Duke. Finally, the key component of melodrama that is celebrated in the film's closing scene is the feeling of 'too late' (see Williams 1998). The sense of loss and human despair in front of the irreversibility of time is what triggers not only Christian's tears as he is holding Satine's dead body in his arms but also the tears in the spectators' eyes.

Overall, *Moulin Rouge!* as a contemporary musical melodrama seems to adopt an archaeological attitude towards the history of the two genres it memorialises. By reshuffling some of their most definitive traits, Luhrmann reminds us that they can remain alive and affective, as long as they are replayed, recycled and reshaped through the updated rules of visual representation and the needs of contemporary sensibility.

The hybrid approach

The majority of films in the sample exhibit a multi-generic construction that contains a hybrid selection of generic qualities that often contradict one another. For instance, Wong Kar-wai's *Chungking Express* combines the crime drama with the romantic comedy, juxtaposing some of their most stereotypical traits in a stark and bewildering manner. Various noir elements such as the glamorous but deadly femme fatale with the raincoat and the sunglasses, the city at night, the killings and the drug deals blend with comic-romantic situations involving canned pineapple, fast food, stolen letters, desperate phone calls to ex-girlfriends, secret visits and chance encounters.

In a similar vein, *The Million Dollar Hotel* is a crime drama or murder mystery with a heavy dose of black humour and satire. The murder, the line of suspects, the hard-boiled detective who is determined to solve the mystery at all costs and the tragic end of the leading character are contrasted with the humourous voice-over commentary and the satire on the media and the art world. It is a film that achieves a delicate balance between the comic side of the story that stems from the eccentricities of the hotel residents and the dark side of their hopeless lives in a derelict place.

An analogous combination is found in *Arizona Dream*, which constantly switches from drama to comedy in a western setting. As the reviewer in *Positif* points out:

> In a *mise-en-scène* of stupefying audacity, he [Kusturica] moulds all the genres of American cinema. *Arizona Dream* adopts the language of what he describes with a staggering skill, which lets us believe that one moment we are in an Arthur Penn western, a Douglas Sirk melodrama or ... a Jerry Lewis comedy. (Bourguignon 1993: 18–19; author's translation)

The film evidently delved into the rich generic pool of classical Hollywood cinema and selectively borrowed competing formulas and conventions, accentuating the vast range of the American genre tradition. In contrast with Luhrmann and Von Trier, who were trying to inventory and rework the historical traits of one or two genres, Kusturica seems to rework various historical elements across diverse genres for the sake of plurality and juxtaposition.

Lastly, the same attitude is manifest in Oliver Stone's *Natural Born Killers* as well as in Tom Tykwer's *Lola Rennt*, as they both combine a wide range of iconographic and plot elements from different genres. The former starts off as a road movie and ends as a thriller with a thick veneer of satire, while the latter contains elements of action movies, lovers-on-the run, gangsters and slapstick comedy combined with a video game logic.[10]

On a concluding note, the analysis of the sample has proven that generic motivation is instrumental in the narrative logic of the post-classical films and the long list of well-established generic qualities from the classical era exert considerable influence on the shape and dynamics of their narration. In that sense, the sample films could easily be classified as 'genre films' similar to their classical Hollywood counterparts. However, a closer look at the genericity of the post-classical paradigm reveals two finer distinctions between the two traditions: firstly, we trace a penchant for memorialising a specific genre through an archaeological investigation into the diverse norms and formulas that emerged in the course of its history, and, secondly, we also evidence an increased tendency towards hybrid and multi-generic films, which combine competing generic formulas playing off against each other.

Artistic motivation

The last type of motivation that can influence the shape of a filmic narration is the artistic motivation, which justifies the presence of a component 'by its power to call attention to the system within which it operates' (Bordwell *et al.* 1985: 21). This formal strategy is also called 'laying bare the device', indicating its intention to expose its own principles of construction. The use of techniques and forms that challenge the 'invisible' and 'transparent' mode of representation was by definition inimical to the classical Hollywood model which, as I previously emphasised, was dominated by a Bazinian notion of realism that excluded any obtrusive technical intervention on the part of the filmmaker. As a result, the presence of artistic motivation was quite limited in the classical tradition and it could only be employed momentarily and restrictedly, unlike in other cinematic modes, such as art cinema or the historical-materialist mode, where it systematically offered its services to the filmmakers' artistic or ideological agendas (see Bordwell *et al.* 1985: 23).

In the case of the post-classical paradigm, I would like to make an important clarification. As I previously argued, the post-classical narration relies
on a type of realistic motivation that entails a break with the seamless Hollywood representation and invites a multilayered cinematic space and a highly
mediated time that both unveil the means of their own construction. The reason I chose to classify these formal strategies as part of a 'realistic' and not an
'artistic' motivation is because the strategy of 'laying bare the device' acquires
a different function in the post-classical cinema from the one it had served
within the art cinema or modernist tradition. In contemporary media, and by
extension in contemporary cinematic practices, the self-reflexive devices that
create a discontinuous and self-conscious act of representation have become
normalised mainstream conventions, which, instead of serving a radical rupture with classical realism, strive to capture the real in new terms.

Yet, 'artistic motivation' is indeed valuable in the framework of the post-
classical cinema not because it can explain some of the technical options in
the films that 'lay bare the device', but because it can accommodate a particular self-reflexive device, the practice of parody, which constitutes one of
the main motivational factors in the post-classical narration. Before looking
at the films, I consider it indispensable to explain what I mean by the term
'parody' by comparing and contrasting some of the most prominent writings
on the topic. Thus, I will try to clarify some of the misconceptions about the
term that have been responsible for its either ambiguous or gratuitous use in
recent film theory and criticism.

First and foremost, I would like to begin with Linda Hutcheon's theory of
parody that, despite drawing mostly on literature and occasionally architecture, remains particularly popular and reliable. According to Hutcheon:

> The collective weight of parodic *practice* suggests a redefinition of parody as
> repetition with critical distance that allows ironic signaling of difference at the
> very heart of similarity. In historiographic metafiction, in film, in painting, in
> music and in architecture, this parody paradoxically enacts both change and
> cultural continuity: the Greek prefix *para* can mean both 'counter' or 'against'
> and 'near' or 'beside'. (1988: 26; emphasis in original)

If we adapt this definition to the cinematic realm, we could argue that parody is the strategy of evoking, recalling and rewriting forms and conventions
from cinematic history in order to establish an artistic dialogue with historical and influential art-works. This parodic dialogue between old and new elements depends on the notion of 'repetition with a difference' and results both
in the critical re-evaluation of old cinematic traditions and in the double-
layering of meaning in the new work. For the purposes of this investigation

of the formal parameters of the post-classical cinema, I would like to clarify that parody should be approached as a *process* or *practice* that bears specific formal and structural characteristics, which create an involvement with and distance from a certain text with ironic or estrangement effects. The reason I raise this point with emphasis is because various theorists have examined parody as a separate genre or often as a sub-genre of comedy, limiting thus the significance and the multiplicity of its functions. For instance, Wes Gehring claims that parody is an American genre that, like other 'comedy approaches', has the fundamental goal of being funny and therefore does not have a determinate time and space (see 1999: 2–3). Despite the fact that he makes some useful observations on the topic, the contextualisation of parody as yet another standard American genre obscures its multifaceted functions in contemporary international filmmaking.

A different take is found in Dan Harries' book *Film Parody* (2000), which presents a thorough theoretical account of how parody operates on textual, pragmatic and socio-cultural levels. By reviewing the writings of the Russian Formalists on the subject and by relying on Linda Hutcheon and Margaret Rose's theories of parody, Harries makes an insightful approach by treating parody as a 'discursive mode'. As he notes:

> For these reasons, I prefer to describe film parody not so much as a 'meta-genre', or conversely, as a textual anti-genre, but rather as a discursive *mode*. This perspective more clearly aims at the *functions* of parody rather than any specific content or thematic. Employing a range of ironic, 'disrupting' techniques, parody therefore becomes more of a methodic 'approach' to re-contextualising target texts and canons than a particular type text. (2000: 7; emphasis in original)

The problem with Harries, unfortunately, is that in order to explore this discursive mode, he resorts to genre theory and its concepts, such as the lexicon, the syntax and the style. He argues that the parodic activity through six different strategies – reiteration, inversion, misdirection, literalisation, extraneous inclusion and exaggeration – aims at transforming these three basic components of each genre film and generates in that way the desired 'difference through repetition'. After a systematic analysis of these diverse formal techniques, he concludes that 'film parody has created a formulaic means to generate its discourse in a standardised fashion' (2000: 37).

Although I consider Harries' theoretical framework, and especially his starting point, to be in the right direction, I have strong objections to his selection of films and, inevitably, to the conclusions he draws from them. It seems that he tried to circumvent the danger of turning parody into another film genre and, yet, his body of films and the consequent analyses led him back to the exact same place as with Gehring. The wrong turn occurred in his attempt to characterise and classify the particular works as 'film parodies' in their entirety, instead of tracing parodic 'moments' and 'relations' in a wider range of films that employ parody in a more subtle and selective manner and, above all, that do not necessarily belong to the category of comedy. Parodic discourses may present the possibility of laughter but the comic elements are not an essential prerequisite. As Gary Saul Morson argues, 'parody recontextualises its object so as to make it serve tasks contrary to its original tasks, but this functional shift need not be in the direction of humour' (1989: 69). By limiting his sample to the films that use parody as an end in itself and even market themselves as 'parodies' to signify a certain type of comedy, Harries inexorably restricts the applicability of his framework and downplays the nuances of the parodic elements in a far wider range of contemporary films.

On the other hand, an all-encompassing perspective is exemplified in Noël Carroll's account of 'allusionism', a term he coined to describe the various ways in which a film can make cinematic references and create this play of 'repetition with a difference'.[11] In the article 'The future of allusion: Hollywood in the seventies (and beyond)', Carroll defines allusionism as follows:

> An umbrella term covering a mixed lot of practices including quotations, the memorialisation of past genres, the reworking of past genres, *homages*, and the recreation of 'classic' scenes, shots, plot motifs, lines of dialogue, themes, gestures, and so forth from film history, especially as that history was crystallised and codified in the sixties and early seventies. (1998: 241)

His analysis exemplifies different kinds of allusion with the close examination of films as diverse as Altman's *McCabe and Mrs. Miller* (1971), Coppola's *The Conversation*, Scorsese's *New York, New York* (1977), Wenders' *American Friend* (1977), Werner Herzog's *Nosferatu* (1979), De Palma's *Blow Out* (1981) and Kasdan's *Body Heat*. Carroll's account is valuable not only for its inventory of various strategies of allusion but also for providing us with a point in history – the 1970s – when this tendency became more and more pervasive. Although parody is a very old artistic practice, in cinema it became systematically employed only when film history and theory were sufficiently developed and a canon of films and filmmakers was formed. From that point onwards, the rich history of cinema would provide an enormous depository of cinematic codes, models, stars and auteurs that younger generations could allude to in order to create repetition with a difference and to generate meaning through a dialogue with the past.

Finally, I would like to refer to the distinction between parody and pastiche. In principle, the main difference between the two intertextual practices lies not in the form but in the intention, mood and tone. On the one hand, parody aims at creating a critical distance and irony through the transformation of a prototext, whereas pastiche imitates for the sake of mere imitation by generating more similarity than difference (see Harries 2000: 31). The fact that this distinction is based on subtle and intangible notions, such as mood and tone, or on degrees of similarity and difference, results in a discrepancy among theorists about whether certain works offer parody or pastiche, with the opposition between Hutcheon and Jameson regarding postmodern art as the quintessential example (see Hutcheon 1988: 26–7). Things become even more complicated when more recent books, such as Ingeborg Hoesterey's *Pastiche: Cultural Memory in Art, Film, Literature* (2001), criticise Jameson's condemnation of pastiche and mount a defence of this formal device as a self-reflexive and critical tool of postmodern cinema. Whether parody and pastiche gradually end up – rightly or not – as synonyms is something I cannot anticipate. In this book, I will favour the concept of parody as a primarily textual practice and steer clear of its potential ideological implications. With these theoretical explanations in mind, I will continue with three film analyses that underline the prevalence of parody in the post-classical cinema as a part of the artistic motivation that foregrounds its filmic texture and acknowledges its historicity.

Europa

Europa takes us back to Germany after World War Two and depicts the story of Leopold, an idealistic young American of German origin who gets a job as a sleeping-car conductor in the German railway company 'Zentropa' in order to participate in the country's reconstruction. During his rather short stay there he experiences the grim situation in Germany and finds himself trapped in an ongoing battle between the American occupiers and the 'Werewolves', a partisan group of ex-Nazis who resist the occupying forces. Slowly, he falls victim to his innocence and, eventually, he sabotages the train that would plunge himself and hundreds of people into death.

The film's thematic concerns and the choice of black-and-white cinematography allude to the numerous films that have represented this key historical moment and have shaped our collective memory. Roberto Rossellini's *Germania Anno Zero* (*Germany Year Zero*, 1947), among others, is an important reference point, since it also portrays the plight of the German people in their zero year following the collapse of the Third Reich. Amid the rubble of Berlin, a 12-year-old boy called Edmund, who struggles to survive and support his family, falls prey to the surrounding madness as he is not old, wise or strong enough for the tasks that the conditions force upon him. Like Leopold, his innocence is marred in a horrifying way: an ex-Nazi seduces him and convinces him to kill his father because he is a burden to the family. When Edmund realises the gravity of his crime he kills himself to put an end to his misery. The atmosphere of insanity, corruption, fear and despair is shared in both films as they portray the trajectory of two similar characters being eliminated in the end by the same work of opposing forces which fight for survival in a derelict country.

The departure, however, from Rossellini's film – and from all other representations of this war – lies in Von Trier's excessive and self-reflexive visual style. Where neorealism used documentary-like immediacy, *Europa* uses extreme stylisation that creates a critical distance from all the events depicted in the story. The images of the ruins and the rubble in the dark-lit streets, as well as the dilapidated interior settings, are constructed to convey the feeling of decay that rules the lives of the characters and deliberately refer us to the dark, stylised and unrealistic *mise-en-scène* of German Expressionism.

What is also interesting in the film's parodic play with cinematic history is its conception of character. In contrast to the classical tradition that relies on the construction of the protagonists as unique individuals, Lars von Trier moulds them as social types defined by a specific environment and a historical condition. By constantly drawing attention to their formulaic typicality, he produces an estrangement effect that prevents them from functioning as suturing agents.[12] For instance, Leo is a young idealist who wants to contribute to the 'rebirth' of a devastated country. He is innocent and naïve and gets caught in the implications of a serious social and political battle. Katharina is the archetypal duplicitous femme fatale, who first seduces Leo, then falls for him and finally betrays him. Leo's uncle, Herr Kessler (Ernst-Hugo Järegard) is the typical obedient and servile person who always abides by the rules and wants to stay out of trouble. For Uncle Kessler 'humility' is the key to the world and his only refuge is to drink secretly, locked in his compartment. Max Hartmann (Jørgen Reenberg) is the corrupted entrepreneur who offered his services to the Nazis by carrying Jews in his trains. He is now collaborating with the Americans but he cannot bear the burden of his guilty past and commits suicide. Katharina's brother, Lawrence (Udo Kier), is the leftist homosexual intellectual who condemns the war and the corruption of both sides. Colonel Harris is the representative of the American occupiers who personifies their opportunistic behaviour as well as their distorted notion of ethics. Finally, the two examiners who chase Leo to test him for his competence in the midst of the dramatic events on the train not only stand for bureaucracy and absurdity as a remnant of the Nazi enterprise but also allude to Franz Kafka's stories that often manifest 'a surreal textuality in which the ordinary slips seamlessly into the extraordinary' (Hoesterey 2001: 59). As Hoesterey comments on the scene:

> the exceedingly banal examinations to which [Leo] Kessler is subjected are hilariously grotesque. 'Your problem is not important', Kessler, in real trouble, screams at his examiners, reminding readers of *The Trial* of a moment in the cathedral when the chaplain admonishes K.: 'Forget such irrelevancies'. (Ibid.)

With such character delineation *Europa* could be regarded as a collection or even a recollection of cinematic stereotypes, represented with remarkable precision in an attempt to memorialise the cinematic past. According to Von Trier, even the faces of the actors seem familiar to us and carry the trace of a certain history, even if we don't know it (see Danton *et al.* 1991: 37).

In addition, various reviewers have traced references to Hitchcock's thrillers and train films like *The Lady Vanishes* (1938), *Strangers on a Train* (1951) and *North by Northwest* (1959), while Von Trier admits his allusions to *Vertigo* (1958) mostly through the musical theme, which is a variation of Bernard Herrmann's musical score. Finally, Orson Welles' play with the filming techniques, and especially *Citizen Kane*'s encyclopaedic technical range and flamboyant visual effects, seem to be an important source of inspiration for the film. Yet, instead of depth of focus and concealed back projections, *Europa* creates the 'ironic signalling of difference at the very heart of similarity' by revealing the seams of the filmic image and playing with their artificiality.

On the whole, the tendency of the post-classical filmmakers to borrow elements from other films and to motivate their stories parodically is illustrated in Von Trier's following statement:

> I steal a lot of things from the cinematic past for making my films. Stealing from cinema is for me like using the letters of the alphabet when writing. I have to look for the elements that will help express myself and these elements are the clichés. (In Danton *et al.* 1991: 38; author's translation)

Natural Born Killers

Oliver Stone's film features the killing sprees of the murderous couple Mickey and Mallory as they drive across America, imitating the famous *Badlands/ Bonnie and Clyde/Gun Crazy* plotline. The misadventures of Mickey and Mallory as outcasts, lovers and serial killers function as a pretext for the film's fierce critique of contemporary culture and the narration employs different visual styles and formats to parody various modes of representation from the history of film and television.

Firstly, one of the most prominent parodic sections in the film is Mallory's flashback, which takes us back to the day she met Mickey. This flashback constitutes a quite distinct segment in the plot, as it is shot entirely in a TV sitcom format and is bound both by opening and closing credits. Its title *I Love Mallory* appears on the screen, as a rather blatant allusion to *I Love Lucy* (1951–57), while the tacky décor of the setting and the nuclear family life that is depicted refer us to numerous American sitcoms, but above all to *Married with Children*. Stone is creating a parody of the sitcom tradition by exaggerating and twisting their basic formulas and conventions. Mallory lives with her parents and her younger brother but life in this family is a nightmare, since her father rapes her with the tolerance of her mother who tries to maintain the 'happy family' façade. The caricature of the family is magnified by the laugh track, which accompanies her father's abusive behaviour and her mother's shallow and imbecilic remarks. The style of this section tries to imitate the look of television by reducing the camera movement and duplicating the traditional TV shots and angles, which accentuate the movement of the characters and their interactions. The television effect is at its most extreme when we see a break for commercials, including a whole Coca Cola spot.

But that is still only the beginning. After this self-contained flashback, Oliver Stone both literally and metaphorically changes the channel to show us the murderous action of Mickey and Mallory that ensues following their meeting in the sitcom. This time we follow the story through the images of a TV magazine show, called *American Maniacs*, which has a special report on the couple. Again, after the credits of the show, we hear the host's stilted commentary accompanied by interviews with people and friends of the victims, black-and-white blow-ups of 'police file photos' and of course a kitschy dramatised restaging of a murder, so common in sensationalistic television shows like *America's Most Wanted* (1988–present) (see Pizzello 1994: 45).

However, television is not the only target of the film's parodic spirit. The overabundance of images derived from different sources, formats and modalities and the bricolage aesthetics of certain scenes refer us to the American avant-garde cinema of the 1960s and to films as diverse as *Scorpio Rising* (1964) and *Berlin Horse* (1970). The allusions to avant-garde experiments are particularly prominent in the sequence in the hotel room where Mickey and Mallory have a fight. The room becomes a surreal setting where different surfaces function as screens for projection. Mickey is zapping on the TV allowing the procession of shots from old films, commercials, cartoons and news programmes while at the same time the window behind him becomes another screen where all sorts of found footage flickers in a back projection.

This extensive use of found images from stock libraries is motivated artistically as a parodic activity that alludes to compilation/collage films while it reframes them in the overall narrative context.

Arizona Dream

Arizona Dream not only embodies a 'European' version of the American Dream, to which the title alludes, but also expresses a candid fascination with the American landscape, both the natural and the cinematic. The film opens in New York, the most popular cosmopolitan American city, and moves to the south where the hustle and bustle of the busy streets gives way to the vast open spaces and small cities of Arizona. The American iconography is also evoked in the selection of the settings, especially the two houses. On the one hand, Leo's pink-painted house is representative of the kitschy style that Europeans consider typical of American taste whereas, on the other, Elaine's country house is reminiscent of scenery in a western, a quintessentially American genre.

The story world is inhabited by characters that oscillate between their fictional identity and the actors' star personas and take part in situations that constantly duplicate famous scenes from classical Hollywood films. For example, Paul Blackmar is a struggling actor who builds his personality by imitating his favourite Hollywood actors. He fakes Al Pacino's New York accent, he expresses himself through the lines of his favourite films and spends most of his time acting out several of their scenes. There is even a moment in the film when he mentions in front of his cousin Axel his admiration for Johnny Depp, creating a very self-referential moment since Axel *is* played by Johnny Depp. Moreover, Leo's character borrows aspects from Jerry Lewis's star persona and his well-known career as a comedian. Despite the fact that he plays a middle-aged car salesman in crisis, there are moments where the narration capitalises on Lewis's comic personality by having him perform tricks and gags in some old home-movies or sell cars using his comic grimaces and gestures.

The parodic references to Hollywood stars are also accompanied by the quotation and restaging of some classic scenes from Hitchcock's *North by Northwest*, Coppola's *The Godfather Part II* (1974) and Scorsese's *Raging Bull* (1980). Paul is fascinated with all three films, he knows all their dialogue by heart and rehearses them at every chance he gets. First, he goes to the cinema to see *Raging Bull* and jumps onstage to play Robert De Niro's part in the quarrel scene with his brother, which also foreshadows the quarrel scene between himself and Axel that follows. Later on, he performs the crop-dusting sequence from *North by Northwest* in a local talent night, and then he duplicates the experience when Elaine chases him with her new plane. Finally, Paul watches *The Godfather Part II* the night that Grace kills herself and, in a way, the particular scene featuring an imminent family tragedy – Pacino's Michael having his brother murdered – prepares us for the other tragedy that is about to occur in the story world. Apart from the allusions that are related to Paul's character, it is important to note that the entire film is punctuated from start to finish by a dream sequence that appears at regular intervals and overtly alludes to Robert Flaherty's historic documentary *Nanook of the North* (1912).

As a whole, it seems that Kusturica has based his own version of the American Dream on a parodic and playful dialogue with classic moments and stars of Hollywood, the quintessential American dream factory. The narration of the film incorporates cinematic representations of the Golden Age and transforms them into an inseparable part of the characters' identities and actions. Thus, parodic motivation becomes here, just as in the previous case studies, a fundamental principle in the constructional logic of the film and is elevated to a key feature in the post-classical narrative model.

POST-CLASSICAL SPACE:
THE CINEMATIC SPACE AND ITS
DIFFERENT ARTICULATIONS

'Space exists only at twenty-four frames per second'
(Edward Branigan in Heath 1986: 389)

In his famous essay 'Narrative Space', Stephen Heath provides a thorough account of the parameters that determine the construction of space in the cinematic medium and the different functions that the narrative acquires in relation to the filmic space. He explains that the study of space in the cinema can be roughly divided into two parts: firstly, the examination of the space 'in frame', of the space that is held and organised within each frame, and secondly, the examination of the space 'out of frame', of the space that is created by the editing of the shots or the camera movements and its reframings (1986: 390). These two distinct dimensions of the cinematic space are constantly welded together in order to serve the process of narrativisation, which is the need, on the one hand, to turn space into place and, on the other, to endow this place with continuity, coherence and unity. As he observes:

> The classical *economy* of film is its organisation thus as organic unity and the *form* of that economy is narrative, the *narrativisation* of the film ... The narration is to be held on the narrated, the enunciation on the enounced; filmic procedures are to be held as narrative instances (very much as 'cues'), exhaustively, without gap or contradiction. (1986: 397; emphasis in original)

Of course, Heath refers specifically to the classical narrative where the cinematic space makes indeed a wholesale commitment to the development of a story without 'gaps or contradictions'. This commitment, however, should not be regarded as a prerequisite for the cinematic space in general but, instead, it should be treated merely as a particular historical option that was favoured within a particular cinematic tradition, namely the classical Hollywood cinema. As David Bordwell explains:

> In making narrative causality the dominant system in the film's total form, the classical Hollywood cinema chooses to subordinate space. Most obviously, the classical style makes the sheerly graphic space of the film image a vehicle for narrative. (Bordwell *et al.* 1985: 50)

This transformation of the 'sheerly graphic' space of the frame into a story space that accommodates the actions of certain individuals is achieved through a set of technical and stylistic devices that crystallised during the studio years and became so pervasive that people often tend to regard them as natural. The classical spatial system offers the filmmakers an unsparing range of options for manipulating the space 'in' and 'out of frame' and for generating the illusion of reality in the classical realist sense.

Firstly, at the level of the image composition, the classical shot accentuates the centrality of the human body in the filmic space, reflecting the position of the human agent in the centre of the narrative. This central positioning is consistently maintained with the help of the camera, which pans or tilts to follow figure movements, or with the use of frame-cutting, which accommodates the entrances of the characters into new story spaces. Moreover, the classical film has specific rules for placing bodies in front of the camera and for approaching the action in a frontal position. For example, the characters can face each other directly with their heads but not with their bodies, or they cannot turn their back to the camera, unless a gesture bears a particular narrative significance. Furthermore, the classical image is founded on the representation of depth that aims at converting the flat screen into a plate-glass window. This impression of depth is created by the meticulous arrangement of the character movements, the colours, the textures, the make-up, the selection of lenses and, above all, the lighting schemes (see Bordwell *et al.* 1985: 50–5).

The same meticulous attention is given to the construction of the space 'out of frame', which results from the joining of the separate frames. When it comes to this spatial dimension, the commitment of Hollywood cinema to classical realism is facilitated by the use of 'continuity editing', an editing style whose primary purpose is to ensure the smooth transition from shot to shot and to prevent the disruption of the narrative action. A sum of practical devices, such as the 180° system, the analytical cutting and the shot/reverse-shot pattern,[1] were established in classical filmmaking practice thanks to their ability to portray action unobtrusively (see Bordwell *et al.* 1985: 55–8).

If we examine all the aforementioned spatial qualities of the classical film in terms of the motivations that we encountered in the previous chapter, we can begin to realise how the two systems – causality and space – become related. In the classical paradigm, the two dimensions of the classical spatial system, the image composition and the editing, work consistently to subordinate space to the compositional and realistic motivations. The compositional motivation requires the prominence of the story information, character development and the centrality of the action, while classical realism begs for an 'ideal' positioning of the viewer in front of a plate-glass window to the fictional world. The dominance of these two types of motivation in the Hollywood cinema has forced the classical space to mask the careful planning behind the seemingly neutral and invisible classical staging and continuity editing.

However, what happens to the spatial system of the sample films when their narrative motivations are reconfigured in the ways indicated in chapter one? What are the specific transformations that their spatial features undergo when hypermediated realism and parody become priorities and the narration no longer needs to be transparent? In the following part I will present an overview of the issues that arise in regard to the spatial formations in the new paradigm and then I will proceed with a number of case studies.

The post-classical shift: from photographic to graphic spaces

According to the sample analysis, the system of narrative space in the post-classical paradigm manifests some considerable divergences from the classical mode. One of the new formal changes evidenced in this domain is the use of 'intensified continuity'. Paradoxically enough, the term was coined by Bordwell who was the first to detect and record a set of new stylistic techniques in the article entitled 'Intensified Continuity: Visual Style in Contemporary American Film'.[2] Adhering to the typical Bordwellian research methods, the article traces four innovative technical options based on the extensive analysis of a large body of contemporary American films from the last four decades. Although Bordwell still aims to prove that the classical paradigm is in place, he makes the following statement:

> Still, there have been some significant stylistic changes over the last 40 years. The crucial technical devices aren't brand new – many go back to the silent cinema – but recently they've become very salient, and they've been blended into a fairly distinct style. Far from rejecting traditional continuity in the name of fragmentation and incoherence, the new style amounts to an intensification of established techniques. Intensified continuity is traditional continuity

amped up, raised to a higher pitch of emphasis. It is the dominant style of American mass-audience films today. (2002b: 16)

The fact that this 'fairly distinct' style of intensified continuity does not negate the traditional continuity supplies sufficient evidence for Bordwell to deny once more the existence of a post-classical cinema. And undoubtedly, this is a tricky argument, given that the majority of American films that he analyses are indeed fairly classical and largely comply with the classical rules of storytelling. On the other hand, his claim becomes rather speculative when he argues about the international baseline of the new trend:

> More broadly, intensified continuity has become a touchstone for the popular cinema of other countries. The new style was a boon for marginal filmmaking nations; close-ups, fast cutting, sinuous hand-held camera moves, long lenses on location, and scenes built out of singles were friendly to small budgets ... It is now the baseline style for both international mass-market cinema and a sizable fraction of exportable 'art cinema'. (2002b: 21–2)

This expansive attitude begins to blur the scope of intensified continuity and its influence in the filmmaking process. I believe that the stylistic options that fall under the umbrella of this new term are too limited in themselves to prove either the persistence of the classical or the emergence of the post-classical.[3] These are merely technical devices that could be easily incorporated in different cinematic traditions, ranging from Hollywood blockbusters to international art films, without determining in a definitive manner whether there is an entire paradigm shift or not. In the case of the post-classical model, the use of intensified continuity appears to be an integral part of the new spatial system that collaborates resourcefully with the post-classical motivations that we have examined so far and the post-classical time that I will discuss in the next chapter. To assess its role in the overall post-classical structure, however, we will have to look more closely to what intensified continuity actually consists of.

The first important change that this new type of continuity has on the look of the films regards the rapid editing pace reflected in the drastic diminution of the Average Shot Length (ASL).[4] While the ASL of a Hollywood film from the period 1930–1960 ranged from eight to eleven seconds, the typical feature today is likely to have an ASL of between three to six seconds.[5] The significance of this modification, however, should be neither overstated nor understated; as a standard characteristic of current filmmaking, the fast cutting rate has not replaced the spatial continuity with visual incoherence and disorientation, as many would have expected. On the other hand, it has led to an elliptical type of editing which eliminates many of the redundancies of classical continuity, such as the many establishing shots and the long two-shots.

The second aspect of this new style is the extensive use of extreme lens lengths. The short (wide-angle) lenses became a popular option amongst young filmmakers in the 1970s, not only as a result of their ability to film expansive establishing shots and bizarre close-ups but also their typical distorting effects, such as the warping on the frame edges and the amplification of distances between the front and back planes. Alternatively, the long (telephoto) lenses with their documentary-like immediacy and the stylised flattening of the screen space were transformed into an 'all-purpose tool, available to frame close-ups, medium shots, over-the-shoulder shots, and even establishing shots' (Bordwell 2002b: 18). The two stylistic devices that were favoured by the combination of the extreme lens lengths were the 'wipe-by' cut and the rack-focus. Instead of the classical deep staging and deep focus cinematography, the filmmakers now employ them as an easy way to shift focus and distance either from shot to shot or within the same shot.

The closer framing of dialogue scenes is the third characteristic of intensified continuity that Bordwell identifies. This paradigm privileges the use of 'singles' that contain in a medium or close-up shot only one person at a time and allow the surroundings to take up the rest of the frame, thus obliterating the need for establishing and re-establishing shots. Moreover, as far as shot scales are concerned the choices have become rather limited; with the abandonment of the *plans américains* and group framings, the filmmakers choose from the range of medium shots to extreme close-ups.

All the above stylistic options are combined with and reinforced by the powerful free-ranging camera movements. It has become a rule that when there is a long take the camera needs to move fluidly in the filmic space. Thanks to lighter filming equipment and flexible cameras, it is common to follow the movement of the characters in all possible places (corridors, staircases, streets and so forth). Whereas the classical spatial system reserved ostentatious camera movements for highlighting the points of dramatic action, the intensification of classical continuity has turned the grandiose crane shots of Orson Welles into a staple of current cinematography. Moreover, the standard shot/reverse-shot pattern is often replaced by dynamic push-ins and pull-outs that emphasise the characters' emotional reactions, while an arcing camera is the most recurrent device in group gathering scenes.

The qualities of intensified continuity are fairly widespread in the sample films but their presence is far from gratuitous. Given that the post-classical paradigm puts an enormous emphasis on hypermediated realism in its attempt to capture the energy of the action and shatter the transparency of the image, the strong expressive power of the camera movements, the fast cutting pace and the contrasting lens lengths become indispensable tools for the new narrative needs of the post-classical narration. The powerful expressive qualities of this new continuity did not escape Bordwell's attention either:

> Intensified continuity represents a significant shift within the history of mov-iemaking. Most evidently, the style aims to generate a keen moment-by-mo-ment anticipation. Techniques which 1940s directors reserved for moments of shock and suspense are the stuff of normal scenes today ... Here is another reason to call it intensified continuity: even ordinary scenes are heightened to compel attention and sharpen emotional resonance. (2002b: 24)

However, the need for hypermediacy, which is so important for the post-clas-sical model, as demonstrated in the previous chapter, is only partly satisfied by intensified continuity. The post-classical spatial system, in fact, proceeds with a much more radical transformation by shifting the emphasis from the photographic to the graphic qualities of the cinematic image. This important shift in visual representation has been articulately theorised in Lev Manov-ich's writings on the 'new language of cinema'. In the book *The Language of New Media* (2001) Manovich takes up a two-fold task: on the one hand he seeks to define and scrutinise the characteristics of the new media in close relation to the cinematic medium and its intrinsic mode of representation, while, on the other, he wants to trace or even anticipate the strong influence of digital technology and computerised representation on the cinematic lan-guage of the present and the future. The second dimension of his project is worth discussing in more detail, as it reveals the underlying philosophy of the post-classical spatial construction.

First and foremost, Manovich's main argument claims that the advent of digital technology imposed a distinct logic to moving images by subordinat-ing the photographic and cinematic qualities to a painterly and graphic spirit. Whereas traditional cinema emphasised its recording capacity by using live-action footage and representing space realistically with the help of continuity editing, digital techniques re-established the features of the rather marginal practice of animation. As he notes:

> The opposition between the styles of animation and cinema defined the culture of the moving image in the twentieth century. Animation foregrounds its artificial character, openly admitting that its images are mere representations. Its visual language is more aligned to the graphic than to the photographic. (2001: 298)

All the technical devices and special effects that were central to animations, such as back projections, matte paintings, miniatures and optical tricks remained peripheral to mainstream filmmaking for fear that they could reveal the constructedness of the moving image and thus contradict the principles of classical realist representation. However, the dominance of computer logic and the abundant use of digital tools in the 1990s brought all these elements back into the limelight and shaped the characteristics of what Manovich calls 'digital cinema'. The principles of this new type of cinema are summarised as follows:

> Live-action footage is now only raw material to be manipulated by hand – animated, combined with 3-D computer-generated images, and painted over. The final stages are constructed manually from different elements, and all the elements are either created entirely from scratch or modified by hand. Now we can finally answer the question 'What is digital cinema?' *Digital cinema is a particular case of animation that uses live-action footage as one of its many elements.* (2001: 302; emphasis in original)

Apart from animation, Manovich acknowledges that digital cinema is strongly affiliated with another marginal tradition, the avant-garde filmmaking practice of the twentieth century. The avant-garde artists had developed various experimental strategies, like collage, painting, scratching and wild juxtapositions of images or text within a single frame. All these revolutionary processes have been 'appropriated' by digital technology and have become common everyday functions of film editing software. And he concludes: 'All in all, what used to be exceptions from traditional cinema have become the normal, intended techniques of digital filmmaking, embedded in technology design itself' (2001: 307).

The key aspect of digital cinema is its preoccupation with the spatial dimensions of the moving image, in contrast to the traditional film practice that favoured the temporal articulations of the cinematic medium. The technique of digital compositing provides numerous spatial possibilities for digital moving images that so far remain unexploited by mainstream Hollywood cinema. Manovich indicates that commercial narrative cinema is still dependent on the classical realistic mode of representation and subordinates the digital tools to the need for invisible effects that create transparency and not hyper-mediacy.[6] However, the power of digital cinema lies elsewhere; as an alternative to the classical temporal montage, the properties of the computer screen have paved the way for a new type of 'spatial montage', defined as follows:

> In general, spatial montage could involve a number of images, potentially of different sizes and proportions, appearing on the screen at the same time. The juxtaposition by itself of course does not result in montage; it is up to the filmmaker to construct a logic that determines which images appear together,

when they appear, and what kind of relationships they enter into with one another. (Manovich 2001: 322)

The spatial montage breaks the logic of one image/one screen and introduces the logic of addition and coexistence, allowing a number of 'texts' to appear simultaneously on the surface of the screen and compete for prominence.[7] Manovich further distinguishes two types of spatial montage based on compositing: the 'ontological' and the 'stylistic'. The former allows incompatible elements to coexist within the same time and space, while the latter facilitates the merging of different media formats, such as 35mm and 8mm film, within the same shot or more generally within the same film. Both these forms of frame construction entail a large degree of information density that outshines the capacities of the classical device of 'depth of field' (2001: 328).

In order to evaluate the role of the digital operation, maintaining a sense of sobriety and historical perspective, Manovich is quick to highlight the fact that the technique of spatial montage or the creation of dense and layered images is not a new invention. The method of compositing is primarily a conceptual operation that can be traced back in the history of very different media such as painting, photography, music, television and video art long before the advent of computer technology.[8] However, the introduction of digital tools not only in filmmaking but also in other media[9] facilitated the creation of spatial montage and invited the widespread use of compositing for constructing spatial images and clusters with more complex narrative and stylistic functions.

However enlightening and insightful Manovich's account of digital cinema may be, one question remains inescapable: where do all these new aesthetic possibilities of digital cinema materialise? Which *cinematic tradition* exemplifies the disruptive qualities of compositing and spatial montage? Manovich's answer is rather ambivalent, as his examples are far too scattered and dissimilar to be able to draw overall conclusions. For example, he discusses Robert Zemeckis's *Forrest Gump* (1994) along with Zbignew Rybczynski's *Tango* (1982)[10] and Czech filmmaker Konrad Zeman's *Na komete* (1970) for their ontological and stylistic montage. Moreover, while arguing that mainstream Hollywood cinema is still latched onto the classical mode of spatial representation, music videos and CD-ROM-based games constitute textbook cases of digital cinema.

My own answer to this question is that we need not go that far nor should we wait that long for the emergence of a full-blown digital cinema. The textual analysis of my chosen films clearly shows that all the properties of digital cinema, as mapped by Manovich, constitute fundamental constructive elements of the post-classical system of space with indubitable potential for further future development. It is not necessary to search for the embodiment of digital cinema in non-cinematic forms like music videos or video games; the post-classical mode of narration has already begun to explore the spatial possibilities of digital technology, instigating the shift from the photographic to a graphic space that defies transparency and challenges the classical distinction of space 'in frame' and 'out of frame'. The ten case studies that follow will elaborate on the manner in which the post-classical filmmakers handle their respective cinematic spaces, hoping to reveal once more the intricate relation of this new paradigm with its predecessors.

Case Studies

Europa

This film is a quintessential case of digital cinema despite not having a single digital image in its entire 110 minutes. Although Lars von Trier strictly refrains from computer technology, he enthusiastically embraces the logic of compositing, as a conceptually creative operation. Aiming at the kind of hypermediated realism described extensively in chapter one, *Europa* offers a rich and impressive play of images by transforming each frame into a complex visual cluster with a highly dense narrative meaning. Instead of abiding by the rules of classical realist representation and the continuity editing of the classical era, Von Trier paradigmatically uses most of the old technical methods in order to construct a screen world that consists of discontinuities, ruptures and excessive visual opacity. However, his aim is not to destroy the classical space and its narrative value; what he purposefully tries to achieve is a playful reworking of the classical techniques and a blatant exposure of their artificiality and constructedness. A careful examination of his stylistic choices will reveal his excellent knowledge of the classical rules and the conscious innovative departure from them in a way that epitomises the post-classical treatment of cinematic space.

Firstly, a classical device that is consistently challenged is the staging in depth that is replaced by the most daringly impressive spatial montage. As a replacement for deep focus cinematography, the combination of multiple back and front projections, superimpositions and the mixture of black-and-white images with colour create an unusually high tension between the different planes of the image and the actions that take place in each plane.[11] As Von Trier has pointed out:

Sometimes we have up to seven layers of images in black-and-white and colour. We can thus combine two or more images filmed with different lenses, such as a background shot with a telephoto lens and a foreground shot with wide-angle. (Quoted in Kennedy 1991: 69)

What is intriguing about the self-reflexive cinematic space that results from the blending of several image layers is that not only does it not relinquish its narrative function but it also adds enormous dramatic value to the story. An illuminating example is the scene of Leo and Kate's first meeting in the train compartment, where we find the two following shots:

fig. 1.1

1. Medium black-and-white shot of the interior of Kate's compartment from a low angle. In the foreground on the left, Leo is on his knees making the bed. In the background on the right, Kate is looking at Leo and she gradually slips out of focus. Leo pulls up the sheets covering the whole frame (figs 1.1, 1.2).
2. Cut to a medium close-up. Leo is in the foreground *in colour* now and Kate in the background in a black-and-white back projection. Kate slowly walks behind his back and leaves the frame for a moment. She then re-enters the frame in the foreground and in colour next to Leo. At this point the two protagonists are both in colour against a black-and-white back projection. Kate starts making the bed herself and Leo leaves the frame. He re-enters the frame in the black-and-white back projection, which appears in the background (figs 1.3–1.5).

fig. 1.2

fig. 1.3

fig. 1.4

This very small fragment illustrates the visual density of the images in *Europa* and the intricate staging of the action in separate planes, projections and colours. The relationship between the two characters and the unbridgeable gap that separates their lives becomes palpable in the scene with the continuous shifting of their places in the foreground/background, foreshadowing the fatal end-

fig. 1.5

fig. 1.6

fig. 1.7

fig. 1.8

fig. 1.9

fig. 1.10

ing of their affair. More specifically, Kate begins the conversation from the background, first out of focus and then in a back projection. She next tries to approach Leo by entering his colour foreground, yet they cannot occupy the same space for very long and she soon 'pushes' him away to the black-and-white back projection, confirming the distance that separates them with the following words: 'What you say seems to come from a place far away.' This type of frame construction is a typical feature throughout *Europa* and displays Von Trier's impressive ability to maintain balance between his artistic virtuosity and the film's narrative exigencies.

Another classical device that is transformed in his hands is the point-of-view shot pattern. One strategy is to ostensibly refuse to show what the characters are looking at. For example, in a scene at the first dinner party with the Hartmann family, Kate's brother asks the guests to come to the window to see the blasts of the allies and they all soon squeeze together to catch a glimpse of the view (fig. 1.6). Nonetheless, the camera denies this view to the spectator and the fact that the characters remain in front of the window for an entire minute makes the lack of the point-of-view shot not only perceptible but also disturbing. The other tendency is to use colour and slow-motion with some of Leo's point-of-view shots, especially when he looks at Kate. We often see him in black-and-white and then we see her as the object of his look in colour, connoting his loving feelings towards her.

Moreover, the analytical editing that typifies the system of space in the classical paradigm is replaced here by spatial montage and the multilayered images of the various projections and superimpositions. Von Trier opens numerous scenes with fairly classical exterior establishing shots but then breaks the realistic effect by fragmenting the interior spaces into different front and back projections and downplaying the feeling of the unity of space that the analytical editing is supposed to achieve. In addition, the function of cutting is significantly altered, as the change of the back projection often indicates the change of the story space in a rather surreal manner. For instance, there is a scene where Leo and Kate are framed in close-up, in colour, against the black-and-white projection of a river. Kate says, 'Marry me please' to Leo and he says 'yes' and kisses her. When the kiss is over, the back projection dissolves into the figure of a priest in a church and the two protagonists turn to face him. A cut to the other side of the axis shows the priest in the foreground and the couple in the back projection in their wedding clothes (figs 1.7–1.9). The use of the dissolve in the back projection to signal the shift of the narrative space not only makes the former even more visible but also demonstrates how the mixed projections equally strive for prominence throughout the film.

In terms of the general framing of the action and the camera movement, *Europa* displays many of the elements that Bordwell has identified as intensified continuity. The dialogue scenes are often filmed in extreme close-up single shots (figs 1.10, 1.11), while the rack-focus often prevents the need for cutting. In the longer takes we find a number of crane shots that move in and out of buildings, while parts of the dinner scenes are shot in long spiralling movements of the camera around the actors. The film is also rich in overhead shots (either stable or accompanied by intense camera movement), which provide impressive views of the action (fig. 1.12). At the same time, amidst the overload of visual tricks, it is quite striking to find some excessively classical shots, such as the classical staging and the deep focus cinematography in figures 1.13 and 1.14, which now seem strange digressions from the mannerist norm.

fig. 1.11

fig. 1.12

fig. 1.13

fig. 1.14

fig. 1.15

fig. 1.16

fig. 1.17

fig. 1.18

fig. 1.19

fig. 1.20

Going back to the visually stunning aspects, however, I would like to underline the director's predilection for figurative, subjective and impossible places. In figure 1.15 we see a low-angle shot from inside the bathtub, which shows the blood coming out of Max Hartmann's hand in colour. This impossible view of the suicide scene took several layers of images, including a very small back projection of the blood, as Von Trier explains (see Sauvaget 1991: 70). In figure 1.16 we have a shot from Leo's dream, while figures 1.17–1.19 are figurative shots that occur in moments of high drama.

Lastly, I would like to refer to two intriguing shots that make particular use of the back projection system to indicate separate places within the same frame. In figure 1.20 we have the handling of a telephone conversation between Kate and Leo who appear together in different projections. In figure 1.21 we have a very ambiguous case of a visual cluster that makes sense only with the help of the voice-over; there is Max Hartmann on the left looking towards the paper *in colour* on the right. However, the voice-over says to Leo: 'You have left the house ... Before you is the questionnaire' and only then does the viewer realise that the paper on the screen is in front of Leo and not in the bathroom, despite Max's misleading look. This is an extremely unusual construction of narrative space that can only become intelligible with the aid of the narrator.

Overall, Von Trier's experiments with the classical stylistic devices and the spatial possibilities of the screen surface result in a consistently disruptive narrative space that shatters the illusion of reality in the classical sense. On the other hand, the consistency of his cinematic language coupled with the simplicity of the basic plot information provides the film with a general narrative coherence. As a result, *Europa* manages to balance the different narrative motivations – the compositional, the realistic and the artistic – by telling a clear-cut story with an expanded spatial repertoire and a dense visual language.

Requiem for a Dream

I have previously discussed *Requiem for a Dream* for its highly subjective realism, which consists of an emphatic and hyperrealistic depiction of the

fig. 1.21

characters' inner emotional and mental states. The attempt to achieve a high dose of hypermediacy and to get as close as possible to their actual experiences demanded a very self-reflexive use of cinematography. As Aronofsky explains:

> We always knew we were going to try to break down some barriers narrative-ly, visually and aurally; we wanted to try to make a film that was completely different from anything that had been done before ... Of course, all of the

special techniques we applied had to advance the story, because we didn't want the film to turn into this self-indulgent, MTV type of thing. (Quoted in Pizzello 2000: 51)

Breaking the barriers and yet serving the story purposes were the two goals that the filmmaker consciously set for himself at the onset and close analysis of the film will reveal that he was, in fact, highly successful.

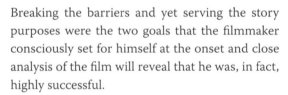

fig. 2.1

Instead of back projections, superimpositions and the old techniques of image manipulation, Ar-onofsky shows a predilection for digital technolo-gies and spatial montage by making widespread use of split-screens. The frame is frequently bro-ken into two separate windows that belong either to two different fragments of the same story space or to two entirely different locales. The function of the vertical or horizontal split-screens is multi-faceted, as they often replace some of the classical devices such as point-of-view shots or crosscut-ting. For instance, in figure 2.1 we see Sara on the top of the frame looking downwards and we si-multaneously see the pills at the bottom, from her own point of view.

fig. 2.2

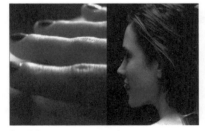

fig. 2.3

fig. 2.4

fig. 2.5

fig. 2.6

fig. 2.7

fig. 2.8

However, the most frequent purpose of the split-screens is to depict the same event from two different subjective positions. Apart from the opening sequence, briefly discussed in the chapter on motivation, there is a scene of an intimate conversation between Harry and Marion that is shot in an unconventional manner. The first shot (fig. 2.2) shows them in close-up next to each other against a black background, creating the misleading impression that they both occupy the same screen space. The next shot, however, reveals that they are actually contained in separate split-screens, which feature shifting close-ups of their faces and bodies (figs 2.3–2.7) for the entire minute-and-a-half-long scene.

The disrupting effect of the split-screens is further enhanced when there is intense camera movement or changes of focal length in one or both frame sections. For example, as Sara tries to refrain from eating, we see a medium shot of her on the left and the object of her thoughts, the fridge, on the right of the screen (fig. 2.8). A slow zoom-in begins in both sections and ends in extreme close-ups (figs 2.9, 2.10). The synchronised zooms into Sara's face and the fridge transform the screen into a particularly subjective space that attempts to capture her increasing fixation on food.

Given that all four protagonists struggle with their addiction to drugs, whether heroin or diet pills, the film often strives to represent their mental states rather than the actual physical place they live in. The attempt to penetrate their minds is heavily assisted by the use of macro and high-speed photography, fish-eye lenses and special body-mounted camera rigs that offer unique views of the action. For example, there is a scene with Sara tidying up her house under the influence of the pills; her hyperactivity is signalled by the exceeding fast-motion of the images, while the overall visual effect is even further accentuated by the fact that the camera pans on these high-speed images (fig. 2.11). Similarly, when the characters take drugs, their state of euphoria is indicated by fast-motion and fish-eye distortion or slow-motion and white fade-outs (figs 2.12, 2.13).

In terms of shot scale, there is a constant juxtaposition of long shots, usually from a high angle (fig. 2.14), with extreme close-ups in order to indicate the passage from the 'real' outer world to a more subjective one. Many conversations are shot in extreme single close-ups, while crane shots and spiralling camera movements are used in the opening and closing moments of various scenes. The pace of the editing becomes gradually frantic, as the film spirals into the living hell of the protagonists. An equally relentless crosscutting within split-screens, especially in climactic scenes, makes it impossible to register all the shots and aims more at conveying the energy of a situation, reminding us of Raymond Durgnat's speaking of the 'headlong, tense, unbroken, "you are there" movement of cameras and cast, the confused imbroglio of bodies, gestures, shouted accusations, the sense of mounting spectacle'.[12]

On the other hand, as Aronofsky explicitly stated in the interview quoted above, the highly stylised camerawork and the digital effects that materialised a subjective and hypermediated type of realism, had to complement and reinforce the progression of the story and its compositional demands. The adventurous filming techniques and the groundbreaking cinematic language succeed in meeting the narrative ends through their dramatically consistent and meaningful use, which is established from the first minutes in the film. Therefore, the viewer can easily grow accustomed to this 'new' style and follow the story, which otherwise develops in a rather linear and unambiguous manner. In other words, the self-reflexive construction of space by no means aims at contra-

fig. 2.9

fig. 2.10

fig. 2.11

fig. 2.12

fig. 2.13

fig. 2.14

dicting plot and character development in order to create ambiguity, as was the case in art cinema. In fact, the fragmentation and deconstruction of the classical realistic space with the help of digital compositing not only do not obliterate the narrative space where the predicaments of the characters unfold, but they also enrich it with several other dimensions.

Moulin Rouge!

The hypermediated realism of *Moulin Rouge!* and Baz Luhrmann's deliberate attempt to achieve a high dramatic energy were briefly touched upon in the chapter on motivation. Here a further examination of the film's spatial composition will bring to the surface in more detail all the principles that govern its post-classical narrative space. These principles are knowingly introduced by the cinematographer Don McAlpine who designed the look of the film in accordance with the director's concept of 'heightened realism'. As he explains:

> There is an unwritten style manual for Hollywood films, but that book doesn't exist when you work with Baz. If he thinks it's best to put the camera at somebody's navel, looking up his or her nostrils, then we do … If you at least know the rules, you know when you're breaking them. And on this film we broke every rule in the book. (In Bosley 2001: 42–4)

Although there are in fact numerous written manuals for the classical Hollywood style, McAlpine's statement raises two crucial points: firstly, they had to break a number of classical rules in order to visualise their core idea, and, secondly, their knowledge of the classical style was fundamental in providing them with norms and principles that they could work against. Both these aspects reflect fairly accurately the intricate relationship of constant reference and contradiction between the classical and the post-classical tradition, which I have been trying to develop.

fig. 3.1

fig. 3.2

Turning to the film itself,[13] I would like to start by commenting on the settings and the iconography that make a powerful impression in their effort to establish the lack of any sense of classical realism. Although the story is set in Paris at the turn of the century, the reconstruction of the city is based entirely on miniatures, models of buildings and matte paintings (figs 3.1, 3.2). Being shot exclusively on soundstages in Australia and Madrid, the film focuses mainly on the interior scenes and leaves hardly any time to register the exterior shots of the Moulin Rouge (fig. 3.3) or Christian's room (fig. 3.4). At the same time, the artificiality of the sets and the sumptuousness of the colours, as for example in the exotic 'Elephant' (fig. 3.5), prevent the viewer from noticing any details in the surroundings and place the focus on the performance of the characters. Furthermore, *Moulin Rouge!* employs numerous digital effects and contains several computer-generated images that contribute immensely to its heightened energy. In figures. 3.6 and 3.7 we see the characters under the influence of absinthe and their hallucinations of the 'green fairy', while in figure 3.8 the two protagonists dance against the Paris skyline under a Méliès moon. The filmmaker resorts several times to digital enhancing techniques and experiments widely with different lighting and colour schemes.

Apart from the spectacular special effects, the film draws enormous visual power from its frenzied editing pace. As a reviewer notes, 'cuts always come just before you expect them to, and there's a wealth of detail, visual and narrative, packed into every one-and-a-half second shot' (Jones 2001: 22). The rapid cutting produces startling effects from start to finish, but reaches its peak in the dance scenes and the spatio-temporal transitions among different segments of the story. For instance, the can-can dance seeks to transmit a massive energy and a 'you-are-there' feeling by cutting frantically from long shots to extreme close-ups and from the dancers to the audience. The same editing speed is repeated every time

fig. 3.3

fig. 3.4

fig. 3.5

fig. 3.6

fig. 3.7

fig. 3.8

fig. 3.9

fig. 3.10

fig. 3.11

fig. 3.12

fig. 3.13

fig. 3.14

Christian initiates a new fragment of his narration and takes us from his attic to the past events at the Moulin Rouge.

Yet, on the other hand, it is notable how Luhrmann holds onto the narrative control of the film and ensures the clear and intelligible progression of the story. The pyrotechnics of the style had to remain 'slave to the story', as he explains,[14] and this goal required not only a tremendous discipline but also recourse to some classical techniques, such as careful character placement and meticulous staging of the action. For example, in the scene where Christian and the Duke go to the Moulin Rouge to meet Satine, some shots aim to maintain a strong narrative function amidst the hectically extravagant movements of the dancers and the loud rhythmic music. In figure 3.9 we have a very balanced and centred composition of the two men sitting separately and yet close enough for Satine to misunderstand who the real Duke is. In figure 3.10 we have a long shot showing Christian in the foreground, Satine in the middle and the audience at the back, as she invites him to dance and prepares the ground for the intimate meeting that is going to follow. These classically-shot moments often serve as punctuation marks that contain the hectic camera movements and the other special effects.

Moreover, the film plays consciously with various classical devices such as establishing shots and shot/reverse-shot patterns. For instance, there is an interior shot of the dance hall where the customers throw their hats in the air and the film cuts to a bird's-eye-view of Paris showing the hats above the sky of the Moulin Rouge (figs 3.11, 3.12). Another interesting scene is the moment Christian embraces Satine for the first time in the elephant because the editing breaks the 180° axis and establishes a 360° space (figs 3.13, 3.14) that nevertheless manages not to destroy our orientation. Additionally, most of the conversations between two or more characters are shot in singles, while there is often a juxtaposition of extreme long shots with extreme close-ups that exaggerates the analytical editing in the scene.

fig. 3.15

The other two stylistic aspects that compete for prominence with the editing are the hyperactive camerawork and the varying speeds of motion. Luhrmann enriches his heightened language with spectacular 360° tracking shots and long upward or downward crane shots that punctuate numerous scenes by taking us from the time and place of an action to another one in the future or the past. For example, the shots in figures 3.15 to 3.17 constitute parts of a long crane shot, which begins with Satine and Christian on the balcony of his hotel room and slowly draws away, giving us a bird's-eye-view of the city. However, the shot continues in order to enter a new space (figs 3.18, 3.19), which reveals a picnic scene with the two protagonists and the Duke. Replacing cutting with long distinctive crane shots to signify the spatial transitions adds to the artificiality of the narrative space and gives it a floating quality. Moreover, there are some camera moves that try to evoke the kinetic zooms of fast-paced electronic games, especially as they race into the night club and then withdraw with the same frantic haste (see Kinder 2002: 35). Another standard strategy is the use of swift 'push-ins' and 'pull-outs' on the actors' faces, which capture dynamically the various facial expressions, whereas recurrent whip-pans augment the energy of the scene. The highly polished look of the entire film is at some point blemished by a shaky hand-held camera that records some personal

fig. 3.16

fig. 3.17

fig. 3.18

fig. 3.19

moments between the two lovers behind the scenes. Although this technical choice seems rather out of place compared to the overall style, it denotes the filmmaker's daring gesture to indeed break the rules, even those of his own personal consistency. Finally, a regular use of fast- or slow-motion and step-printing cinematography[15] succeeds in sensationalising the action and captivating the viewers' attention.

On the whole, it seems that *Moulin Rouge!* follows the example of *Requiem for a Dream* and *Europa* in the way it breaks most of the classical Hollywood rules and experiments with the wide range of technical options that old and new media provide. This language builds a hypermediated space that defies notions of classical realism both in terms of the pro-filmic (settings) and filmic (editing) events. The film's 'spatial effects' constantly acknowledge their constructed nature and, yet, do not abandon their narrative strength. Instead, the large amount of discontinuities, slanted camera angles, rapid-fire cutting, impossible shots and relentless camera movements remain faithful to their ultimate goal: to tell a heart-wrenching love story that remains engaging and moving from beginning to end.

The Million Dollar Hotel

fig. 4.1

fig. 4.2

fig. 4.3

fig. 4.4

Wim Wenders' *The Million Dollar Hotel* is a visually beautiful film that takes advantage of digital technology to create a poetically intense atmosphere. Compared to the three preceding case studies, it is essential to point out that the German filmmaker, unlike Luhrmann or Aronofsky, did not set out to break 'every rule in the book' and remained closer to some fundamental principles of the classical spatial system. For example, a large part of the film consists of centred and stable compositions that are punctuated by continuity editing techniques in a fairly conventional cutting rhythm. However, the film diverges from the classical norm on several occasions and in different ways that are worth a detailed examination.

First and foremost, Wenders put enormous emphasis on the visual qualities of the film, especially the lighting schemes, in order to transform a dilapidated hotel into an enchanting Edward Hopper-style environment (figs 4.1–4.3). Moreover, the numerous night scenes, both interior and exterior, are exceptionally dark and most of the time the figures of the actors are hardly discernible. The play with the dark lighting becomes even more prominent in the scene of Geronimo's arrest that takes place in the lobby. In figure 4.4 we have an extreme high-angle shot of the lounge where we barely see a policeman arresting Geronimo. As soon as he puts on the handcuffs, the frame rate increases and the characters start fighting with the policemen in fast-motion, while the camera cuts to a ground-level angle (fig. 4.5). As the fight goes on, the shot in figure 4.6 slowly freezes and the lights are switched off, except for a spotlight on Tom Tom's body as illustrated in figure 4.7.

Apart from the lighting, there are various other mannerist elements that add to the film's visual riches. For example, Wenders likes to sporadically insert images from other sources, such as photo stills (fig. 4.8) or TV extracts (fig. 4.9), indulging in what Manovich would call 'stylistic montage' (2001: 158). Moreover, in another scene he fuses the story space with Tom Tom's mental images by superimposing his thoughts in the window frame by his bedside (fig. 4.10). He also shows a preference for extreme low- or high-angle framing and overhead shots, while often emphasising the fluid camera movements and aerial shots from the roof of the building. However, the most frequent violation of classical continuity comes from his repetitive jump-cuts, especially during the meetings between the two protagonists or when Tom Tom dances alone in his room. Similarly, the regular use of fast- or slow-motion endows the scenes with high energy or romantic aura respectively. As the film's cinematographer, Phedon Papamichael, observes:

> Tom Tom and Eloise are always involved in a sort of dance, with each moving back and forth and around while checking the other out, almost like animals sniffing one another out ... This was used especially in Tom Tom/Eloise scenes to create a different reality around them, suggesting a unique kind of perception. (In Martin 2001)

The slow-motion combined with the sound effects and the digital enhancing during the encounter

fig. 4.5

fig. 4.6

fig. 4.7

fig. 4.8

fig. 4.9

fig. 4.10

scenes in the corridor result in a semi-subjective space that illustrates the dynamics between the two characters and their subjective experience of the situation.

Taken as a whole, *The Million Dollar Hotel* creates a distinctive narrative environment that blends in facets of hypermediated and subjective realism. Although it does not attack the viewer with the force of *Moulin Rouge!* and it does not deconstruct its images with the audacity of *Europa*, Wenders' subtle amalgamation of the continuity system with discontinuous techniques and digital effects not only produces a visually arresting film but also contributes significantly to an understanding of the post-classical system of space construction.

Natural Born Killers

Can we still talk here about shots? We should find a new word to characterise these incessant passages of images that are both subliminal and convulsive.

Electrons as well as projectiles but certainly not shots anymore. A space where everything is on the surface, like in a baroque sphere, where the images do not cease to accelerate towards the eye and to glide on top of each other, instead of the eye being the one to move, like in early cinema, towards the scrutiny of the shot. (Jousse 1994: 50; author's translation)

fig. 5.1

fig. 5.2

fig. 5.3

This extract from *Cahiers du cinéma* is representative of the commentaries and reviews that accompanied the release of Oliver Stone's film and the sensation caused by its visual style. In the previous chapter, I commented on its episodic narrative structure, its hypermediated realism and its superfluous parodic motivation, all of which constitute a highly self-conscious narration. Here I will investigate the film's construction of space and explain why it stirred such a fervent discussion regarding the limits of filmic representation.

Beginning with the idea of 'breaking every law of cinematography' (which sounds rather old-fashioned after what we have encountered in the previous case studies) Stone set out to make a film that would portray the madness of the century as it is encapsulated in the killing spree of two psychopaths. Using the styles of filmmakers as diverse as Antonioni, Jean-Luc Godard, Stanley Kubrick and Sam Peckinpah as a construction kit – to employ Bordwell's term[16] – he built a polystylistic film that not only renders an external version of Mickey and Mallory's story but equally aims at capturing their inner mental states (see Pizzello 1994: 38–40). Given the visual wealth of the film and the overabundance of special effects, it would be impossible to analyse in detail many segments and discuss all the optical tricks Stone utilises. For that reason, I will present selectively some typical shots and then conduct a shot-by-shot analysis of a key scene, the marriage between the two protagonists.

Firstly, the discontinuous cutting and the slanted camera placement are the most persistent elements of the film. In figure 5.1 there is an extreme close-up on Mickey's mouth from a skewed high angle, which cuts to an equally skewed but low-angle shot of a church nearby (fig. 5.2). As the camera pans slightly along the church, the face of a dead man is superimposed on the wall (fig. 5.3). This type of framing, cutting and superimposition amounts to a standard device in Stone's cinematic vocabulary, which soon becomes familiar and predictable during the viewing process. Moreover, the scene in the motel room constitutes an interesting case of spatial montage with back projections playing through a multi-paned window by the bed to visualise Mickey's mental chaos (fig. 5.4). In figures 5.5 and 5.6 we see the opening and closing credits of the 'I Love Mallory' section as mentioned earlier, which forms a distinct episode in the film. This part is shot mostly on video and tries to emulate television style with its traditional singles, master and over-the-shoulder shots. Finally, in figures 5.7 and 5.8 we have a small sample of the film's relentless play with colours and lighting techniques.

fig. 5.4

fig. 5.5

fig. 5.6

fig. 5.7

fig. 5.8

fig. 5.9

fig. 5.10

fig. 5.11

fig. 5.12

fig. 5.13

fig. 5.14

fig. 5.15

fig. 5.16

fig. 5.17

fig. 5.18

fig. 5.19

fig. 5.20

fig. 5.21

fig. 5.22

fig. 5.23

fig. 5.24

fig. 5.25

fig. 5.26

fig. 5.27

fig. 5.28

fig. 5.29

fig. 5.30

fig. 5.31

fig. 5.32

fig. 5.33

Secondly, I chose to analyse closely the marriage scene because it demonstrates the two core aspects of the film's overall style. On the one hand, it presents a remarkable stylistic freedom and experimentation with different discontinuous techniques, while, on the other, it maintains an essential narrative coherence and contributes to the progression of the story. More specifically, the scene contains 28 shots with an average shot length of 6.2 seconds, which is fairly close to the standards of intensified continuity.[17] These shots are the following:

Shot 1 (figs 5.9, 5.10): close-up of a hand dropping a red puppet into a gorge. We see the puppet falling until it becomes a red dot (colour, 35mm).

Shot 2 (fig. 5.11): cut to an extreme long shot of the bridge over the gorge from a completely different angle (black-and-white, 16mm, digitally enhanced).

Shot 3 (fig. 5.12): medium shot of Mickey and Mallory on the bridge. The camera cranes up over their heads and moves freely in a 360° space (colour, 35mm).

Shot 4 (fig. 5.13): jump-cut to high-angle shot and the camera keeps floating (colour, 35mm).

Shot 5 (fig. 5.14): cut to an establishing shot of the bridge from a slanted angle (colour, 35mm).

Shot 6 (fig. 5.15): cut to a medium close-up on Mallory's profile (colour, 35mm).

Shot 7 (fig. 5.16): cut to a reverse-shot of Mickey (colour, 35mm).

Shot 8 (fig. 5.17): cut to a medium shot of Mallory putting on a wedding headband from a slanted angle (colour, Super 8).

Shot 9 (fig. 5.18): cut to a medium close-up on Mickey slashing his hand (colour, 35mm).

Shot 10 (fig. 5.19): cut to a medium shot of Mickey, as the camera pans to include Mallory in the shot (colour, Super 8).

Shot 11 (fig. 5.20): cut to Mallory again (colour, 35mm).

Shot 12 (fig. 5.21): cut to a high-angle double shot of the characters (colour, 35mm).

Shot 13 (fig. 5.22): cut to Mallory again (colour, 35mm).

Shot 14 (fig. 5.23): cut to a medium shot of the characters. The camera is hand-held and tilts up to show Mickey's face (colour, Super 8).

Shot 15 (fig. 5.24): jump-cut, similar camera movement as in shot 15 (colour, Super 8).

fig. 5.34

Shot 16 (fig. 5.25): 360° cut to a medium close-up of Mickey (colour, 35mm).

Shot 17 (fig. 5.26): overhead shot of the characters (colour, 35mm).

Shot 18 (fig. 5.27): analytical cut to a close-up of their clasped hands (colour, 35mm).

Shot 19 (fig. 5.28): dissolve into a sequence showing their blood transforming into snakes (colour, animation).

fig. 5.35

Shot 20 (fig. 5.29): dissolve back into an overhead shot, as in shot 18, but this time the camera moves slowly and stops in front of the two characters (colour, 35mm).

Shot 21 (fig. 5.30): cut to a close-up of Mallory's hand as Mickey puts the wedding ring on (colour, 35mm).

fig. 5.36

Shot 22 (fig. 5.31): cut to a medium double shot. Mallory is looking offscreen (colour, 35mm).

Shot 23 (fig. 5.32): eyeline cut to the car that passed by and a whip-pan that takes us back to Mallory's face looking angry (colour, Super 8).

Shot 24 (fig. 5.33): cut to her face from a different angle and then the camera focuses on their rings (colour, 35mm).

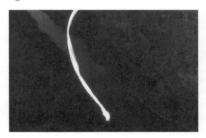

fig. 5.37

Shot 25 (fig. 5.34): cut to the two characters while the camera begins to move unsteadily around them in 360° (colour, Super 8).

Shot 26 (fig. 5.35): cut to a medium close-up as they kiss (black-and-white, 16mm).

Shot 27 (fig. 5.36): cut to a medium double shot (colour, 35mm).

Shot 28 (fig. 5.37): cut to the headband falling down the gorge (colour, 35mm).

At first glance, the construction of space in this particular scene transgresses most of the principles of classical continuity and particularly the 180° system. From the editing choices to the camera movements and from the alternation of the film stocks to the digital effects, Oliver Stone triumphantly displays his intention to break the rules and to subjugate the story world to the logic of density found in digital cinema. On the other hand, the visual overload and the optical tricks do not block our understanding of the basic narrative information, which is the fact that Mickey and Mallory are on a bridge over a gorge and they get married in their own unusual manner. One could even trace symmetries between certain shots, such as the opening and closing shots that both feature items falling down the gorge or the use of black-and-white cinematography in the beginning and the ending of the scene. Although the film contains several segments that are more rapidly cut or use more disrupting effects, it can be argued that the cluttered spaces of *Natural Born Killers* are only momentarily disorienting and ambiguous. In fact, maintaining an overarching sense of organisation was amongst the filmmaker's central concerns. As the cinematographer Robert Richardson points out:

> Many of our shots were so experimental that we would often duplicate them another way if we had fear about whether it would be too excessive or whether it would line up with another, more conventional shot. We had to find a way to make the connection between the shots, or our compositing rhythm might have been entirely thrown off. Much of the success of our approach was in the layering, and we had to make a great number of decisions based upon that consideration. (In Pizzello 1994: 42)

Similarly, Stone was confronted with the problem of 'coherence' in an interview with Gavin Smith when he was asked if the film is only superficially incoherent. His answer was: 'I think it's coherent, but it's evolving too, with open-ended imagery at points which throw you off kilter' (in Smith 1994: 12). This statement aptly describes the overall style of the film and touches upon its double-faced play with the rules of classical filmmaking. The important issue is that the space in *Natural Born Killers* maintains its narrative capacity and does not thwart the development of the story or the causal relations of the events. The fact that it accomplishes a fine balance between experimentation and coherence baffled the critics and was one of the reasons that led to some conflicting reviews. However, the contradiction is resolved if we come to realise that the film's hypermediated space serves equally successfully all the four different narrative motivations that are at work, despite the outward tension that it causes. Therefore, if we keep in mind the different narrative levels, as explicated so far, it becomes easier to understand the workings of a film like *Natural Born Killers* and to identify the characteristics of the post-classical paradigm through a seemingly chaotic territory of similarities and discontinuities.

Amélie

fig. 6.1

Jean-Pierre Jeunet's film offers without doubt an archetypal case of post-classical space where classical compositions, intensified continuity techniques and digital effects form a very richly textured screen world. Amélie's magical environment could not be portrayed accurately if Jeunet did not emphasise hypermediated realism and especially its subjective dimensions. 'Each shot had to be a new idea', he explained in an interview, and this principle is plainly visible in his finished project (in Vincendeau 2001: 24).

fig. 6.2

As an initial observation, I would like to note that the rules of classical frame construction constitute a solid foundation for the film's spatial system from start to finish. For example, in figure 6.1 there is a typical long establishing shot of a platform in the Parisian metro, while figure 6.2 shows a conventional medium shot of Amélie with her father. The graphic balance and the centredness of the action in these shots amount to two basic recurring features of the overall shot composition. One interesting variation of the analytical editing, however, is the opening of a scene with an extreme long shot, followed by a slow zoom-in on a section of the frame to focus on the incident that takes place. Moreover, most conversations are filmed in the classical pattern of shot/reverse-shot but with tighter framings according to the style of intensified continuity. It is also quite characteristic to find shots where Amélie looks directly into the camera and explicitly addresses the viewer, endowing the narration with a high degree of self-consciousness (figs 6.3, 6.4).[18]

fig. 6.3

fig. 6.4

fig. 6.5

fig. 6.6

fig. 6.7

fig. 6.8

fig. 6.9

fig. 6.10

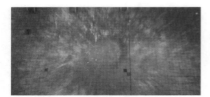

fig. 6.11

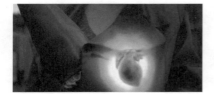

fig. 6.12

One of the numerous spectacular assets of *Amélie* is the relentless movement of the camera that blatantly plays the role of the guide by lurking around the characters and capturing the best possible view of their actions. Apart from the view, however, the camera tries to emulate the mood of each scene rendering, for example, the feeling of excitement with violently brisk moves or the romantic atmosphere with fluid breezy movements. This expressive use of the camera is also complemented with some standard techniques, such as push-ins, whip-pans, extravagant crane shots and spiralling overheads.

As far as the space 'out of frame' is concerned, the film makes an unsparing use of both traditional and spatial types of montage. The cutting pace in the linear editing is generally fast but on certain occasions it becomes impossible to follow as the images flash only for split seconds on the screen. This is particularly common in the sequences that introduce the various characters in the beginning, as well as in the various flashfowards and flashbacks. Although the temporal montage does not require further mention, the spatial kind is too bold and innovative to be ignored. Imitating the logic of cartoons and animation in general, Jeunet constructs the screen as a multi-windowed surface that depicts different types of reality simultaneously. In figures 6.5 and 6.6 we have two shots of a conversation between Amélie and the shop assistant at the erotic store where Nino works. As Amélie listens to some of Nino's odd pastimes, such as dressing as Santa Claus or recording funny voices, her mental images of these actions are superimposed on the left side of the frame. In a similar cartoon-like manner, the shots in figures 6.7 and 6.8 show her fantasies taking shape on the upper left corner as she is standing in front of the kitchen counter. The shot in figure 6.8 in particular is a very daring cluster of imaginative and real space with a *mise-en-abyme* structure. In addition, the entire film comprises numerous examples of stylistic montage where different types of image formats, especially black-and-white film clips, are combined either sequentially or within the same frame, as in figure 6.9.

The virtues of digital compositing are further explored in order to render on the screen the sense of heightened and subjective reality, which is an important aspect of the film's realistic motivation, as noted in chapter one. Jeunet uses different special effects and computer-generated images in order to be able to represent the seemingly unrepresentable and thread the seemingly unthreadable. The emotional status of the characters is the most obvious case; when Amélie sees Nino walking away from her, she dissolves into water (figs 6.10, 6.11) or when she is excited to see him, the camera appears to penetrate her clothes to let us catch a glimpse of her heart beating fast (fig. 6.12). In another aforementioned scene, Amélie takes a blind man by the hand and gives him a crazy tour in the nearby streets filling him with feelings of elation (fig. 6.13). Apart from the characters' subjective states, however, Jeunet has tried to visualise other processes such as Amélie's conception (fig. 6.14) or the distance that separates her house from Nino's (fig. 6.15). In addition, the frame often behaves more as a computer screen or a notebook, on which the filmmaker has taken the liberty of writing phrases or circling things so as to highlight the details that the viewer should take notice of, such as the fly on the window or Monsieur Poulain's upper lip (figs 6.16, 6.17). Lastly, the magical realism of the film is completed with certain animated scenes where objects take a life of their own and interact with the characters (figs 6.18, 6.19).

In conclusion, *Amélie* could be regarded not only as a textbook case of digital cinema in Manovich's terms but also as a typical example of post-classical space construction with its fine bal-

fig. 6.13

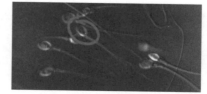

fig. 6.14

fig. 6.15

fig. 6.16

fig. 6.17

fig. 6.18

fig. 6.19

ance between classical rules and innovative elements. The multi-dimensional spaces of the film employ all the technical means possible in order to be able to provide a dense and hypermediated portrayal of Amélie's romantic story.

Trainspotting

> British cinematic culture has a very strong tradition of dogged realism, and that's something we fought against. (Danny Boyle in Thompson 1996: 80).

An adaptation of Irvine Welsh's 1993 novel, *Trainspotting* was released in the United Kingdom in February 1996 and was followed by rave reviews, on the one hand, and a public controversy on the other. Working against the grim and ascetic documentary style of the British cinematic tradition, Danny Boyle tries to bring to prominence the visual qualities of his work and to reinforce his narrative with the sense of heightened realism. The film seeks an authentic approach to drug addiction from the point of view of the addicts and, as a result, the notion of hypermediacy proves to be extremely accommodating for representing their turbulent emotional states. The construction of space becomes engaged in the attempt to portray the subjective experiences of a group of young drug addicts and thus relies on the post-classical recipe that blends the classical and intensified continuity with special effects.

fig. 7.1

fig. 7.2

fig. 7.3

fig. 7.4

Firstly, the frame construction generally combines the classical elements of centredness and balance with frontal and direct address of the viewer as in figures 7.1 and 7.2. In terms of shot scale, Boyle shows a clear preference for graphic extreme long shots (figs 7.3, 7.4), while he emphasises two opposing camera positions: on the one hand he places it on the ground level (figs 7.5, 7.6) imitating the drug addicts who tend to spend a lot of their time lying on their backs on the floor, while on the other, he inserts several overhead shots (figs 7.7, 7.8).

The intensified continuity in the film is mostly found in the long lurking movements of the Steadicam, as well as in the varying pace of the editing. The scenes that want to transmit the feeling of excitement, such as when the characters play football or when Renton (Ewan McGregor) moves to London, are shot as short video clips with fast cutting, freeze-frames and jump-cuts. One remarkable case is Spud's (Ewen Bremner) interview where his amphetamine-driven energy is portrayed by the rhythmic alternation of a medium with a long frontal shot (figs 7.9, 7.10). On the contrary, the scenes that show the routine of the life of a drug addict have a fairly long ASL and are more classically edited.

Although Boyle openly admits that he is not fond of digital technology and remains faithful to the traditional techniques,[19] he nevertheless embraces computer screen logic at least in one scene. When Renton urgently needs to use a bathroom, he enters a bar and heads directly to the toilet. Before showing us how filthy that place is, Boyle makes an overt extradiegetic commentary by bracketing the toilet sign with the words 'the worst in Scotland' (fig. 7.11). In addition, the emphasis on subjective realism requires various special and spatial effects that provide access to the characters' inner conditions. For example, in figures 7.12 and 7.13 we see shots of a surreal scene during which Renton dives into the toilet to retrieve his suppositories in an ultimate act of despair. Moreover, on two other occasions the film tries to capture the influence of drugs on Renton's perception. Firstly, in the scene of his overdose he is lying on a red carpet and is taken over by the feeling of sinking into the ground. This feeling is portrayed in a series of subjective point-of-view shots like the one illustrated in figure 7.14. Secondly, when his parents lock him in his room in

fig. 7.5

fig. 7.6

fig. 7.7

fig. 7.8

fig. 7.9

fig. 7.10

fig. 7.11

fig. 7.12

fig. 7.13

fig. 7.14

fig. 7.15

order to detoxify him, he suffers from hallucinations that take over the screen space (fig. 7.15).

As a whole, *Trainspotting* exemplifies various elements of intensified continuity combined with a graphic treatment of the spatial dimensions that break some of the constraints of the classical realist conception of space found in Hollywood cinema. Although more restrained than some of the previous cases, Boyle's film offers many interesting types of spatial construction that are valuable for understanding the workings of the post-classical paradigm.

City of God

Fernando Meirelles and Kátia Lund's film was previously highlighted for its exuberant sense of hypermediated realism and the examination of space here spells out in more detail the mechanics of this particular motivation. The City of God is inhabited by dozens of characters and the filmmakers accordingly devised numerous ways to record the grim everyday reality.

The opening hits the ground running with a rapid montage of close-up images from a market: a knife is sharpened against a black granite surface, chickens are plucked and chopped, vegetables are sliced and people are dancing the Samba. A few seconds later, a half-plucked chicken manages to free itself from its leash causing a chaotic chase through the streets, edited with a frantic cutting pace matching the rhythm of the music. The chase comes to an end when the chicken stops in front of Buscapé, who suddenly finds himself caught in a compromising situation. On the one side, there is Lil' Ze and his gang yelling at him to grab the chicken, while on the other, the policemen line up ready to square off against the gang. The dramatic tension that rapidly builds is captured by repeated speeded-up swish pans, moving from left to right on Buscapé's still body, as he struggles with indecision. When he explains in the voice-over that 'it has always been like that', the camera whirls around him and a graphic dissolve takes us back to the 1960s in a similar confrontation during a football game. In this sequence the combined forces of intensified continuity emulate the violent and conflicted nature of the story producing the desired heightening effect.

But that is merely the beginning. Throughout the film the images are obedient to the logic of hypermediacy and are constantly transformed into overflowing vessels of narrative power. All four techniques of intensified continuity team up with the vast options of spatial montage in an effort to compress three decades of slum life and myriads of killings into 135 minutes of screening time. The examples are numerous but for analytical purposes, I have singled out four intriguing moments. The first comes from the story of the Tender Trio and the hotel robbery incident. After the three gangsters have left the hotel with their loot, the screen goes dark for a couple of seconds and then a slow pan begins revealing the aftermath of the attack. The panning of the camera glides over one single composite image that comprises different shots from various parts of the hotel. In figures 8.1–8.4 we see fragments of this spatial montage which collates the dead couple in the room with the massacred bodies in the kitchen area and the fleeing car belonging to the gang in the far end. The choice of this spatial construction generates a narrative gap regarding the culpability of the Tender Trio and the murders, which will only be filled halfway through the film when we enter 'The Story of Lil' Ze'.

The second case is a sequence entitled 'A historia da boca dos apês', which condenses the several-year-long history of a drug joint into two-and-a-half minutes. Instead of the classical montage sequence, which would connect the various phases of a long process with the use of temporal editing, the filmmakers preferred spatial montage and the startling effects that it can achieve. The shot in figure 8.5 is a very balanced medium shot

fig. 8.1

fig. 8.2

fig. 8.3

fig. 8.4

fig. 8.5

fig. 8.6

fig. 8.7

fig. 8.8

fig. 8.9

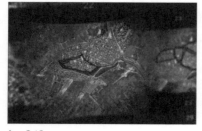

fig. 8.10

composition that suddenly freezes and dissolves into the image in figure 8.6, which bears the title of this episode. From then on, the framing of the scene remains static but the content continually shifts, as colours, people and props appear and disappear like spectres from the past (figs 8.7, 8.8). This long chain of dissolves emphasises the graphic and painterly qualities of the cinematic space, without giving up on the progression of the story. The voice-over as well as several snippets of diegetic dialogue accompany these densely layered images ensuring the necessary narrative coherence.

The mannerist treatment of cinematic space is further pursued in another unusual montage sequence that consists of overhead shots of brutal killings appearing in fast-motion. It is the time when Lil' Ze gains control over the drug trafficking in the *favela* without breaking stride and his rapidly expanding turf is visualised in figures 8.9 and 8.10 in the form of satellite shots. In these shots, red markings indicate the areas upon which he gradually seizes power, demonstrating quite graphically the impetus of this fearless gangster.

Finally, I would like to refer to the recurring use of split-screens that replaces the traditional crosscutting and reinforces the logic of addition and coexistence that typifies the post-classical system of space. The standard type of split-screen that cuts the frame in two equal spaces is used, for instance, when the narrator wants to compare Lil' Ze to Bené. Each character occupies one half of the screen and their diegetic actions unfold simultaneously, while the voice-over underscores their enormous differences in personality. On another occasion, however, the split-screen divides the frame into two unequal surfaces that exaggerate even further the disrupting effect of the horizontal wipe (figs 8.11–8.12). The larger space contains a loud exchange between Sandro Cenoura (Matheus Nachtergaele) and Mané Galinha (Seu

Jorge), two of Lil' Ze's principal enemies, while the smaller tries to frame the chase of the little boy. Instead of crosscutting between the scenes, the filmmakers chose to show the two actions simultaneously, using the screen space as a win-dowed slate.

To sum up, the cinematic space in *City of God* is emblematic of the key transformation that oc-curred in the shift from the classical to the post-classical mode, namely the move from photo-graphic to graphic spaces. The exhausting use of intensified continuity and the resourcefulness of the spatial montages endow the filmic narration with a new sensibility that makes the action erupt with energy and vigour.

fig. 8.11

fig. 8.12

Oldboy

The complexity and the density of the plot in *Oldboy*, which has already been discussed, is in parallel with the intricate treatment of the cinematic space and time in the overall narration. Park Chan-wook's choices in the handling of space and time on the screen mirror the twisted nature of the story and enrich the classical options with a long list of new stylistic devices. The ex-amination of the temporal traits will be reserved for the next chapter, but the analysis of the spatial features here will enable me to underline once more the defining qualities of post-classical space.

First and foremost, one should not underestimate the presence of a number of classical devices that are still in use and could be regarded as a solid foundation underneath the flamboyant effects and the hypermediated images. For instance, several exterior scenes are carefully balanced compositions as in figure 9.1, while a number of interior scenes bear an elaborate stag-ing in depth that amounts to a treatise on classical staging as in figure 9.2. The excessive classicism of these shots almost becomes parodic when con-trasted with a long array of post-classical stylistic choices that mould space into a palpable and yet fluid entity that interacts with the characters at every step they make.

fig. 9.1

fig. 9.2

In *Oldboy* the four techniques of intensified

fig. 9.3

fig. 9.4

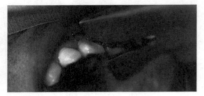

fig. 9.5

fig. 9.6

fig. 9.7

continuity are recruited by the South Korean filmmaker in his attempt to capture the violence, cruelty and perversity of the story and accomplish a heightening impression. The graphic qualities of the filmic image are accentuated both by the expressive lighting schemes as well as the framing of the action, which offers seemingly impossible views and allows the camera to affirm its presence. The overhead shots are a frequent choice as indicated by figures 9.3 and 9.4, while the extreme close-ups on props or body parts occasionally create strong physical reactions (fig. 9.5). Equally disturbing are some of the editing options, which tend to juxtapose extreme close-ups with extreme long shots. For example, in figure 9.6 the overhead view of Oh Dae-Su's release on the rooftop is immediately followed by the extreme close-up of his eye reacting to the daylight (fig. 9.7). This type of framing and editing in some instances becomes particularly demanding, as the viewer is required to swiftly adjust to the changes in distance and perspective, as shots come and go in an accelerated tempo.

On the other hand, the scenes that are shot in longer takes rely on fluid camera movements that generate the experience of the floating of the narrative space. The first arresting manoeuvre comes four minutes into the film to stage one of the key moments in the story, namely Oh Dae-Su's kidnapping. A medium shot shows him in a telephone booth talking to his wife and daughter. His friend asks to talk to them too and Oh Dae-Su steps out of the kiosk. The camera slowly pans to the right, pushing him into the offscreen area, and does not stop until it makes a 180° turn. As soon as it reaches that point, Oh Dae-Su's absence is suddenly made perceptible and his friend anxiously cries out for him. The medium shot then cuts to an overhead view of the booth and the camera begins to hover over the area in the dark, augmenting the enigmatic nature of the incident.

In addition, the mannerist handling of the spatial co-ordinates of the action is aided by the spatial montage and the graphic explorations of the movie screen. One such case is evident in figure 9.8, where a red dotted line is drawn on a freeze-frame to indicate the distance between the hammer and the head of a villain. Similarly, in figure 9.9 the red subtitles emphasise the words he struggles to utter as he sits bound and gagged. Another type of hypermediated space is found in figure 9.10, which shows a composite shot made of several layers superimposed on top of each other. Lee Woo-Jin is placed on the right supposedly looking through the mirror. Oh Dae-Su is seen in the background on the left holding up a picture in front of a wall covered with framed photos. This intricate arrangement of characters and props in the shot emulates the classical staging in depth while, in fact, constitutes a *mise-en-abyme* display made feasible only with the aid of superimpositions.

fig. 9.8

fig. 9.9

Finally, the spatial montage is made even more explicit in figures 9.11 and 9.12, which belong to a sequence consisting exclusively of split-screen shots. On the right, Lee Woo-Jin with a smirk on his face reveals the role of hypnosis and replays some of the key events of the plot – such as the ringing of Oh Dae-Su's phone in the restaurant – on the left. The presentation of the flashback with the help of spatial montage in this case replaces traditional temporal editing, which would place the shots in a linear fashion, one after another, in order not to break the transparency of the frame. The striking effect of the split-screen is even amplified by the graphic match of the two sides, as Lee Woo-Jin knowingly takes on the same posture as his victim on the other side (fig. 9.12).

fig. 9.10

fig. 9.11

fig. 9.12

All in all, Park Chan-wook's stylistic choices are on a par with those we have encountered so far in the previous case studies and attest to the consistency of the parameters of the post-classical paradigm. The examples singled out reveal how a new inventory of devices for staging and shooting the action is increasingly superseding the classical norms and establishing a novel approach to filmmaking that is gaining momentum across the globe.

Arizona Dream

I am closing the series of case studies in this chapter with Emir Kusturica's film because it will help me raise some critical issues regarding the 'spaciousness' of the narrative paradigms in general and the post-classical type in particular. Given that the purpose of this book is to conduct a bottom-up type of research and to allow a number of close analyses to lead to general conclusions without disregarding possible exceptions or discontinuities, I have purposely chosen to investigate the construction of space in *Arizona Dream*, as it is rather different from the other 13 films in the sample.

fig. 10.1

fig. 10.2

fig. 10.3

It has been clearly established in the previous chapters that *Arizona Dream*, as its title suggests, is a world full of dreams and fantasy-like situations. The surreal elements of the dreams that haunt the characters are constant and ubiquitous from beginning to end, creating a highly subjective narrative. Nevertheless, compared to all the other filmmakers discussed in this chapter, Kusturica is significantly less flamboyant and energetic. He uses very long takes and, for the most part, relies on the general rules of classical composition and continuity editing. Balanced establishing shots (fig. 10.1), careful and semi-frontal positioning of the actors (fig. 10.2) and the staging in depth of the action (fig. 10.3) are some of the main spatial characteristics of the film.

fig. 10.4

fig. 10.5

On some occasions, however, Kusturica treats his classical spaces with a remarkably unclassical freedom facilitated by digital technology. For example, in the scene where Elaine and Axel talk about their childhood dreams, the former's fantasy about flying materialises on the screen as their table leaves the ground and swirls around in the air (fig. 10.4). Similarly, Grace's feeling of lightness and serenity at her mother's birthday party is visualised when her chair starts ascending and descending gracefully against the wall (fig. 10.5).

Moreover, Axel's obsession with fish is regularly highlighted when a fish appears wandering through the landscape as in figures 10.6 and 10.7. Lastly, the surreal atmosphere is completed with some mannerist shots, such as a slow pan in an evening scene outside in the garden. In figure 10.8 we see the beginning of the shot showing Alex, Grace and Paul on the right side of the trunk of a tree, then the camera slowly pans to reveal Elaine in figure 10.9 and finally the pan ends by showing the three characters on the left side of the tree (fig. 10.10).

Overall, *Arizona Dream* clearly avoids the pyrotechnics of style and the intricate spatial effects that were evidenced in the other sample films. Kusturica adorns his narration with digital effects and spatial montage in a more selective and subtle manner that seeks to reflect the melancholic mood and feelings of his characters. By selecting this film and not *Chungking Express*, *Fight Club* or *Magnolia* for the section of case studies in this chapter, I want to explain how the post-classical paradigm is a relatively flexible structure that allows the films to follow its rules and conventions to varying degrees. Just as the classical model contains films that embody classical continuity to a larger or lesser extent, similarly the post-classical mode gives leeway to its films to apply the post-classical principles of spatial construction at different levels of emphasis. Therefore, the more subtle spatial features of *Arizona Dream* should not disqualify it from being a post-classical film nor should they jeopardise the consistency of the wider post-classical system of space.

fig. 10.6

fig. 10.7

fig. 10.8

fig. 10.9

fig. 10.10

A concluding note

In spite of the differences between the personal styles of the various directors discussed, the close analysis of their work has proved that the overall system of post-classical space constitutes a distinct paradigm with particular constructive principles that once again sustain individual creativity. It is arguably a far richer and wider paradigm than the classical but the unifying logic behind its copious devices is the construction of a cinematic space that can simultaneously satisfy a specific ensemble of narrative motivations. I cannot stress enough how intricately interdependent the various systems of this paradigm are and how narrative logic exerts enormous influence on the shape of the time and space co-ordinates. The persistence of the compositional motivation in the post-classical model still requires a place to accommodate the stories of the characters – hence the partial use of classical continuity for the achievement of an overarching sense of spatial coherence. But this is not the *only* aim. The increased emphasis on the motivations of hypermediated realism and parody necessitates a space fit for a heightened reality, on the one hand, and for intertextual references, on the other. For that purpose, the post-classical system of space recruits the logic of density and simultaneity embodied in computer technology and transforms the cinematic frame into a surface hospitable to a wide assortment of images.

All things considered, I would like to argue that the post-classical model of narration subordinates space to its various narrative motivations and causes it to serve its multifaceted narrative exigencies, whether that is a plot element or a subjective emotional state. Close textual analysis has shown that whether it is *Europa*'s back projections, *Requiem for a Dream*'s split-screens, *Moulin Rouge!*'s miniatures or *Arizona Dream*'s surreal flying scenes, the post-classical system of space consists of a depository of spatial devices that perform, above all, the same conceptual operations and fulfil the same functions.

POST-CLASSICAL TIME:
THE TEMPORAL QUALITIES OF
THE CINEMATIC IMAGE

The exploration of the temporal features of the cinematic medium has been a remarkably problematic issue for film theorists. In contrast to the perceptibility and measurability of the spatial co-ordinates of the moving images, the intangibility of time on the screen has resulted in a long-lasting controversy about how – if at all – cinema can express temporal relations. One of the sources of this dispute could be the tendency to compare cinema with literature, particularly around the theme of adaptation. The strategy of various film and literary theorists to compare the two different media according to the medium-specificity thesis, trying to reveal what each medium excels at, has often resulted in misleading observations.[1] For example, George Bluestone asserts that 'the novel has three tenses; the film has only one. From this follows almost everything else one can say about time in both media' (quoted in Cardwell 2003: 82). Similarly, if more elaborately, Alain Robbe-Grillet claims that:

> The essential characteristic of the image is its presentness. Whereas literature has a whole gamut of grammatical tenses which makes it possible to narrate events in relation to each other, one might say that on the screen verbs are always in the present tense ... by nature, what we see on the screen is in the act of happening, we are given the gesture itself, not an account of it. (Quoted in Dagle 1980: 47)

Bluestone and Robbe-Grillet's arguments, made in the late 1950s and early 1960s, were met with fierce criticism by various writers who felt that the comparison of cinema with literature and the emphasis on the lack of tenses in linguistic terms was too short-sighted (see Dagle 1980; Currie 1995; Cardwell 2003). As a result of this critique, the next concept that appeared on the theorists' agenda in replacement of 'presentness' was that of 'tenselessness'. It was Brian Henderson in his influential article 'Tense, Mood and Voice in Film' who claimed that 'cinema has no built-in tense system as language does' and, therefore, it is possible to create a shot or an entire film without indicating tense (1983: 6). On the other hand, another group of scholars argued that, even if we consider a separate film shot as inherently tenseless,[2] the multi-channelled textuality of the cinematic medium offers a far wider range of temporal articulations than those found in the written text. The combined forces of imagery, dialogue, voice-over and sound are capable of expressing intricate temporal relations and thus endowing the filmic narrative with the subtlest nuances of time (see Sesonske 1980; Cardwell 2003). In fact, it is quite challenging – hence so rare – to restrict all the filmic possibilities to a single tense, whether that is past, present or future. Joan Dagle insightfully observes that the example of Alain Resnais' *L'Année dernière à Marienbad* (*Last Year in Marienbad*, 1961), written by Robbe-Grillet himself, in fact proves the multifaceted temporal capacities of the cinematic medium. As she ironically points out, 'the timeless present of Marienbad reveals that film narrative can speak entirely in the present tense only with great difficulty' (1980: 57).

Having established the capacity of cinema to express time, despite the lack of grammatical tenses, most film theorists considered Gérard Genette's work on time-relations in literary narratives as an invaluable manual for identifying these relations in cinematic narratives as well. In his book *Narrative Discourse* (1980), Genette focused on Proust's novel *À la Recherche du Temps Perdu* (1913–27) with the aim of examining and theorising what he called the 'tense', the 'mood' and the 'voice' of the text. Although Henderson tried applying all these three aspects to the filmic discourse in his aforementioned article, it was mostly Genette's typology of tense that prevailed in the writings of the most prominent film narratologists, such as Seymour Chatman and David Bordwell.[3] The latter has dedicated an entire chapter to narration and time in his *Narration in the Fiction Film*, which constitutes the most detailed and informative description of cinematic time in the field. For that reason and also to maintain the conceptual and methodological consistency of this book, I will adopt Bordwell's account as the principal theoretical framework that will enable me to identify the temporal qualities of the post-classical mode of narration. But before laying out the post-classical treatment of time, it is essential to flesh out the intricate formal properties of the cinematic medium that are rarely appreciated in full in the various relevant writings.

First and foremost, the features of temporal construction in a film can be classified along three broad categories: order, duration and frequency. Each category contains different options for building the temporal aspects of the

narration, and more specifically for manipulating the temporal relations between the fabula and the syuzhet.[4] By borrowing the distinction between recounting and enactment from Chatman's work, Bordwell argues that the fabula events taking place over an inferred time period can either be recounted
through character dialogue and other expositional means or enacted directly
in the syuzhet in various configurations.[5] Focusing mostly on events that are
actually presented onscreen, he introduces two ways of looking at temporal
order: one includes questions of simultaneity and successivity, while the other
deals with the matter of chronology. It is quite common for theorists to over-
look the capacity of the cinematic medium to handle simultaneous events
due to the limitations of the sequential projection of the images. However,
the strength of Bordwell's typology lies in its ability to address the issue and
propose the following four possible combinations in the filmic narration:

1. simultaneous events in the fabula can be depicted simultaneously with
   deep space compositions, split-screens, etc.
2. successive events in the fabula can be presented simultaneously with split-
   screens or sound effects.
3. simultaneous events in the fabula can be presented successively with
   crosscutting.
4. successive events in the fabula can be depicted successively with regular
   editing techniques. (see Bordwell 1985: 77)

Without a doubt, not all four options have been equally popular in the history of mainstream filmmaking practices. The vast majority of films prefer a
successive presentation of events whether they actually happen successively
or simultaneously, thus making a recurrent use of the third and fourth combination.

Regarding the element of chronology, the syuzhet can stage the events
of the story in chronological order or choose to deviate from it by moving
backward or forward in time.[6] In the former case, the film presents a 'flashback', which depicts sections of the fabula that took place in the past. These
filmic segments that interrupt the linear flow of time in the story world can
either appear autonomously or be justified compositionally as the personal
recollections or recountings of the characters in the film. Depending on the
way a flashback is presented, the narration handles this unnatural reversal of
time with a higher or lower degree of self-consciousness respectively.[7] On the
other hand, the device of the 'flashforward' moves forward in time and offers
a glimpse of future events. This break in chronology creates a fairly disruptive
effect since the shift to a future time can rarely be explained realistically and
can only become intelligible to the viewers in retrospect. The obscurity and

uneasiness that the flashforward tends to cause means its appeal has been relatively low and it has been excluded entirely from the repertoire of classical filmmakers.

The second major category of time is the duration. The cinematic duration consists of three variables: the fabula duration, the syuzhet duration and the screen duration or 'projection time' (see Bordwell 1985: 81). The latter type of duration is strictly governed by the style of the film, and, more specifically, by a range of cinematic techniques, such as *mise-en-scène*, cinematography and editing. For example, the action of the fabula might cover a period of twenty years, of which the syuzhet will dramatise six months in 97 minutes of screen time. These three different types of duration can form various relations among themselves depending on the narrative needs of each movie, the predilections of each filmmaker or even more broadly of each cinematic tradition. These relations can be inventoried as relations of equivalence, reduction and expansion.

Firstly, in the case of *equivalence* the duration of fabula, syuzhet and screen time are equal. Although it would seem a very natural type of temporal construction, in fact complete equivalence throughout an entire film is a rather unusual occurrence that can be found either in primitive narratives or alternative forms of filmmaking. Instead, equivalence is mostly maintained during the various scenes of the syuzhet, especially those that are shot with long takes. Several scenes, however, can be constructed or connected with the help of *reduction*, a very common and widespread strategy for the co-ordination of the temporal qualities of the film. The reduction can be achieved either with ellipsis or compression. The former omits segments of the fabula from the duration of both syuzhet and screen time, while the latter condenses the fabula and syuzhet duration in the duration of the screen time. Although the device of ellipsis constitutes a normative practice in mainstream cinema and can serve various different narrative functions,[8] the strategy of compression is significantly rarer, as it is mostly achieved with the aid of fast-motion or meticulous tricks in the *mise-en-scène*. Lastly, there is the exact opposite option of *expansion*, which inflates the fabula duration either through insertion or dilation. The insertion takes place in the editing process and entails the interruption of the action with non-diegetic shots, such as intertitles or other images seemingly irrelevant to the diegetic scene. In contrast, in the case of dilation the screen duration stretches out the depicted action through the use of slow-motion effects.

In addition to all these variations, the cinematic duration includes the possibility of the pause. Although in technical terms the screen time never pauses during the course of the projection, the use of 'freeze-frames' has always been an option for some filmmakers. During the freeze-frame the fabula time stops but not necessarily the time of the syuzhet, since the frozen image is often accompanied by voice-overs, music or other sounds that might add information about the story world. According to Chatman, this pause frequently serves descriptive purposes and, as such, it constitutes the most explicit type of description in the cinematic medium (see 1990: 49).

Finally, the third general category of time, the temporal frequency, involves the manner in which the syuzhet represents the regularity or singularity of the fabula events. By applying Genette's literary analysis to the cinematic medium, Brian Henderson distinguishes between four types of possible relations: 1. the singulative that narrates once what happens once; 2. the multiple-singulative that narrates n times what happens n times; 3. the repetitive that narrates n times what happened once; and 4. the iterative that narrates once what happened n times (see Henderson 1983: 10). Unfortunately, this direct application of literary categories for the cinema becomes rather crude if we take into consideration the intrinsic differences between the two media. In contrast to the ability of written language to express time with precision through the use of tenses and other temporal expressions, the capacity of cinematic language to articulate meaning through a complex arrangement of image, dialogue and sound leads to an augmented difficulty in discerning the various types of frequency in the filmic discourse. To solve this issue, Bordwell resorts again to Chatman's distinction between recounting and enacting to construct an elaborate table of nine possible ways that the syuzhet can handle the fabula information in terms of frequency. This table focuses on the two levels of expression, recounting with words and enacting with images, and illustrates how many times a fabula event can be either recounted or enacted (see Bordwell 1985: 79). Although this typology is not entirely unproblematic either, it is a rather safe observation that the majority of mainstream films do not explore unusual types of frequency and tend to recount the events several times while enacting them only once.

Now if we turn to the classical paradigm of narration and look at the construction of temporality in most Hollywood films, we realise that time, along with space, follows the rules of classical realism and strives to represent the action of the story as if it unfolds naturally before our eyes. The reliance on a linear chronology and the masterful combination of ellipsis with equivalence through continuity editing produce an unobtrusive depiction of the story, shunning any flamboyant effects that could endanger its verisimilitude. Overall, the temporal qualities of a classical film do not seek any prominence and are completely subordinate to the other classical narrative requirements, namely the need for tight and clear cause-and-effect relationships. As Bordwell observes, 'Time in the classical film is a vehicle for causality, not a process to be investigated on its own' (Bordwell et al. 1985: 47).

The post-classical shift: from real to mediated time

When we enter the realm of the post-classical, once again we are confronted with a far richer structure of temporality that can no longer be regarded as a mere 'vehicle for causality'. The questions that I will strive to investigate are: what are the principles of the system of time in this new paradigm? How have the changes in the narrative motivations and the spatial construction affected the representation of time? What is the conceptual driving force behind the specific temporal devices that comprise the post-classical temporal scheme?

I would like to start with the last question because it involves the conception of time that underlies the narration in the post-classical films at the broadest level. Given that the system of time is very closely related to the system of space analysed in the previous chapter, one would expect that Lev Manovich's account of 'digital' cinema would discuss the changes in temporality that took place with the introduction of digital logic into cinematic practices. However, a close reading of his work shows that he fails to tackle the issue, as he becomes utterly absorbed in the spatial possibilities of the digital moving images. In regard to questions of time, he presents a brief, sketchy argument about the technique of the loop as 'a narrative engine' by drawing his examples from non-cinematic forms, such as video games and CD-ROMs (see 2001: 314–22). It is evident why he could not include cinema in this discussion, given that the loop as a model for temporal construction in mainstream contemporary films is not yet applicable, at least in the technical sense, due to the lack of interactivity in the film viewing process. On the other hand, the impact of computer logic cannot be restricted to the spatial construction of the filmic image, regardless of the prominence of space in the digital environment. The embrace of digital concepts and tools in current filmmaking has had important effects on the temporal structure of contemporary films that certainly require further elaboration.

First and foremost, to begin to trace these effects, it is helpful to keep as a springboard Manovich's main observation that digital cinema has generated a shift from photographic to graphic representations, following the long lineage of two marginal cinematic traditions, animation and avant-garde practices. I would like to argue that this conceptual transformation in the construction of space entails a parallel transformation in the representation of time, and, more specifically, a shift from the representation of 'real time' to 'mediated time'. Whereas the photographic images of classical cinema are devoted to the faithful and realistic depiction of analogue time as the time closest to our human experience, the graphic images of the digital cinema are freed from such obligation and can explore the numerous possibilities of the 'mediated' or 'manipulated' time. Timothy Murray eloquently comments upon this comparison between photographic and digital images in the following passage:

> You might recall, in this context, how cinema was praised by its influential French theoretician, André Bazin, for freeing time from its 'embalmment' in photography. In contrast to cinema, he writes, 'photography liberates its object from temporal contingency in a way that 'embalms time' in the click of the instant and thus heightens the photograph's ontological value or 'presence'. It's hard not to be amused by how this logic has come full circle, in that digitality, the medium of virtuality, could be said to free time from the hallucination of analogue movement, from the hallucination of cinema's temporal movement from point A to point B to point C. (1999: 6)

Yet the power of digital technology to free moving images from the analogue movement does not signify the abolition of analogue time; it merely transforms it into one option among many. Yvonne Spielmann explains, in more technical terms, the nature of simulation as follows:

> Two aspects of simulation become visible: first, in the forward movement as an affirmation of moving, filmic images; and second in the reversal of this movement, moving backwards, and also in the still point of movement that both dissolves and negates the first feature. *Because moving is possible in both directions it becomes optional.* The reversibility of moving images indicates that transformation is possible in both ways, either to affirm analogue tools or to transgress those in digital manipulation. (1999a: 146; emphasis added)

Of course, the temporal manipulations of digitality – just as in the case of spatial collages and complex digital compositing – perform above all a conceptual operation, which is not a new invention per se. If we look at Bordwell's description of cinematic time, we can confirm that all the different temporal options have already been registered for the reason that they were tried before, however partially, either in mainstream or experimental films that strove to transgress the representation of analogue time with the analogue tools themselves. With the advent of digital technology, however, these intermittent attempts of the past became increasingly popular, as the new technical means rendered the process of manipulation particularly effortless and accessible. But even now, under these conditions of exceptional creative freedom, the value or significance of analogue time is never abandoned. In other words, the introduction of digital logic in contemporary filmmaking has simply magnified, multiplied and intensified the codes of analogy by re-

negotiating the relationship with 'real time' in a way that only the most experimental artists would have dared in the past (see Turim 1999: 51).

This renegotiation of 'real time' lies at the heart of the new mode of narration that I am trying to demarcate here. According to the sample analysis,
the post-classical system of time is permeated by the technical innovations
of digital technology and exemplifies this crucial conceptual shift in its approach to the representation of time. Just as post-classical space emphasises
the graphic qualities of the cinematic frame, post-classical time accentuates
the mediated nature of the cinematic time by exploring multiple means of
temporal manipulation, rendering time more palpable than ever before. On
many occasions, the post-classical films dare to re-materialise the temporal
signifiers and 'mediate' the linear progression of time, thus transgressing the
classical prerogatives of the Hollywood paradigm.

But this general conception of time is not a mere abstraction; it is the
underlying principle of a very precise formal structure in the post-classical
system of time, which is fully integrated with the other two systems, causality and space. And this brings me to the second question that I previously
posed regarding the effects of the new motivations and spatial construction
on the representation of time. I think it is essential to embed the functions
of the temporal system into the wider narrative structure in order to understand how the different systems and levels of generality interact with each
other to create a narrative model of considerable depth and complexity. For
that purpose, I would like to stress that, at the broadest level, the system of
post-classical time is affected equally by the compositional and the realistic
motivation of the narrative logic. The change from the classical realism of the
Hollywood films to hypermediated realism has led to new temporal needs
to portray a story in the post-classical mode. The power of the logic of hypermediacy has allowed the multiplication of mediated images that are both
spatially and temporally related in a complex and multilayered manner. Yet,
these formal manipulations of the cinematic properties do not negate the
need to visualise time realistically; just as in the case of post-classical space,
the approach of the 'real' is effectuated here through the path of hypermediacy that treats technological interventions as an extension of our human
experience of reality.

In addition, the novelties of compositional motivation in the post-classical
model, such as the use of multiple characters, spliced plots and multiple story drafts, allow the films to fragment their temporality and treat the natural
passage of analogue time as one option among many others. And when this
option is preferred, the classical relations of equivalence or linear chronology are there to help satisfy the basic constructional needs of the story and
establish the cause-and-effect relations of the plot. Evidently, the role of the

post-classical temporal system in this broad scheme becomes multi-dimensional, as it is required to maintain a symmetry between the competing motivations and accomplish the ultimate goal, namely to produce a narrative film. The freedom of contemporary filmmakers to explore and expand cinematic language, as I have described here and in previous chapters, is still used for storytelling and, hence, requires a fine balance between the various narrative systems and their often contradictory goals.

Finally, we have to face the last question, which regards the specific features of the post-classical system of time and the way the narration handles the aspects of order, duration and frequency. This question can only be answered properly through the meticulous textual analysis of the selected films that provide ample evidence of a rich and intriguing temporality that problematises not only the nature of the new narrative mode but the nature of the cinematic medium in general. In fact, all the questions around the ability of filmic images to express tenses and to articulate temporal distinctions, which were presented in the opening of this chapter, find concrete answers in the works of the post-classical filmmakers who play with cinematic time with enormous ease and creativity. In the following pages I will explore the characteristics of temporal construction in the post-classical paradigm, using my film selection as a copious source of textual information. Instead of presenting selective case studies, this chapter will provide an analysis and classification of all 14 films according to the three broad temporal categories.

Temporal order

The post-classical paradigm offers contemporary filmmakers numerous choices for ordering the story events and arranging their presentation in the syuzhet. Whether they actually employ digital tools or not, they adopt the theoretical freedom of the digital technology and the computer screen to manipulate time in all directions. Liberated from the limitations of straight chronology, their films demonstrate that the linear movement in time becomes merely an option that can prevail at will. Out of the 14 sample narratives, 11 contain an intricate temporal order that outshines some of the most intriguing examples of complex chronology in cinema. My analysis of the post-classical temporal order will divide its focus into the two analytical areas: the issue of chronology and the possibility of simultaneity.

Starting with the questions of chronology, I would like to refer to *Fight Club*, as it certainly flaunts a complicated plot structure with heavy doses of suspense until the closing moments. The overt narration of the film (which will be extensively analysed in the next chapter for its excessive self-consciousness) relies on the playful and flexible treatment of time as a type of narrative loop. The plot opens at a climactic point in the action showing us the protagonist with a gun in his mouth. As soon as the gun is removed, he begins to explain his situation, described as Project Mayhem. After this short introduction, he initiates a brief flashback that stops abruptly after a few seconds to give way to another one that goes even further back in time, at the point when it all supposedly started. This narrational liberty, jumping back and forth in the fabula time, is a constant feature of the film, emulating the non-serial access of information in the digital environment. The second flashback indeed takes us to the source of the protagonist's problem and carries on the portrayal of the events in a largely linear order with several occasional shorter flashbacks, as for instance in the case of the explosion at the condo, the meeting between Tyler and Marla, and especially the realisation of the former's mental disorder. After all the twists of the plot are revealed, the loop of the film is finally completed with the return to the exact moment of the opening sequence where the protagonist has a gun in his mouth. The voice-over of the film says, 'I think this is about where we came in', to emphasise the closure of the loop, while Tyler Durden makes a joke about the flashback and states openly his awareness of the narrative device.

Similarly, Baz Luhrmann's *Moulin Rouge!* portrays a love story in the years around 1900 at the Moulin Rouge with its syuzhet constructed as a loop. A singing Toulouse-Lautrec hands over the narrative voice to Christian who sits forlornly in his room thinking about the loss of Satine. As he decides to write down the story of their tragic love affair, he initiates a flashback to the moment he arrived at the train station in Paris a year before. Throughout the film, the image of Christian tapping on his typewriter reappears to highlight the presence of the flashback, while the back-and-forth movements in the story materialise on the screen with the flamboyant pull-outs from and push-ins to the long establishing matte shot of Paris. Unlike the classical flashback that seeks to hide its traces, the post-classical narration of *Moulin Rouge!* returns to the present regularly without any concerns for the disruption of the linear procession of the fabula time. After the death of Satine onstage and her plea for their story to be told, we see Christian conclude both his novel and the film by typing 'the end' on the paper. Luhrmann's navigation into the wild life of the Parisian cabaret oscillates constantly between the present and the past, trying persistently to remind the viewers of the inescapable fate of the lovers and the tragic ending of their affair.

The use of the loop is also Park Chan-wook's preferred technique in *Oldboy*, as it enables him to orchestrate the plot twists and the riddle-solving of the story. A closer look at the first twenty minutes of the film is illustrative of the complex chronology that governs the entire narration. A pre-credit sequence welcomes us *in medias res*, as the silhouette of a person appears to be holding another one by a neck-tie on a roof-top ledge. The one holding the tie is Oh Dae-Su who introduces himself by initiating a flashback. The story events follow in the order below:

1. Cut to a police station where Oh Dae-Su has been arrested for being drunk and disorderly. He is bailed out by his friend, Joo-Hwan.
2. Oh Dae-Su calls his daughter from a phone booth. Joo-Hwan takes over the phone and, as he speaks, Oh Dae-Su is kidnapped by persons unknown.
3. credit sequence with various types of clocks ticking and turning.
4. Oh Dae-Su is held captive in a private prison resembling a shabby hotel room. He has been held captive there for two months with no indication of who is holding him there or why.
5. he describes his routine, which includes regular visits by his captors who clean the room and cut his hair. During those visits he is gassed into unconsciousness.
6. a year after his imprisonment, he watches on the news a report of his wife's murder and finds out that the police consider him to be the prime suspect. He has a nervous breakdown.
7. a montage sequence compresses the time Oh Dae-Su has spent watching television, using it as a watch and a calendar and relying on it as his only friend and companion.
8. one day he begins to write an autobiographical diary in his attempt to maintain his sanity and trace his captor. He fills several notebooks.
9. as time passes his boiling anger forces him to train by shadow boxing, punching at the walls of his prison until thick calluses form on his knuckles.
10. after the first six years, he decides to mark the passage of time on his hand by tattooing one straight line for each year that goes by. At the same time he begins to slowly dig a hole into one of the walls with the help of a metal chopstick.
11. a montage sequence compresses the years from the sixth to the fourteenth. With the use of a split-screen, the film shows us in the right half of the frame some of the key historical moments that took place in those years, such as the 9/11 attacks or Korea's participation in the football World Cup, while in the left half Oh Dae-Su is seen carrying out his daily activities.
12. by the fifteenth year Oh Dae-Su manages to dig through the wall and feel the rain in his hand. Filled with excitement, he estimates that it will take him another month to escape.
13. soon after, though, a woman enters his room and hypnotises him.
14. Oh Dae-Su is set free on a rooftop with a new suit of clothes and his prison diaries. He sees another man sitting on the edge of the building with a

small dog in his lap and he tries to communicate with him by touching and smelling him. That man is suicidal and attempts to jump off the edge, but Oh Dae-Su grabs his neck-tie, saving him from death. He asks him to postpone his death in order to listen to his story. This takes us back to the exact opening moment of the film and sheds new light on the scene.

The return to the opening scene does not only complete the temporal loop but it also helps us reinterpret the event before our eyes: the man holding the neck-tie is not trying to kill the other one, as it appeared the first time; instead, he is trying to forestall his death. This deception results from the staging of the action and foreshadows the broader sense of deception that the narrative performs, as regards the relations of the characters and their goals. Thus, the temporal ordering of the events becomes an ally in twisting the story and withholding its key secrets.

Moving on to *The Million Dollar Hotel*, we find the entire story enveloped in the flashback of the dead protagonist in a mode reminiscent of Billy Wilder's *Sunset Blvd*. As Tom Tom falls off the roof of the Million Dollar Hotel, he not only realises that 'life is the best' but also tries to present viewers with his reason for committing suicide. Hence, the unusual and unrealistic backward movement in time, which sets the clock of the syuzhet two weeks prior to the day of his fatal jump. A brilliant graphic match connects the present to the past and the moment that Tom Tom lost his life to the moment that life became meaningful to him – when he met Eloise. From that point on, the entire film depicts the story events chronologically, leading up to the revelation of the mystery and the character's motivation. Throughout this flashback, Wenders keeps the protagonist's voice on the voice-over track commenting on the action and reminding us of the finality of his demise in the film's resolution. Moreover, a brief flashback within this overarching flashback takes place before the closing moments to portray Tom Tom's memories of his friend's murder on that same roof. With the return to the present and the formation of the temporal loop, *The Million Dollar Hotel* reverses the classical Hollywood linear structure and emphasises the possibilities of the moving images to transcend the limits of analogue movement and to manipulate narrative time in the most improbable ways by giving life and voice to the dead.

On a similar note, the characters in *Lola Rennt* are not simply granted the opportunity to return to life but also the chance to alter their fates. Tykwer builds his film with a parallel plot structure that contains three forking paths. After a short introduction to the main compositional elements, such as the characters and their goals, the film narrative diverges into three possible narrative threads with three different outcomes. In this case, the notion of the loop materialises more than once; as soon as the first plotline reaches a conclusion, the film returns to the same point in the fabula time and starts an entirely new plotline all over again. Thus, the temporal order emulates the functions of video games containing various options of time and story manipulation. However, the temporal complexity of the film is not reduced to this multiple-draft narrative. On the contrary, the vast opportunities of the digital technical language are relentlessly explored throughout all the various parts of the film, manipulating the time of the syuzhet in the most exhilarating fashion. For example, the initial phone call between the two protagonists, Lola and Manni, is intertwined with two flashbacks depicting what went wrong that morning and they failed to meet. As they recount their respective experiences, the syuzhet visualises the information they exchange in a disjointed and abrupt manner, crosscutting between the colour images of the present and the black-and-white images of the past. Furthermore, as their discussion reaches a climax and Manni begins to panic, he remembers his boss's violent behaviour and starts another brief flashback in black-and-white. This pattern is repeated several times in the course of the film, interrupting the chronology of the story and creating a fragmented temporal order.

The same is also true in the case of *Natural Born Killers*, a film that has been extensively analysed for its spliced plot, extreme hypermediated realism and densely constructed cinematic spaces. Regarding the temporal relations of the narrative, the opening sequence plunges us into the story world *in medias res*, showing the slaughter of several customers in a diner by the murderous couple, Mickey and Mallory. As soon as the scene is completed, the film makes a backward movement in time in order to describe the history of this couple, beginning from the day they met. This flashback is initiated by Mallory's memory and is visualised in a highly self-conscious manner in the form of a television sitcom episode (as repeatedly noted). Although the start of the flashback is clearly signalled, the closure is slightly more ambivalent and could be positioned after the marriage. However, the syuzhet does not return to Mallory and her reminiscing but makes another odd temporal leap by cutting to the *American Maniacs* television show, which is dedicated to the killing sprees of the protagonists. The show itself is located chronologically after the marriage but in fact functions as another flashback on their actions, those that occurred between the marriage and the preparation of the programme. This unusual covert flashback is completed when the syuzhet takes us to the editing room where Wayne Gale consults with his assistants and from then on the story continues in a linear order until the end.

The few examples of flashbacks that I have described reveal that the sample films exhibit not only numerous but also extremely inventive ways of breaking chronology and creating a bifurcating temporal order. Another device that contributes to this purpose is the flashforward, which has now become a possible option in the repertoire of the post-classical filmmakers. Although it still remains less popular than the flashback, it is worth noticing the different ways that the syuzhet of the films makes a forward movement in the fabula time. For instance, among the flagrant convolutions of the plot in *Amélie* we find a flashforward that is both recounted in the voice-over and visualised on the screen. When Amélie arrives in Paris to begin a new life, the voice-over narrator announces, 'It is August 29th. In 28 hours, her life will change forever. But she doesn't know it yet', while a series of shots flash rapidly prematurely revealing some of the scenes that will follow and will indeed change her life. Another example is found in *Lola Rennt* where the future fate of some secondary characters is unveiled through the flashing of several still photos that capture future occurrences. These flashforwards appear frequently throughout the film and change from plotline to plotline in order to emphasise the difference that Lola makes to the world around her as she runs her twenty-minute course. The photos are introduced by an intertitle with the words 'Und dann' and they are accompanied by the sound of the flash that renders the use of the device fairly intelligible. Lastly, *Trainspotting* contains an interesting case of forward movement, which constitutes part of a larger and more complicated scene construction that exhibits an enormous narrative freedom and fluidity in time and space.[9] The flashforward is initiated by the protagonist, Mark Renton, who blatantly freezes the progression of a scene in order to shed light on the true version of a past incident. More specifically, after his friend Begbie (Robert Carlyle) has bragged about winning a pool game, Renton moves the syuzhet a few days forward to show us how he found out that Begbie had been lying. As soon as the truth is established, the flashforward ends and the film resumes from the scene that had been frozen. It is worth noticing how the flashforwards in all three films are signalled by non-diegetic sources of information, such as the voice-over commentary or intertitles that facilitate audience comprehension. In contrast to the total lack of flashforwards in classical Hollywood and the highly ambiguous and obscure flashforwards of art films, the use of the device in the post-classical paradigm becomes more frequent and more communicative than ever before.

Yet, the most innovative element of the construction of time in the post-classical era is its emphasis on the portrayal of the temporal relation of simultaneity. This particular characteristic of the temporal system is closely dependent on the post-classical system of space, which favours the spatial montage and the creation of visual clusters, as underlined in the previous chapter. The principle of spatial montage is to combine several images on one screen and to reinforce the logic of addition and coexistence. The simultaneous arrangement of visual information on the same surface creates a new type of story ordering that is entirely incongruent with the rules of the classical cinema. As soon as the frame becomes freely occupied by a number of separate representations, the narrative function of the cluster becomes extremely dense with intricate temporal nuances. If we return to Bordwell's typology of order, and specifically the four relations of simultaneity and successivity, we will realise that the post-classical paradigm gives equal prominence to all the options by promoting the role of simultaneous depictions. However, a close analysis of the clusters and the spatial montage in my sample films demonstrates that the relations between syuzhet and fabula events in the state of simultaneity become more complex and ask for a more careful classification. Towards that end, I would like to suggest the following four types of temporal relations that can be distinguished in a cinematic cluster:

1. simultaneous events in the fabula can be depicted simultaneously.
2. successive events in the fabula can be presented simultaneously.
3. a single event in the fabula can be presented simultaneously with non-diegetic information such as graphics, titles or other signs.
4. a single event in the fabula can be broken into several fragments and be presented simultaneously from different diegetic levels.[10]

The dominance of the spatial dimensions of the moving image and the power of cinematic techniques such as digital compositing, split-screens and back projections, develop new temporal patterns that are no longer constrained by the linear, sequential passage of analogue time. The films that I have chosen as archetypes of the post-classical cinema offer a rich inventory of such new patterns that are worth a closer look.

Starting with Lars von Trier's *Europa*, we can look at the shots analysed in the chapter on space and find several relations of simultaneity. The shots in figures 1.1, 1.3 and 1.5 contain a single event – the first encounter between Katharina and Leo in the train compartment – but its depiction is built out of different projections that fragment the spatio-temporal qualities of the shot without such fragmentation occurring in the actual story. On the contrary, the transition from the shot in figure 1.7 to the one in figure 1.8 signifies a shift in the time and place of the events – the first shot is by a river and the second in a church – but the actors do not move in time. In figure 1.8 we simultaneously see the priest and the protagonists, despite the fact that for that brief second these two images exist in different time locations. Moreover, in figure 1.20 there is a more conventional representation of a telephone conversation during which we see the people at the two ends of the line appearing together in separate projections. Lastly, the shots in figures 1.16–1.19 would fall under the third category that I have created, as they contain visual information that belongs to different diegetic levels. In all four cases, Leo acts at the story level – dreaming, shooting, drowning or running – while the back projection shows simultaneously other images that are clearly non-diegetic.

In *Requiem for a Dream* the relation of simultaneity is visualised with the ubiquitous use of split-screens. One of the intriguing functions of this device is to break down a single event into two different views. In figure 2.1 we see Sara on the top looking down, while the object of her look appears as a point-of-view shot on a different screen at the bottom. Similarly, the intimate moment between Harry and Marion is split into two separate takes on the same action (figs 2.2–2.7). Where Lars von Trier employs the traditional back projections to separate the action into distinct planes, Darren Aronofsky divides it into horizontal or vertical split-screens.

On the other hand, the images from *Natural Born Killers* demonstrate how the visual clusters can combine the story events with non-diegetic elements and create tension between the various narrative levels. For instance, the shot in figure 5.3 replays Mickey's point-of-view shot in figure 5.2 coalescing it with his mental imprint that shows another murder. Along the same lines, the dense image in figure 5.4 displays simultaneously both the diegetic act of making love and the internally focalised reflections on the window that represent the characters' inner state of mind.[11] The entire film employs a wide range of technical means, and particularly digital compositing, to build images that allow different aspects of time to coexist in the same cinematic space.

Numerous examples are also found in *Amélie*, a film that flaunts highly complicated and rich temporal articulations. Regarding the issue of simultaneity, we often see the characters' thoughts being visualised while the action is taking place, as in figures 6.5–6.8. Other times the extra-diegetic commentary interferes with the story in order to emphasise certain aspects, such as the spermatazoa that led to Amélie's conception or a fly on the window (figs 6.14–6.16), to name just a few.

In addition, I would like to bring into this discussion two films not analysed in the chapter on space for reasons of economy and organisation. Both *Lola Rennt* and *Fight Club* contain intriguing examples of spatial montage that call attention to the possibilities of simultaneity as outlined above. In Tykwer's film the parallel itineraries of Manni and Lola beg for a synchronised depiction of their action, which materialises with the use of split-screens instead of the traditional crosscutting. In figure 11.1 we see Manni waiting on the left, while Lola runs frantically on the right. As time runs out, the frame is divided into three parts to accommodate a close-up view of the hands of the clock (fig. 11.2). The shot in figure 11.3 is particularly remarkable as the three sections of the screen depict the same event from different angles: starting from the right, we have Lola's point-of-view shot of Manni who appears on the left in closer view as he looks up at the clock, which appears as his own point-of-view shot at the bottom of the screen. Tykwer captures the action by fragmenting the screen and thus emphasising the importance of time and simultaneity for the progression of the story.

fig. 11.1

fig. 11.2

Finally, an intriguing case of simultaneous depiction of distinct visual elements is found in *Fight Club*. The images in figures 12.1–12.3 are part of a long tracking shot that is digitally composed in order to fuse the IKEA catalogue with the apartment of the main character. The meticulously selected furnishings appear gradually on the screen along with the captions that accompany them in the catalogue while at the same time Edward Norton is shown walking in the midst of them. The story action is thus complemented with very explicit non-diegetic information to create images that exist in entirely separate time locations.

fig. 11.3

On the whole, the analysis of the films according to the principles of temporal order brings to the surface the significant departure of the post-classical paradigm from the classical rules of temporal articulation. The various examples prove that the ordering of the fabula events in the syuzhet of the post-classical films has become significantly more complex and varied than the one we find in the classical tradition. The filmmakers appear to be freed from the tyranny of linearity, as they handle the narrative time with the flexibility and omni-directionality that is embodied in digital technology. In practical terms, this means that the story events are frequently shuffled and portrayed in random or reverse order. At the same time, this freedom creates an intense need for temporal precision in the staging of the events and their explicit positioning in their fabula world. The forward and backward movements in time do not aim to create ambiguity or confu-

fig. 12.1

fig. 12.2

fig. 12.3

sion for the viewer and for that purpose the narration uses multiple devices, such as voice-overs and intertitles, that consistently inform spectators about the temporal shifts and breaks in the portrayal of the action.

Temporal duration

The parameter of duration in the post-classical paradigm offers even more possibilities for innovative creation and experimentation. The fact that the cinematic duration is divided into three separate but intertwined variables – fabula, syuzhet and screen duration – provides opportunities for multiple combinations, which are indeed fully explored in this new model. With a variety of technical and stylistic devices the filmmakers manipulate the temporal duration by constantly alternating the rhythm of the narration and relentlessly shifting the relations of equivalence, reduction and expansion. The duration thus becomes a palpable filmic element that contributes not only to the basic compositional needs of the story but also to the hypermediated realism that motivates the construction of these films.

This section will investigate the characteristics of temporal articulation in the sample along the categories of equivalence, reduction and expansion in order to understand how the fabula, the syuzhet and the screen duration work together. As an introductory observation, I would like to note that if we look at the three types of cinematic duration independently of each other, we will realise that the post-classical paradigm maintains several of the classical elements. This means that both the fabula and the plot duration are governed by deadlines that ensure the forward movement of the story, just as in the classical model. As far as the screen duration is concerned, the films tend to have an average length of approximately 120 minutes, which is slightly longer than the typical Hollywood film of the studio era. However, the significant differences between the two modes can be traced if we study the relations of these three durational types and the patterns they have developed in the post-classical treatment of time.

Starting with equivalence, it is evident that all the films contain several scenes, during which all the variables have an equal duration. On the other hand, the frequent use of fast editing and abundant optical effects has seriously curtailed the number and the length of these scenes and has privileged, instead, the strategies of reduction and expansion. Firstly, the tactic of reduction allows the fabula duration to be narrated in an abridged fashion either by means of ellipsis or compression. The pervasive role of ellipses and montage sequences that characterised the Hollywood narration is explored even further in the new paradigm, which multiplies the functions of these devices and accentuates their role as punctuation marks.[12] On the other hand, the strategy of compression that was all too marginal in classical films and was typically reserved for comic situations now becomes a staple in the narrative process. Imitating the recurrent use of fast-motion in the tradition of animation, the post-classical filmmakers choose to compress both the fabula and syuzhet duration on the screen for several purposes, as some selective examples will demonstrate.

In *Requiem for a Dream* there are plentiful scenes that are compressed with the use of fast-motion for the reason that the accelerated tempo of the screen duration aims at emphasising the addictive states of the four protagonists and their subjective experience of time. For instance, the fabula events that are usually portrayed in fast-motion include parties under the influence of drugs and Sara's hyper-kinetic daily routine caused by the diet pills. Moreover, when Sara begins her diet, Aronofsky uses the technique of pixilation in order to condense the consumption of the egg, the coffee and the grapefruit into a fleeting second and thus capture Sara's impression of the passage of time. In a parallel fashion, Wenders plays with fast-motion on several occasions in *The Million Dollar Hotel* and manipulates the natural duration of the scenes to produce a type of aura around some characters. For example, when Tom Tom spends time in his room alone listening to music, a combination of fast-motion and jump-cuts create a dynamic visual moment, while in another scene, the arrest of Geronimo by the police, Tom Tom's resistance is accentuated by the accelerated pace of the image track. Similarly, in *City of God* the potential of fast-motion to intensify the dramatic resonance of the action is exploited in several scenes of violence, especially those that involve confrontations with Lil' Ze's carnivorous gang. In the celebrated opening sequence, the camera swirls around Buscapé's body in fast-motion to indicate the dizzying emotion that takes over him in that menacing situation. In other cases, the gang's brutal attacks on the inhabitants of the *favela* are compressed in fast-motion both for dramatic and economical purposes. Lastly, I will refer to *Moulin Rouge!* and its extensive use of compression in numerous scenes that contributes to the overall excessive style of the film. Luhrmann indulges frequently in fast-motion projection for three basic purposes: to accelerate the transitional shots between places and particularly the entrance to the Moulin Rouge; to caricature some character movements and gestures; and to heighten the spectacular dance numbers in the cabaret. Overall, the technique of fast-motion has become a favourite option in contemporary filmmaking for its ability to accentuate certain events or characters, to capture some aspects of the psychological experience of time and to generally produce dynamic and playful sequences.

On a parallel note, the second type of temporal manipulation, the durational expansion, enjoys enormous popularity in the post-classical narratives and is effectuated both through the technique of insertion and dilation. The former expands the time of the fabula by inserting non-diegetic frames or longer excerpts that do not belong to the actual story events but serve as a commentary or a means of association. Even though all the films are crammed with such examples, in some cases the insertions are so impressively long and autonomous that they are worth a special mention. In *Fight Club* the voice-over narrator suddenly interrupts the progression of the action in order to make an illustrative introduction to Tyler Durden and his activities. When the two characters stand outside the bar after their first drink together, the scene literally freezes and a long non-diegetic extract takes up the screen for a few minutes to present information about Tyler's life.[13] Once the insertion is completed, the scene continues to unfold from the point where it had stopped. Furthermore, there is the case of *Europa* where an overhead shot of the railway tracks and a non-diegetic voice-over take over the syuzhet of the film for the first two minutes and twenty seconds without allowing the opening of the fabula time. These images return several times throughout the entire screen duration, interrupting the flow of the story in a consistent manner. In a similar fashion, the opening of *Magnolia* expands the time of the syuzhet by using material that is related to the main action only by way of association. For five minutes and thirty seconds, an entirely non-diegetic prologue depicts three different events that are all characterised by deadly coincidences and could be compared to the events of the fabula that will be depicted. This remarkable retardation of the story is repeated once more right before the closing moments and functions again as an additional commentary on the meaning of the stories that the film portrays. Moreover, there are shorter inserts throughout the film in the form of intertitles that give information about the weather forecast and can be understood only in relation to the rain of frogs that takes place at the end.

At the same time, there is a kind of expansion by insertion that applies to the lower levels of narration, and particularly that of deep internal focalisation. In this case, the duration of the fabula time is expanded by the addition of a subjective version of a story event between two scenes of the actual action. For instance, in *Natural Born Killers* Stone uses what he calls 'vertical cutting' between an 'inner moment' and an 'outer moment' in the opening scene at the diner when the waitress serves Mickey and Mallory at the bar. The objective reality of the woman bartending, which appears in colour, is briefly intercut with a black-and-white shot of her coming on to Mickey, which functions as the portrayal of her subjective state of mind.[14] The same technique is also found in *Requiem for a Dream* where the syuzhet misleads the viewers momentarily by depicting the fantasies of the characters instead of the real incidents. One such case occurs when Harry and Tyrone are eating in a canteen next to a cop. We see Harry managing to grab the latter's gun and tossing it back and forth to Tyrone in order to ridicule the exasperated cop. However, their play is suddenly interrupted by the return to reality where we understand that Harry was merely fantasising about playing a trick on the cop and that his fantasy does not materialise. With the insertion of the imaginary act into the film Aronofsky engages the screen with extremely focalised images and delays the progression of the fabula.

On the contrary, the other sort of expansion, the technique of dilation, overtly 'delays' the forward movement of both the fabula and the syuzhet with the help of slow-motion or step-printing cinematography. As in the case of fast-motion, this temporal option is now considered as a typical dramatic effect of contemporary filmmaking that serves different expressive needs. For example, it is interesting to look at Wong Kar-wai's use of step-printing in various scenes in order to slow down the portrayal of fast-moving action, such as the chase in the opening sequence. Likewise, Luhrmann employs it to achieve a blurry impressionistic view of the cabaret dances, while he prefers plain slow-motion for dramatising Satine's fainting spells and eventually her death. In Wenders' film slow-motion, apart from the suicide scene, is also found in the first encounters of the two leading characters, as they meet in the corridor of the hotel and engage in a sort of romantic dance with the help of the optical printers and sound effects. With the exception of *Arizona Dream*, all the other sample films resort regularly to the technique of dilation in their attempt to heighten the depiction of the story, to highlight specific scenes or character movements and to create images with a strong affective undercurrent.

Lastly, before closing the discussion of duration and the complex grid of temporal relations in the post-classical narratives, it is essential to call attention to their ever-increasing use of the temporal pause. Freeze-frames constituted a rather marginal option in mainstream cinematic traditions but now they are merely another ordinary device employed for a range of narrative or stylistic purposes. The impressive use of the freeze-frame in *All About Eve* (1951), which has been so extensively analysed for its narrative boldness and exceptionality (see Kozloff 1988; Chatman 1990), pales by comparison with the examples of frozen images that we find in the sample. One of the recurring functions of the freeze-frame is to mark the ending of the film, as in *Lola Rennt*. Along the same lines, Wong Kar-wai uses a freeze-frame in the middle of *Chungking Express* in order to signal the ending of the first plot and the beginning of the second. Yet, the ability of this device to suspend cinematic time and act as a boundary is explored in a more piecemeal manner right in the heart of the story both in *Fight Club* and *Trainspotting*. In the former, the narrator pauses the diegetic time with the intention of making a non-diegetic tour into the life of Tyler Durden, while in the latter the leading character stops the progression of the scene with Begbie's tale about the pool game and uses the freeze-frame as a boundary for the flashforward that exposes his unreliability. On other occasions, as in *Moulin Rouge!*, the plentiful freeze-frames serve the expressive needs of the film and its overall flamboyant style. For instance, when Christian is asked to write a play about love for Toulouse-Lautrec and his company, he suddenly realises that he has never been in love. His bewilderment and hesitation are portrayed on the screen not only with the help of Ewan McGregor's acting skills but also with the palpable contribution of the temporal pause. On the other hand, in several cases the image freezes to facilitate the descriptive purposes of the narration and to allow the viewers to comprehend certain aspects of the images. For that reason, the still frame is almost invariably accompanied by an explanatory voice-over that conveys the necessary information to the audience. In *City of God* the narrator pauses on many faces along the way in order to introduce them and anticipate their actions before the plot moves frantically forward. In contrast, in *Oldboy* Park Chan-wook resorts to the freeze-frame discussed in chapter two (fig. 9.8) in order to give us time to register the position of the characters and the impending attack. However, the most extravagant example is found in the introductory sequence of *Magnolia*, which features the story of an unsuccessful suicide attempt that became a successful homicide. The absurd incident is portrayed with the help of multiple intermittent freeze-frames showing the young man landing on a net, his mother pulling a shotgun and his father standing by the window (figs 13.1–13.3), while the voice-over simultaneously describes the situation in detail. The use of the freeze-frame becomes even more extreme when the narrator pauses on the long shot of the suicidal jump and turns the frame into a drawing surface upon which he is free to draw the itinerary of the falling body and emphasise the extraordinariness of the event (figs 13.4–13.6).

fig. 13.1

fig. 13.2

fig. 13.3

Overall, the investigation of the characteristics of the temporal duration of the sample has revealed the intricate relations of reduction and compression as well as the power of the pause that endow the post-classical system of time. As in the case of order, the filmmakers appear to opt for a highly manipulated duration that entails complex configurations of fabula, syuzhet and screen time. Even though the importance of equivalence and of the 'natural' progression of analogue time is not abolished, the post-classical time shows how these temporal relations are merely some options in a wider repertoire of possibilities for shaping the representation of time in the cinema.

fig. 13.4

Temporal frequency

fig. 13.5

The category of frequency has been considerably less popular in theoretical discussions of time, partly because Henderson's four types are not always easily identifiable and partly because the singulative form is the dominant type of frequency in most narratives. On the other hand, if we use Bordwell's typology and distinguish between the recounting and the enacting of the fabula events, then it becomes too complicated to keep track of all the combinations of frequency that appear in a film. The study of this parameter, however,

fig. 13.6

becomes interesting if we single out which cases are more accepted or forbidden in each cinematic tradition and we investigate how this particular temporal aspect relates to some broader narrative concerns. For instance, in the classical Hollywood paradigm it is an ordinary practice to have the story events mentioned in the characters' dialogue once or several times, depending on their importance to the action, whereas it is highly improbable for the syuzhet to dramatise the same occurrence more than once. The repetition of a dramatisation is difficult to justify in a realistic manner, as it rarely serves any compositional needs, with the exception of some detective stories where repetition is often required for solving a murder or other mysteries.

In the post-classical cinema the taboo on the repeating form is frequently broken, as the compositional motivations become more flexible and the spatio-temporal co-ordinates become multi-functional. In eight out of 14 sample films, there are various repetitions that assume different constructional roles in the story each time. In *Lola Rennt* several scenes or smaller segments of the first plotline are repeated in the subsequent two, while there are some shots, such as the red phone ringing or the bag falling from Lola's hands, which are replayed a few times within the same scene. In *Natural Born Killers* Oliver Stone habitually replays many moments in the story by modifying the stylistic properties of the shots. Furthermore, the opening scene of *Trainspotting*, showing Renton and his friends being chased by the police, is repeated in the course of the film with a different voice-over without any significantly different narrative purpose. The first showing functions as an autonomous introduction to the main character – hence the freeze-frame on Renton's smirking face – while the second showing is integral to the diegetic world. Another repetition is found in *The Million Dollar Hotel* with Tom Tom's jump off the roof in slow-motion appearing in both the opening and closing moments of the film. Lastly, the replay of certain scenes becomes more spectacular in *Fight Club* and *Magnolia*; in Fincher's film the repetition of many story events from an objective angle is essential for the revelation of the plot twist and it is executed in a highly ostentatious manner. In an equally exhibitionist style, Paul Thomas Anderson makes several repetitions throughout the film with the suicide/homicide story being the most obvious one. In order to accentuate the peculiarity of the incident, he shows it in its entirety from three different angles in the beginning of the film, while he repeats a short fragment a fourth time before the ending.[15]

Broadly speaking, the traits of temporal frequency in the post-classical paradigm are admittedly less daring or groundbreaking than those witnessed in the category of order and duration. The films largely depend on the singulative form in Henderson's terms, enacting each event once even if they recount it more times. On the other hand, the emergence of the repeating form in various instances should not be understated, as it clearly supports the broader tendency of contemporary filmmakers to treat cinematic time autonomously of strict compositional motivations and to display their control over the narrating act. The strategy of repeating certain scenes or shots, however partially and moderately, contributes to their attempt to update cinematic language according to the principles of digital technology and to emulate the latter's inherent ability to rewind and replay the same images over and over again.[16]

POST-CLASSICAL NARRATION: SELF-CONSCIOUSNESS, KNOWLEDGEABILITY AND COMMUNICATIVENESS

The main focus of this book has concentrated so far on the exploration of the post-classical mode of narration along its three main narrative systems: causality, space and time. A close textual analysis of a sample of contemporary films has brought to the surface the workings of a new narrative model and revealed several fine distinctions and particularities that distinguish it from the other cinematic traditions of the past and especially from the classical Hollywood cinema. This chapter will carry on the attempt to map the parameters of this model but the focus will shift slightly to a different set of concepts, which describe the way the narration functions as a transmitter of information. More specifically, I will pursue the analytical agenda that David Bordwell put forward in his account of the classical Hollywood cinema[1] and examine the characteristics of the post-classical narratives along three evaluative scales: self-consciousness, knowledgeability and communicativeness. Bordwell borrowed these conceptual tools from Meir Sternberg's work in order to elucidate the workings of the classical narration and to contradict the common prejudice that a Hollywood movie is simply a transparent and illusionist mechanism (see Bordwell *et al.* 1985: 25). Similarly, I will employ these terms to examine the post-classical paradigm and understand how the three systems – the narrative logic, space and time – operate at a different level as vehicles for the transmission of information about the story.

But before anything else, I would like to explain what these qualities mean in order to clarify their contribution to understanding narration. Firstly, a narration can be *self-conscious* to different degrees, depending on how much it acknowledges the fact that it is presenting information to an audience. The core question one asks in order to evaluate this self-consciousness is: how aware is the narration of addressing the audience? Secondly, a narration can be more or less *knowledgeable* in relation to how much information it has about the story. The question here is: how much does the narration know? Thirdly, a narration is *communicative* at various levels according to how much information it communicates to the viewer. Now the question becomes: how willing is the narration to tell us what it knows? A classical narration manifests all three qualities with systematic fluctuations that can be codified precisely and can differentiate it quite clearly from other types of narration, especially the one developed in European art cinema. What Bordwell does to codify these different aspects of the narrative is to analyse his sample films from start to finish in order to trace how their self-consciousness, knowledgeability and communicativeness varies during the progression of the story. According to his overall observation on classical films:

> In the opening passages of the film, the narration is moderately self-conscious and overtly suppressive. As the film proceeds, the narration becomes less self-conscious and more communicative. The exceptions to these tendencies are also strictly codified. The end of the film may quickly reassert the narration's omniscience and self-consciousness. (Bordwell *et al.* 1985: 25)

More specifically, a classical film opens with a credit sequence, which is a self-conscious device that addresses the audience directly, introducing the cast and often setting the tone of the film. The first sequences are usually highly expository and omniscient as they intend to provide information about the time and place of the story and the principal characters. Gradually, the narration tries to phase itself out and to communicate information only through the characters' dialogue and interaction. This is a crucial strategy that works effectively to build an integral diegetic world and to efface any narrational manipulation from the outside. Despite the fact that the camera is spatially omnipresent in a technical sense, the narration controls its omniscience by using the characters to motivate the movement both in space but particularly in time. For instance, the flashbacks are always motivated through a character's memory, even though the actual information of a flashback exceeds that character's consciousness. Moreover, the protagonists are responsible for revealing or suppressing information and they are charged with repeating decisive cues, so that the viewers can follow the story. However, the classical narration does not restrict its knowledge to a single person's subjective view. It becomes more communicative by smoothly moving from one character to another, by occasionally employing impersonal sources of information, such as the media, and by maintaining continuity in time and place. Finally, in the closing moments of a Hollywood film there is a very clear sense of closure, into which the film steadily and efficiently builds, and this closure is further accentuated by an epilogue that confirms the stability of the narrative state. At this stage, the narration can risk a modest degree of self-consciousness with non-diegetic titles or an occasional direct address to the camera, but, as in the beginning, these devices wield very little influence on the actual closing of the story, which has explicitly resulted from the characters' actions.

In addition to this epigrammatic overview of classical narrative traits, I would like to refer to another side of narration: the process of creating and filling gaps.[2] Bordwell again borrows some of Sternberg's concepts to demonstrate how classical film handles the development of the story and the spectators' expectations by calling attention to informational gaps and by inviting the formation of certain hypotheses. Even though creating gaps seems to be a fundamental and indispensable goal for all narrative films in cinematic history, what typifies the Hollywood film is that it steadily leads to the filling of these gaps, to the confirmation of the hypotheses and to the creation of the feeling of certainty. While European art-film directors close their films leaving some, if not most, questions unanswered, the classical Hollywood conventions dictate the need for the classical film to show it all, to tell it all and to know it all by the time it reaches the end.

With these theoretical issues in mind, in the next section I will begin to explain how the post-classical narration manifests Sternberg's three narrative qualities, leading the post-classical films to adopt new strategies for handling the transmission of story information.

The transformations of the post-classical narration

The features of self-consciousness, knowledgeability and communicativeness are moulded primarily by the motivations that govern the system of narrative logic of a film, as delineated in chapter one.[3] The transformations that took place as we moved from the classical to the post-classical mode produced a different balance among these three qualities and refashioned the manner in which the films conduct their storytelling capacity. First and foremost, the post-classical narration is characterised by the prominence of hypermediated realism and parody as key motivational factors, which entail by definition the foregrounding of the act of representation and the awareness that they are performing a narrating operation. As a result, an extremely high degree of self-consciousness becomes a vital trait of the post-classical film that acknowledges in every instance its constructed nature. In sharp contrast to the solid diegetic world of the classical film and its unobtrusive visual style, the post-classical counterparts dare to break the diegesis and the 'window to the world' in order to explore the numerous possibilities of the storytelling act.

On the other hand, when we turn to the traits of knowledgeability and communicativeness, the differences between the classical and the post-classical are subtler. The post-classical narration is as knowledgeable as the classical, in the sense that we understand that the film has most of the story information at its disposal. The influence of the soaring self-consciousness, however, allows the post-classical film to disclose its knowledgeability more freely than the classical, which would normally use the characters' interactions as pretexts for hiding its ability to know everything and move without constraint in the story world. Similarly, the self-consciousness affects the manner in which the post-classical narration manifests its communicativeness. Although, both the classical and the post-classical are fairly communicative types that increasingly transmit more information as the plot develops, the post-classical films do not hesitate to reveal crucial secrets of the story even from the very beginning. Therefore, the intriguing side of the post-classical self-consciousness is that, instead of thwarting the knowledgeability and communicativeness of the narration for the sake of obscurity and ambiguity,[4] it reinforces them to such an extent that it produces a rich and multifaceted narration that 'knows it all' and 'tells it all' very explicitly.

These preliminary observations will certainly be supported by detailed examples from the sample films. Yet, before proceeding to the textual evidence, I would like to dwell on the issue of self-consciousness and the different shapes it acquires. My emphasis is purposefully placed on this particular quality, as it is the one that marks a clear-cut differentiation between the classical and the post-classical, while it also has a bearing on the materialisation of knowledgeability and communicativeness.

Self-consciousness in focus

The aspect of self-consciousness, or reflexivity as it is commonly labelled, has a long tradition in artistic practices. According to a broad definition, 'artistic reflexivity refers to the process by which texts foreground their own production, their authorship, their intertextual influences, their textual processes, or their reception' (Stam *et al.* 1992: 200). Reflexivity as a narrative strategy aims at revealing the principles of the construction of a film or, in other words, at 'laying bare the device', as noted earlier in the section on artistic motivation. Consequently, the viewers are encouraged to regard the portrayed events as merely a fictive account and to see through the conventions that regulate it. In his book *Reflexivity in Film and Literature* (1992) Robert Stam dedicates a chapter on the 'genre of self-consciousness' and presents some enlightening arguments on the subject, which I would like to use as a guide for my brief overview.[5]

Starting with a concept by now familiar to us, Stam observes that parody is a key expressive tool of self-conscious texts in their attempt to 'defiantly call attention to their artifice and operations'. Given that I have already analysed rather exhaustively the workings of parody as a strong artistic motivation in the post-classical films in chapter one,[6] at this point it would suffice to summarise his central argument. In agreement with most of the theorists discussed, he argues that parody 'can be seen as an ever-present tendency which renders explicit the intrinsic processes of textuality' (1992: 134). As a reflexive strategy, parody highlights art's historicity and constructs itself on the destruction of cinematic codes that have become outmoded and may be superseded. This justifies convincingly why parody has become such a crucial weapon in the self-reflexive artillery of the post-classical narratives in their endeavour to outgrow the classical and other cinematic traditions.

Furthermore, self-reflexivity in the cinema aims at exposing or experimenting with the narrative process itself and the diverse structures it can assume. One significant aspect of reflexive films is the overt manipulation of the temporal and spatial co-ordinates of the story. While the classical narration favours continuity and smooth transitions from place to place and from one point in time to another, in order to limit its omniscience and to minimise its self-consciousness, the post-classical narration accentuates its reflexivity, and by extension its high knowledgeability, by calling explicit attention to the treatment of time and space through editing discontinuities, visual effects and hypermediated images. The filmmakers enjoy the freedom to play with temporal devices by moving back and forth in the story or by freezing, slowing down and speeding up the image track in order to reaffirm their narrative power. At the same time, the self-conscious construction of space presents no limits or prohibitions; the camera can be anywhere, it can move in all possible ways and, above all, it can visualise anything. The same concept of the overt manipulation characterises the entire visual style of self-reflexive films, as they refuse a transparent self-effacing cinematic language and opt for a 're-materialisation of the filmic signifiers' (Elsaesser 1998b: 205).[7]

What should not go unnoticed is the affinity of these reflexive techniques with what Tom Gunning (1990) has codified as the 'cinema of attractions'. Early cinema until 1906 flaunted a set of stylistic elements that were distinctively diverse from the narrative films of the later years inasmuch as they emphasised the exhibitionist qualities of cinema. Big close-ups, recurring looks at the camera and cinematic manipulations, such as slow-motion and double exposure, were employed in order to address the audience directly and to rupture the self-contained diegetic world. With the passage of time, the storytelling ability of the cinematic medium prevailed and the 'cinema of attractions' went underground either as a component of avant-garde practices or as a momentary aberration in classical narrative films (see Gunning 1990: 57). This parallel between pre-classical and post-classical narratives was also observed by Miriam Hansen who claimed that they are both characterised by 'a measure of instability that makes the intervening decades look relatively stable, by contrast, for they are anchored in and centred by the classical system' (quoted in King 2000: 30).

However, in my account of post-classical narration both Gunning and Hansen's claims about the affinities of contemporary cinema with the 'cinema of attractions' are not taken without caution. My textual analysis shows that the post-classical works weigh upon such an intricate formal structure that any oversimplifying opposition like spectacle versus narrative or any over-statement about the death of storytelling simply rings hollow. Despite the deployment of a wide range of anti-illusionist devices that problematise the image and its sources, the sample films appear to be equally clinging to the narrative strength of the medium in order to explore more complex and challenging ways of telling a story.

In fact, the obsession with the very act of 'telling a story' is embodied in the way self-reflexive films challenge the role of the narrator/author. According to Stam, reflexive artists tend to emphasise the narrative by employing overt narrators as authorial stand-ins, who show off their omniscience and boast their authorial interventions (see 1992: 149–50). This will be precisely the focus of the close analysis of my sample films in this chapter, as they all constitute very intriguing cases of ubiquitous and powerful voice-over narrators that test the limits of narrative theory. As Robert Burgoyne observes:

> One of the most daunting problems for film narrative theory centres on the status of the cinematic narrator, understood as the illocutionary source or instance of emission of the narrative discourse. Because film is a visual rather than a verbal medium, and does not imply a literal speaker or hearer, some theorists argue that the need to designate a narratological source for the representation of the fictional world is obviated: the events of the fictional world simply 'tell themselves', in the words of Emile Benveniste. (1990: 4)[8]

This is a strong point of contention among film narratologists and, unfortunately, Bordwell's own work reflects the conundrum in question. He has adopted a rather inconsistent attitude on the issue of the cinematic narrator, as he uses the concept simply as another aspect of differentiation between classical and art cinema narration. More specifically, he claims that the need to identify a narrative voice is merely an 'anthropomorphic fiction'. As he explains:

> I suggest, however, that narration is better understood as the organisation of a set of cues for the construction of a story. This presupposes a perceiver,

but not any sender, of a message ... Most films do not provide anything like such a definable narrator, and there is no reason to expect they will ... I need only signal that we need not build the narrator in on the ground floor of our theory. No purpose is served by assigning every film to a *deus absconditis*. (Bordwell 1985: 62)

On the other hand, the presence of an authorial figure seems to be essential in the case of art cinema where the filmmaker is considered to be the creator who wants to communicate a message or express a personal vision. Bordwell notes emphatically:

I argued that there was no good reason to identify the narrational process with a fictive narrator. In the art cinema, however, the overt self-consciousness of the narration is often paralleled by an extratextual emphasis on the filmmaker as source. Within the art cinema's mode of production and reception, the concept of the author has a formal function it did not possess in the Hollywood studio system. (Bordwell 1985: 211)

The idea that a narrator should be identified only when the filmmaker possesses a well-established artistic persona that explicitly intervenes in the filmic text rightfully met with fierce criticism on the part of the theorists who underlined that the concept of the narrator was logically and pragmatically indispensable for all fiction films, regardless of their production values or their institutional setting (see Burgoyne 1990; Chatman 1990). At a very general level, the activity of a narrator is a prerequisite for a film text to come into being and to acquire a certain narrative form. Every film presents a fictional world comprising both visual and aural information that has been carefully selected and arranged by someone. However, the distribution and presentation of this information is not a simple or clear process, as it tends to instigate complex narrative voices and employ diverse narrative levels, which are usually responsible for the confusion and lack of consensus among film theorists. One of the theories that provide a comprehensible and inclusive outline of the levels of narration that are usually at play in *all* films comes from Edward Branigan in his book *Narrative Comprehension and Film* (1992).[9] Branigan proposes a narrative schema with eight levels of narration in order to demonstrate that the story data of a film is organised hierarchically along several levels that function simultaneously with varying degrees of explicitness and compatibility. He writes:

A text is composed of a hierarchical series of levels of narration, each defining an epistemological context within which to describe data. A particular text may define any number of levels to any degree of precision along a continuum from the internal dynamics of a character to a representation of the historical conditions governing the manufacture of the artifact itself. (1992: 87)

The narrative levels that he identifies are the following:

1. *Historical author*: the biographical person and his public persona.
2. *Extra-fictional narrator*: the outer limit of the narration, the transitional level between non-fiction and fiction.
3. *Non-diegetic narrator*: it gives information *about* the story world from outside the diegesis. Examples would include intertitles or non-diegetic music (only the audience can hear it).
4. *Diegetic narrator*: information limited by the laws of the story world.
5. *Character (non-focalised narration)*: the character as an agent.
6. *External focalisation*: it gives us the information that a character is also aware of. For instance, an eyeline match is usually externally focalised.
7. *Internal focalisation (surface)*: we see through a character's eyes.
8. *Internal focalisation (depth)*: we see in the character's mind.

The importance of this narrative schema lies in its ability to accommodate all types of narration, even the most intricate and peculiar ones. Classical Hollywood filmmaking tended to centre the narration on the middle levels (4–6), resorting only occasionally and momentarily to the extreme ones (1–3, 7–8) in order to maintain a low degree of self-consciousness. As previously noted, classical narration limited its self-consciousness and its knowledgeability by delegating the transmission of information to the characters, their dialogue and external behaviour. For instance, we would learn about their personalities by witnessing their typical activities or they would communicate their goals and wishes through their conversations. On the other hand, I would like to argue that post-classical narration boasts about how self-conscious and knowledgeable it is by switching emphasis from level to level in an abrupt and explicit manner and by combining non-diegetic voice-overs with the most internally focalised images. In the analysis that follows, Branigan's theory is going to prove an invaluable tool for identifying the various narrative voices and for tracing the sources of the extreme self-consciousness and knowledge-ability in the sample films. In this chapter, I will discuss the films as separate case studies as I would like to provide a dense and multifaceted investigation that will justify all the aforementioned arguments about post-classical narration. As in the case of the system of space, I decided not to analyse the entire sample in order to avoid repetitions and redundancies that would add little to the expositional strength of my theory.

Case Studies

Europa

Lars von Trier's film is what I often call the 'archetype of the post-classical cinema', as it provided me with the inspiration to work on this topic. My focus here will be on its use of voice-over narration, a recurrent device in contemporary cinema that contributes to a high degree of self-consciousness. According to Sarah Kozloff's definition:

> ...'voice-over narration' can be formally defined as 'oral statements, conveying any portion of a narrative, spoken by an unseen speaker situated in a space and time other than that simultaneously being presented by the images on the screen'. (1988: 5)

For a long time the technique of the voice-over was frowned upon by film critics and filmmakers alike, on the grounds that cinema as a visual medium should privilege images over words and should avoid literary devices that emphasise the 'telling' rather than the 'showing'. The voice-over was considered redundant and was rejected as the 'last resort of the incompetent', as it was, apparently, a facile way to convey information about the story world (Kozloff 1988: 22). In the classical Hollywood tradition, voice-over narration was never a prominent narrative choice; it invariably depended on the predilection of some key figures, like Orson Welles, or on the peculiarities of certain genres, such as film noir in the 1940s. On the contrary, it was more warmly embraced in French cinema, as the films of Bresson, Resnais and other *nouvelle vague* directors indicate (see Kozloff 1988: 38). From the 1970s onwards, however, voice-over narration seems to have gained unprecedented ground in international filmmaking – from the New Hollywood directors to Wim Wenders and Wong Kar-wai – having apparently deflected all previous reservations and criticisms. In the hands of contemporary directors, the voice-over technique has been transformed into a powerful tool for increased self-consciousness and complex narrative mastery.

In *Europa* the voice-over constitutes an exceptionally dominating source of narrative power, a true emulation of the voice of God. The deep hypnotic voice of Max von Sydow functions as an unusual type of non-diegetic narrator who seems to be entirely in control of the diegesis and the protagonist's fate. His absolute power in this film is established from the opening sequence, which shows overhead images of a railway track while a compelling voice says:

> You will now listen to my voice. My voice will help you and guide you still deeper into Europa. Every time you hear my voice, with every word and every number you will enter a still deeper layer, open, relaxed and receptive. I shall now count from one to ten. On the count of ten, you will be in Europa. I say one ... and as you focus your attention entirely on my voice, you slowly begin to relax. Two ... your hands and your fingers are getting warmer and heavier...

It takes exactly two minutes and twenty seconds to complete the countdown until the state of hypnosis is supposedly reached. However, the film has not yet shown us anything but the rails and, therefore, it is not clear whether the voice addresses the audience or a character in the story world. On the count of ten, the diegetic narration begins by opening up to a fictional world where we see the addressee of the voice-over: a young man who arrives on a rainy night in Germany in 1945 after the end of the war. But still, the non-diegetic voice-over refuses to withdraw and continues with the following lines:

> You are listening to the noise of rain beating against a large metal drum. Go closer. There is a fence and you have to stop. You are walking across the rail yard and you have been travelling by a train from Bremen and before that on a ship from New York. You are in Germany. The year is 1945.

As he pronounces the last words, an intertitle – another type of non-diegetic narrator – appears on the screen saying: 'Frankfurt Germany October 1945'. Evidently, *Europa* deliberately creates narrative redundancy with all these narrative levels conveying more or less the same information. The flamboyant style and the playfulness that I discussed in the previous chapters as a sign of hypermediated realism is equally manifested in the way Lars von Trier handles his narrative voices. Throughout the film the voice-over narrator consistently dominates the overall filmic narration, thus resulting in an extreme type of self-consciousness which constantly evokes the role of the filmmaker. He flaunts his narrative omniscience and omnipotence by explicitly performing a wide range of functions, such as setting the time and place of the story, linking the different segments of the plot and giving Leopold instructions and advice. For example, there is a scene with an overhead shot of the character of Leo lying in his bed looking at the ceiling, while the camera slowly spirals around him. The narrator talks to him:

> You are in Germany just after the war. You are cold, you are covering yourself up with clothes you have in your suitcase. You are to start your training as a

sleeping-car conductor. When you've rested, you'll be on your way to your new job. Get up! Get up and be on your way!

Leopold is fully overwhelmed by the authority of the voice-over narrator who is in charge of the development of the story and can penetrate even his innermost thoughts and feelings. The extreme omniscience and omnipotence of this illocutionary force, in a way, parodies the filmmaker's power over the characters' destiny. The closing sequence emblematically reasserts the superiority of the author via the non-diegetic voice on the soundtrack as follows:

> You are in a train in Germany. Now the train is sinking. You will drown. On the count of ten, you will be dead. One, two, three, four, five, six, seven, eight, nine, ten. In the morning, the sleeper has found rest on the bottom of the river. The flush of the stream has opened the door and is leading you on. Above your body, people are still alive. Follow the river, as days go by. Head for the ocean that mirrors the sky. You want to wake up, to free yourself of the image of Europa. But it is not possible.

The use of the second person in the voice-over is overtly incompatible with the classical mode of narration and it is even rare in the art cinema paradigm. A similar use of 'you' in the voice-over is found in Resnais' *La guerre est finie* (1966) but the influence seems to come not so much from art cinema as from television commercials. According to Lars von Trier, an advertisement addresses the audience directly because its ultimate goal is to hypnotise the public and lure them into buying a certain product. For that reason he claims that:

> It would be great to be able to hypnotise the public with some images and then not to have to show them a film but only the word 'end' waking them up after an hour and a half. That would really be the absolute film. (In Danton *et al.* 1991: 37; author's translation)

The statement above indicates how other contemporary media forms, such as television, have affected the cinematic language, encouraging a hypermediated mode of expression. In sharp contrast with the classical cinema where the narration depends on the notion of the invisible observer and the film effaces the marks of enunciation, the direct address of the narrator in *Europa* purposefully makes the narrational act exceptionally self-conscious and knowledgeable. By drawing so much attention to the voice-over narration and by emphasising the use of 'you', the film acts out the process of enunciation and interpellation that classical cinema is thought to perform in a concealed way. The dominating voice that controls the narration can be regarded as hypnotising and guiding Leopold to a certain time and space, imitating the cinematic apparatus that is considered to hypnotise and guide the viewers to the story world.

Overall, this intriguing type of voice-over commentary, along with other devices, endows the narration with a high degree of self-consciousness and knowledgeability. In a way, the film confesses from the start that it will tell us a story and that it possesses all the information about it. These two qualities then sustain the function of communicativeness that reveals more and more facts as time progresses and facilitates the viewers in constructing a clear understanding of the story. As a whole, *Europa* exemplifies how the post-classical narration plays with the higher levels of narration in order to become more self-conscious and knowledgeable, while it maintains an increased level of knowledgeability from start to finish.

Lola Rennt

Tom Tykwer's film was previously discussed at length for both its compositional and realistic motivations, as it constitutes a particular case of episodic structure or 'forking-path' narrative with an overtly hypermediated visual style. These two principal characteristics result inescapably in an increased narrative and stylistic self-reflexivity that exposes the seams of its cinematic language.

Firstly, the three parallel plotlines and the story variations demonstrate how a filmmaker can shape the destinies of his characters in numerous ways and can give different endings at will. Although Lola is seemingly empowered with the ability to change the outcome of the action and get her own way in the end, it is in fact the extra-fictional narrator who flaunts his powers through the three separate drafts. Secondly, the multiplicity of narrative plots is paralleled with an even more intense multiplicity of styles that struggle for prominence. The 'bricolage aesthetics' that Bordwell indicated[10] is exemplified in the variety of visual images that Tykwer employs in his attempt to exhaust the possibilities of cinema. His following statement is indicative:

> A film about the possibilities of life, it was clear, needed to be a film about the possibilities of cinema as well. That's why there are different formats in *Run Lola Run*; there is colour and black-and-white, slow-motion and speeded-up motion, all building blocks that have been used for ages in film history. (Quoted in Whalen 2000: 37)

The self-consciousness of the narration in terms of the different plotlines and visual formats emphasises the constructed nature of the film and invites the viewer to realise that everything we see onscreen 'could have been done otherwise', had the director wished for it.

The authority of the filmmaker is equally asserted in the pre-credit sequence of the film where various extra-diegetic sources of information function as a prelude to the diegesis. First, there are the following two epigraphs:

1. After the game is before the game. (S. Herberger)
2. We shall not cease from exploration/And the end of all our exploring/Will be to arrive where we started/And know the place for the first time. (T. S. Eliot)

After the epigraphs, we see a clock's pendulum swinging back and forth across the screen, while the camera slowly tilts up to plunge into the mouth of the clock, as if it were a tunnel. When it emerges on the other side, it enters a fuzzy world full of people in soft focus and begins to wade frantically through the crowd. Occasionally, it slows down to select some individuals, who stand out in bright colours and sharp focus. These are going to be the secondary characters of the story, although we do not know that at the time. The wandering movement of the camera and the selection of faces are accompanied by these words on the soundtrack:

Man, probably the most enigmatic species on our planet. A mystery of open questions. Who are we? Where do we come from? Where are we going? How do we know what we believe we know? Why do we believe anything? Innumerable questions searching for an answer, an answer that will generate a new question and the next answer the next question, and so on, and so on. But in the end, isn't it always the same question, and always the same answer?

When the voice-over ends, a man from the crowd wearing a guard's uniform and holding a soccer ball looks directly into the camera and says: 'Ball is round, game lasts ninety minutes. That much is clear. Everything else is theory. And here we go!' As he kicks the ball into the air, the camera cranes up, giving us an overhead view of the crowd that coalesces into the film's title 'Lola Rennt'.

This extra-fictional introduction that lingers on the outskirts of the fictional world is a highly self-reflexive commentary on the film and its thematic concerns. All these diverse narrative voices redundantly seek to demonstrate that what follows is a type of game akin to the game of life that begins and ends, trying in vain to answer the same question about the meaning of existence. Tykwer ostensibly addresses his audience in order to anchor his film on this philosophical premise and to prepare them for the narrative choices that follow. The logic of the game, and particularly the video game, is further pursued in the credit sequence, which is more typical of video games than of fiction films. An animated sequence shows us a redheaded girl running in a tunnel and smashing all the clocks on her way. The names of some collaborators such as the set decorator, the costume designer, the editor and, finally, the director appear on the screen but we still do not know the actors. The latter are introduced in a separate sequence as if they were players in a video game; their snapshot pictures are shown from the front, the side and the back and they are accompanied by their real and fictional names. Already from the first few minutes, the film adopts in the most blatant manner the hypermediated logic of contemporary media that guarantees an intensive deployment of self-reflexivity.

Although the film remains exceedingly self-conscious throughout its 81 minutes, it is important to note that the narration simultaneously maintains a high degree of knowledgeability and communicativeness. Even though we mainly follow Lola's trajectory in all three episodes, the film repeatedly informs us about Manni's situation and crosscuts to other secondary characters as well. This spatial and temporal omniscience is flaunted by the use of either crosscutting or split-screens, which regularly present the progression of the story from different angles and transmit information about the separate spots of action. At no point in the film does the excessive self-consciousness of the visual style jeopardise the functions of knowledgeability and communicativeness; on the contrary, all three qualities reach their apex, producing a highly complex and pleasurable narration.

Magnolia

In an astounding pre-credit sequence that lasts for five minutes and thirty seconds, Paul Thomas Anderson flaunts his mesmerising power as a storyteller by recombining and 'repurposing' a wide range of cinematic possibilities from different moments in the history of the medium. This prologue contains three short vignettes that depict three separate outwardly bizarre occurrences, which prepare the ground for the equally peculiar stories that are going to follow in the main part.

The film begins with a black screen and a voice-over saying: 'In the New York Herald, 26 November 1911, there is an account of the hanging of three men'. An iris-in opens to a black-and-white sequence shot entirely with a Pathé camera from 1909 to evoke 'early cinema'. This is the story about the murder of a pharmacist who was stabbed outside his *Greenberry Hill* pharmacy by three vagrants with the names Joseph *Green*, Stanley *Berry* and

Nigel *Hill*. This short episode is completely narrated by a non-diegetic narrator who delivers the crucial pieces of information in the voice-over and accompanies them with precise visual proof. The images comprise a mixture of 'cinema of attractions' strategies, such as close-ups on the key protagonists, tableaux compositions and looks into the camera, as well as more contemporary filming techniques, such as dynamic camera movements, crane shots and rapid zoom-ins.

The non-diegetic narrator proceeds swiftly to the second incident saying, 'As reported in the Reno Gazette, June of 1983, there is a story of a fire, the water it took to contain the fire and the scuba diver named Delmer Darion'. In this slightly longer episode, the voice-over narrator informs us about the odd mixture of coincidences involved in this story by combining his 'telling' with the 'showing' of the events in great detail with the help of many exhibitionist strategies. He moves freely back and forth in time and dramatises the story by means of slow- and fast-motion cinematography, freeze-frames and mannerist camera manoeuvres.

The third section of this introduction is dedicated to the death of a young man called Sydney Baringer who tried to commit suicide by jumping off the roof of a nine-storey building but was accidentally killed by a bullet that was fired from one of the apartments. As the film shows his fall, the narrator freezes the frame and takes over the narration saying: 'The coroner ruled that the unsuccessful suicide had suddenly become a successful homicide. To explain' and he goes on to give us all the details of this absurd case. For example, he rewinds the free fall and shows us the detail of the suicide note that Baringer had in his hand. Then, he explains that the bullet was fired by the victim's mother who, at that moment, was having one the regular fights with her husband. He shows us the whole incident from inside the apartment and includes some of the diegetic dialogue that took place. In the end, he even shows us a long shot of the building and re-enacts the story by indicating on the screen the various steps with a yellow marker, as noted earlier (fig. 13.6). At this point the narration reaches the limit of its self-consciousness and celebrates the omniscience and the omnipotence of the non-diegetic narrator who emulates the filmmaker's absolute control over the images and the sounds of the film. Finally, this extended prologue ends with the narrator's personal remark on these stories:

> ...and it is the humble opinion of this narrator that this is not just 'Something That Happened'. This cannot be 'One of those things'. This, please, cannot be that. And for what I would like to say, I can't. This was not just a matter of chance. Oh ... These strange things happen all the time.

The function of this long and self-reflexive introduction is to set the tone for the multiple and intricate stories that follow. The lives of the numerous characters are constantly connected by coincidences and accidental incidents that often compete in uncanniness with the three opening vignettes. The narration moves continually and explicitly between different narrative levels – autonomously from the characters' actions – in order to connect the different plotlines and thus it remains omniscient, ubiquitous and communicative throughout the film. It gives us information that the characters themselves ignore and provides all the insights into their personal situations. Furthermore, there is the regular non-diegetic intrusion of the weather forecast (previously discussed as a type of durational expansion), whose meaning we can only infer retrospectively after the frog rain.

In addition, the film plays with its fictional constructed nature in a scene where Phil Parma, the nurse who takes care of Earl Partridge, is trying to trace Earl's son Frank in order to reconcile them. He is talking on the phone to one of Frank's assistants saying that the scene looks like the numerous ridiculous scenes in the cinema when 'a guy is trying to get hold of a long lost son' but that is exactly what he wants to do as well. So he pleads with him with these words: 'This is the scene in the movie where you help me out … this is that scene.'

Moreover, Anderson exhibits his authorial powers in another inventive sequence when the camera captures every character while they sing along to Aimee Mann's song 'Wise Up'. After countless moments of emotional tension and physical pain, *Magnolia*'s characters are united by the wry lyrics of this song in a highly melancholic atmosphere. Claudia begins to whisper the words, as she sits alone in her apartment, and then each character picks it up consecutively. The non-diegetic song brings them all together, as does the help of the all-powerful narrator.

Lastly, an epilogue appears right before the final resolutions, closing the parenthesis that opened in the prologue. An intertitle with the phrase 'So Now Then' is followed by brief images of the three strange stories, as the voice-over addresses the audience directly for one last time:

And there is the account of the hanging of three men, and a scuba diver and a suicide. There are stories of coincidence and chance and intersections and strange things told and which is which and who only knows. And we generally say: 'well, if that was in a movie, I wouldn't believe it.' Someone so and so met someone else so and so, and so on. And it is in the humble opinion of this narrator that strange things happen all the time. And so it goes and so it goes and the book says we may be through with the past but the past ain't through with us.

With these thoughts, the film creates a symmetry between the beginning and the ending and concludes its impressively self-conscious narration. As a whole, *Magnolia* provides us with another valuable example of how the post-classical narration uses the high level of self-consciousness to reinforce the qualities of knowledgeability and communicativeness in a steadily increasing manner until the final resolution.

Fight Club

David Fincher's film is undoubtedly one of those that present serious challenges to narrative theories. *Fight Club*'s story is built on a complex narrative structure and is dominated from start to finish by a highly subjective voice-over narration. In contrast to the three films already discussed, the voice in this case belongs to a homodiegetic narrator who recounts his innermost experiences and transforms the film entirely into his visual stream of consciousness. The role of the voice-over is decisive in guiding the viewer through the vicissitudes of the story and ensuring we are engrossed in the protagonist's struggle. The enthusiastic appeal of this narrative device for the post-classical filmmakers, as one can conclude from the case studies so far, is also reflected in Fincher's comments:

> The first draft had no voice-over, and I remember saying, 'Why is there no VO?' and they were saying, 'everybody knows that you only use the VO if you can't tell the story'. And I was like, 'it's not funny if there's no voice-over, it's just sad and pathetic'. (Quoted in Smith 1999: 61)

Apparently, Fincher not only overcame this common prejudice but also put all his energy and imagination into creating a fascinating voice-over that holds the film together and takes the spectator on a bumpy ride into the protagonist's mind. The self-consciousness of the narration is constant in both the visual style and the narrator's account that enjoys complete freedom to play with words and images. To begin to untangle the plot of the film and explicate the puzzles it poses for narrative theory, I need to resort to Branigan's narrative levels and make full use of their fine distinctions.

As I have already noted, *Fight Club* begins from the fear centre of the narrator's brain and, as the camera emerges in the outer world, we see him in a close-up with a gun barrel in his mouth, telling us in the voice-over: 'People are always asking me if I know Tyler Durden.' With a brief non-diegetic tour, our narrator promptly informs us about his situation by having the camera drop thirty storeys below, go through the sidewalk into the underground garage, pass through the bullet-hole in the van with the explosives and then move out to the side. These images are accompanied by his voice explaining:

> We have front row seats for this theatre of mass destruction. The demolitions committee of Project Mayhem wrapped the foundation columns of a dozen buildings with blasting gelatine. In two minutes primary charges will blow base charges and a few square blocks will be reduced to smouldering rubble. I know this, because Tyler knows this.

As soon as the camera returns to the top floor, the narrator tries to remember how the story began, thus initiating a flashback that shows him hugging a man named Bob with 'big tits' in a support group for men with testicular cancer. Yet, a few seconds later he changes his mind and stops the flashback saying, 'No wait! Back up! Let me start over.' Then a new flashback begins and takes us further back in time when his problem with insomnia first appeared. As Robert Stam observes, this kind of 'self-correcting style' is a common self-reflexive device in the works of self-conscious fabulists who are incapable of telling stories straight, 'both in the sense of telling them with a straight face and in the sense of telling them linearly, sequentially' (1992: 152–3).

The new flashback, which contains almost the entire film, is a particularly intriguing segment that baffled viewers and critics alike. The key characteristic of this flashback is that it constitutes an extreme type of deep internal focalisation and depicts the narrator's subjective psychotic state. This means that when he creates his imaginary alter ego, named Tyler Durden, we cannot know that he exists only in his mind and not in reality. When the narration is internally focalised, we have access only to the character's mind and not to the objective world. The screen is taken over by his mental images and his subjective views, shutting us off from 'real' events. In this sense, the narrator is neither unreliable nor deceptive, as many critics observed. In fact, he is completely truthful to his inner visions and seeks to transmit his personal experience of the story. The only trick is that he does not reveal his mental problem from the beginning, since it is precisely the suppression of this information that creates suspense in the plot.

In the flashback, our narrator suffers from insomnia and starts attending a number of support groups for people with deadly diseases. On one of his business trips, his double personality disorder fully manifests itself and his alter ego appears in flesh and bone with the name Tyler Durden. The same night an explosion in his condo destroys all his possessions and he moves into an old dilapidated house on Paper Street with Tyler. The presentation of Tyler's character to the audience is an extremely self-conscious, knowledgeable and communicative moment because it amounts to a separate, highly informative non-diegetic insert, as noted before. More specifically, as the two friends come out of a bar and Tyler asks the narrator to hit him as hard as he can, the latter freezes the frame and says: 'Let me tell you a little bit about Tyler Durden.' In the sequence that follows, the narrator looks at the camera and informs us about Durden's night activities. The extract from their dialogue below is very enlightening:

Narrator (*looking directly in the camera*): Tyler was a night person. While the rest of us slept, he worked. He had one part-time job as a projectionist. See, a movie doesn't come all on one big reel. It comes on a few. So someone has to be there to switch the projectors at the exact moment that one reel ends and the next one begins. If you look for it you can see these little dots come in to the upper right-hand corner of the screen.

Tyler (*pointing with his hand at the upper right-hand corner of the screen where a small circle is momentarily drawn on the frame to indicate the dots*): In the movie industry, we call them 'cigarette burns'.

Narrator (*looking at the camera*): That's the cue for a change-over...

Tyler (*looking at the camera*): Why would anyone want this shit job?

Narrator (*looking at the camera*): Because it affords him other interesting opportunities.

Tyler (*looking at the camera*): Like splicing single frames of pornography in the family films...

When this two-minute non-diegetic insert ends, the film continues the progression of the story with the two friends fighting in the street for the first time. Some months later, after dozens of fight clubs have sprung up all over the country, Tyler disappears. The narrator tries to find him by visiting the various places where Tyler had travelled and gradually realises that *he* is Tyler. While in a state of shock, Tyler returns to play with his mind and take charge of the situation. During their confrontation, which I should point out is once more imaginary and takes place completely in the narrator's mind, the narrator tries to see some of the past events from a clear perspective. At that point, the film replays some key events from a diegetic level, albeit in a disjointed style and in slow-motion – techniques that are traditionally reserved for the subjective moments in the lower levels of narration.

As the flashback reaches the end, there is a scene with the two 'protagonists' fighting in the basement of the building in Franklin Street. Now that the secret is revealed we can witness the incident both from the internally focalised images that show Tyler fighting with the narrator, as well as from the surveillance cameras that give us the diegetic view of the situation where the narrator is fighting alone. When we approach the time of the opening moment, his voice says, 'I think this is about where we came in', and this is the last time he talks to us.

The closing scene portrays the narrator's struggle to free himself from his hallucination, which is finally accomplished when he shoots himself in the face. When his girlfriend Marla comes to find him, he reassures her that everything will be fine in the future. As the buildings explode, a shot of a penis flickers for a split second on the screen, reminding us of the extra-diegetic authorial figure that can tamper with the film just as Tyler tampered with the cartoons earlier.

On the whole, *Fight Club* is an extremely intricate and multilayered self-conscious narrative that my analysis here could not possibly fully explore. However, the selective moments described and the overall structure delineated demonstrate that this film could never fit into the classical paradigm of narration. The complex narrative levels, the play with subjective and objective images, the continuous voice-over commentary and the direct address of the audience would never be justified in a classical film. On the other hand, what is it that differentiates *Fight Club* from a film such as Resnais' *Last Year in Marienbad* that also contains all the aforementioned qualities? I believe that the difference can be traced to the fact that the former plays with the self-reflexive devices but does not abolish the causality of the events and, hence, the need to tell a story. The narration in Fincher's film maintains a high level of knowledgeability and communicativeness, revealing the secrets and filling the gaps to a sufficient degree, while Resnais' film is so suppressive that it renders the construction of a story impossible. And therein lies the duplicitous nature of the post-classical narration, which is simultaneously self-conscious, knowledgeable and communicative, and combines reflexivity with accessibility.

Moulin Rouge!

Baz Luhrmann's film is also very far from boasting an 'invisible', 'transparent' and 'seamless' narration. In chapter one I analysed its opening sequence to illustrate the hypermediated realism that motivates the post-classical narrative logic. Then, in chapter two I showed how this strong motivational factor resulted in a highly self-conscious system of space that privileges discontinuity, multiplicity of technical devices and an artificial iconography. *Moulin Rouge!* is thus lushly wrought as an excessive spectacle that freely acknowledges and inventories the variety of its expressive means.

The act of narration is openly exposed with the blatant use of multiple levels of narration that both open and close the film in complete symmetry. As I already noted, in the opening scene the reflexive setting of an old movie palace is followed by an expository intertitle, which then gives way to the song of the first non-diegetic narrator, a white-faced clown who is identified as Toulouse-Lautrec. With the words 'There was a boy, a very strange enchanted boy' from the classic song 'Nature Boy', Lautrec introduces us to Christian, the writer who sits in his room in Montmartre and decides to tell the world about his tragic love affair. As Christian begins to tap the first words of his novel, his voice-over initiates a flashback that takes us back to the time when he first arrived in Paris from England. From that point onwards, the voice-over narration reappears frequently to punctuate the key events of the story and to remind the viewers that Christian is our framing narrator. As we approach the ending, after the death of Satine onstage, the camera cranes up out of the theatre in order to leave the diegetic world both literally and metaphorically. We see again the white-faced Lautrec singing 'There was a boy…' and then Christian in his room typing his closing words:

> Days turned into weeks, weeks turned into months. And then, one not-so-very special day, I went to my typewriter, I sat down and wrote our story. A story about a time, a story about a place, a story about the people. But above all things, a story about love. A love that will live forever. The End.

The theatre stage is then superimposed on these last words and, as we see the red curtain falling, Lautrec sings the last sentence of his song: 'The greatest thing you'll ever learn is just to love and be loved in return.' Thus, the film closes with the same successive narrative layers that it opened with, signalling the end of the narrative act in a consistently outspoken manner.

In addition, the self-consciousness of *Moulin Rouge!* is equally demonstrated in the *mise-en-abyme* construction of the plot. According to a broad definition, *mise-en-abyme* 'refers to the infinite regress of mirror reflections to denote the literary, painterly or filmic process by which a passage, a section or sequence plays out in miniature the process of the text as a whole' (Stam *et al.* 1992: 201). The film takes advantage of its backstage rhetoric and the production of the musical show to play out the intricate relationships between the characters in the story. The French Duke transforms into a Maharaja, the British writer into a sitar player while the setting is transferred to exotic India. Moreover, the two young lovers try to ensure a happy ending for their love affair by first manipulating the story of the play where the beautiful courtesan chooses the poor sitar player over the evil Maharaja. The happy resolution in the show becomes a serious point of contention between Christian and the Duke, which in turn causes the break-up of the couple in their 'real' life. Finally, the song 'Come What May', which was written for the play in order to function as a secret code for the lovers, performs this function outside the show in the closing moments, when Satine sings it to Christian to show that she still loves him.

Lastly, as a musical, *Moulin Rouge!* contains various musical numbers that usually halt the narration so that the characters can burst into song and dance. Although this is a typical generic code of all musicals, the novelty and the exceeding self-consciousness of *Moulin Rouge!* could be attributed to the overt parody that characterises the musical numbers. As Marsha Kinder observes, 'the film is distinguished primarily by its humorous audio pastiche: a promiscuous poaching of familiar words and music from a diverse melange of songs from different decades that acquire new meaning within this new narrative context' (2002: 54). When we see Satine onstage for the first time she sings 'Diamonds Are a Girl's Best Friend' with a detour to Madonna's 'Material Girl', while later she and Christian sing a medley of love songs, including 'All You Need Is Love', 'I Was Made For Loving You', 'One More Night' and 'I Will Always Love You', to name just a few. The familiar lyrics and tunes make it impossible for the viewer to miss the allusions, while some musical numbers also compositionally evoke the original artists. For example, as Harold Zidler sings Madonna's 'Like A Virgin' to the Duke, he grabs a pair of aspics to imitate Madonna's Jean-Paul Gaultier cone bras.

Overall, the self-conscious handling of the love story between the two protagonists not only lays bare the artificiality of the narrating act but also increases the levels of knowledgeability and communicativeness. From the first minutes the film shares with us the knowledge that a tempestuous love affair will end with the death of the heroine, diminishing the traditional notion of suspense. In contrast to the classical model that reveals the resolution of the story at the very end, the post-classical narration dares to reverse the process and unravel the mysteries from the beginning.

Amélie

With the help of a 'veritable arsenal of *cinéma du look* motifs and techniques', as Ginette Vincendeau observes (2001: 24), Jean-Pierre Jeunet creates a film that exults at self-conscious hypermediated play. Previously, I commented on the clear and overt presentation of the characters, the multiple storylines and the ample use of spatial effects. Here I would like to highlight the narrative and stylistic devices that pertain to the self-conscious aspects of its narration.

First and foremost, a powerful non-diegetic voice-over is in charge of both the 'showing' and the 'telling' in this film, providing an aural stand-in for the filmmaker. This omniscient and omnipotent narrator competes with the images for prominence and wields his supernatural powers over the limited knowledge and abilities of the characters. His non-diegetic interferences significantly confine the **diegetic world to such an extent that we have to wait** for eleven minutes after **the film has started for a strictly diegetic scene to** occur. A close description of these first eleven minutes is quite illuminating regarding the various self-reflexive means that Jeunet efficiently deploys. A fast-paced voice opens the film with the following words:

> On September 3rd 1973, at 6:28 pm and 32 seconds, a bluebottle fly capable of 14,670 wing beats a minute, landed on Rue St. Vincent in Montmartre. At the same moment, on a restaurant terrace nearby, the wind magically made two glasses dance unseen on a tablecloth. Meanwhile, in a 5th-floor flat, 28 Avenue Trudaine, Paris 9, returning from his best friend's funeral Eugène Colère erased his name from his address book. At the same moment, a sperm with one X chromosome, belonging to Raphael Poulain, made a dash for an egg in his wife Amandine. Nine months later, Amélie Poulain was born.

With this startling preface accompanied by corresponding images, the film not only introduces us to our heroine from the moment of her conception, but also prepares the ground for a rich and playful narration that explicitly seeks to draw attention to itself. Once the credit sequence is over, the narration thrusts forward with a very self-reflexive portrayal of Amélie's family. A long shot of a man in a doctor's uniform standing in front of a building and looking at the camera comes along with a voice-over explaining: 'Amélie's father, an ex-army doctor, works at a spa in Enghien-Les-Bains.' The camera rapidly zooms into his face while the phrase 'tight lips, sign of hard heart' with an arrow pointing at the man's lip is superimposed on the left of the screen (fig. 6.17). This exhibitionist style continues, as the narrator flaunts not only his knowledgeability but also his fondness of the 'cinema of attractions' mentality. He tells us assertively:

> Raphael Poulain dislikes: peeing next to someone else. He also dislikes: catching scornful glances at his sandals, getting out of the water with clingy wet swimming trunks. Raphael Poulain likes: peeling off large strips of wallpaper, lining up all his shoes and polishing them, emptying his toolbox, cleaning it out and putting everything back.

The same eccentric presentation is then repeated for Amandine Poulain, Raphael's wife, and then continues with some key events of the family's life until Amélie comes of age and leaves for Paris. After completing the description of her childhood, the narrator moves on to the present but still refuses to hand over the narration to the diegesis and the characters. His voice informs us: 'Five years later, Amélie is a waitress at Les Deux Moulins. It is August

29th. In 48 hours, her life will change forever but she doesn't know it yet.' As he utters the word 'forever', a flashforward shows us swiftly a string of images that will appear again later on (the car crash, the photo album and Amélie dressed as Zorro) but neither Amélie nor the viewer can understand their significance. For the moment, the narrator seems to have more characters to introduce before letting the story begin, so he picks one by one the employees and the regular customers at Les Deux Moulins and gives us a summary of what they like and dislike. Whereas a classical film would let these characters unfold their traits to the audience through their diegetic interactions, the post-classical film, as we have seen clearly so far, needs to draw attention to the process of giving information and therefore emphasises the higher levels of narration and the non-diegetic sources.

Although the entire film is unvaryingly self-conscious, one of the noteworthy self-reflexive moments comes when Amélie's routine is presented by both the narrator and the heroine together. The voice-over begins: 'Some Friday evenings Amélie goes to the cinema' and then Amélie – sitting in a film theatre in the middle of a screening – looks at the camera and says quietly: 'I like turning around and looking at people's faces in the dark.' After confessing her favourite habit, she continues, saying: 'I like noticing details that no one else ever sees.' As we catch a glimpse of the film showing on the screen, the French classic *Jules et Jim*, the camera zooms in on a shot of a female face by a train window to reveal a fly that surreptitiously entered the scene. And as if the zoom-in were not enough, a red circle appears around the fly to highlight even more explicitly the sort of 'detail' that the heroine likes noticing (fig. 6.16). Then, Amélie looks conspicuously into the camera, which is now placed beside her (fig. 6.4), and says: 'But I hate it in old American movies when drivers don't watch the road', while a relevant clip from Vincente Minnelli's *Father of the Bride* (1950) is projected on the screen.

After some more habits are described, the voice-over finally reaches the beginning of the story with the words: 'Finally, on the night of August 30th 1997, comes the event that will change her life forever.' I would like to underline a small paradox here, as the last time the narrator signalled the time was the morning of 29 August and he warned us that in 48 hours Amélie's life would change forever. That point in time, however, has no diegetic significance in itself because the narration then makes an entirely non-diegetic detour in order to present the characters' routine, which is certainly not meant to occupy these 48 hours. A close narrative analysis indicates that the diegesis actually begins on the night that 'changes Amélie's life forever', which is 30 August, and everything that preceded was a highly self-conscious exposition of some important background information about the story and the people who would participate in it.

From that point onwards, the numerous plotlines gradually develop diegetically with regular non-diegetic interventions until they reach a final resolution and the central heterosexual couple is formed. The epilogue of the film echoes the prologue:

> September 28th 1997. It is exactly 11 a.m. At the funfair, near the ghost train, the marshmallow twister is twisting. The same moment, on a bench in Villette Square, Felix Lerbier learns that there are more links in his brain than atoms in the universe. Meanwhile, at the Sacre Coeur the nuns are practising their backhand. The temperature is 24° C. Humidity 70% and the atmospheric pressure is 999 millibars.

Overall, for an hour and 52 minutes Jean-Pierre Jeunet displays his storytelling abilities and enjoys the freedom to play with the actors, the images, the voices and the audience without any concern about breaking the classical notion of the 'window to the world'. *Amélie* is a continuous play with multiple 'windows' that compete for attention and prominence. For all these reasons, it is a film that astutely embodies the post-classical features that were evidenced in the previous case studies.

Chungking Express

Chungking Express features two separate stories about how people deal with the vicissitudes of love. The relatively simple and light-hearted storylines are metamorphosed into a whimsical romance thanks to Wong Kar-wai's beguiling visual style and his remarkably acute use of the voice-over. As far as the former is concerned, the photography of the film as well as the editing opt for self-reflexive devices such as fractured compositions, jump-cuts, different colour schemes, freeze-frames and jerky camera movements. Wong experiments with disruptive visual effects and refuses to be constrained by the specific and limited options that classical continuity allows. His directorial style is described below:

> People are always very curious about the visual effects in my works. The not so romantic truth is that lots of those effects are in reality the results of circumstantial consideration: if there is not enough space for camera manoeuvring, replace the regular lens with a wide-angle lens; when candid camera shooting in the streets does not allow lighting, adjust the speed of the camera according to the amount of light available; if the continuity of different shots does not link up right for a sequence, try jump-cuts; to solve the problem of colour incontinuity, cover it up by developing the film in black-and-white ... Tricks like that go on forever. (In Ngai 1997: 113)

In contrast to the carefully and strictly coded classical style that 'escapes observation by dint of being excessively obvious' (Bordwell *et al.* 1985: 11), Wong Kar-wai often prefers the 'circumstantial consideration' that offers unlimited choices and results in images that call attention to their own construction. The wide variety of the self-conscious stylistic devices that appear in the film creates a continuous confusion between diegetic and non-diegetic levels and keeps the viewers aware of the presence of the camera.

At the same time, the filmic images are invested with frequent, dominant voice-overs that navigate the narration through both the external and internal lives of the characters. All the four main protagonists in *Chungking Express* are given the opportunity to speak out in the voice-over, confiding their views and their feelings, while also giving away information about the future developments. It is rather unusual for a film to give all the main characters this chance and it is even rarer to switch from person to person so rapidly and randomly. Some examples from the first episode are enlightening.

The whole opening scene is shot with the step-printing method that gives it a captivating sense of simultaneous animation and suspension and creates a blurring impressionistic look. An intense musical score accompanies the camera as it follows a mysterious woman in a blonde wig, sunglasses and raincoat while she is walking into Chungking Mansions. After a few seconds, the title of the film appears briefly on the screen and then gives way to a tilted-up shot of the sky and the chimneys, openly reminiscent of Ozu. We see dawn breaking in fast-motion and we hear the voice of Officer 223 say: 'We rub shoulders with each other everyday. We may not know each other. But we could become good friends some day. I am a cop. My name is He Qiwu. Serial number 223.' The next shot shows the cop in plain clothes chasing somebody in Chungking Mansions and when he bumps into the woman with the blonde wig, he says, 'At our closest point, we're just 0.01 cm apart from each other.' As she turns and looks at him running away, the frame freezes and his voice informs us: '57 hours later, I fell in love with this woman.' In this first sequence, the voice-over plays a crucial role in identifying the two main characters, the blonde woman and the cop, and helps us make sense of the incredibly blurry and unsettling images. However, despite the fact that the narrator is homodiegetic and participates in the story of the film, the voice-over appears to be explicitly omniscient and communicative, to a degree that transcends the actual knowledge of the character.

Moreover, throughout the film the voice-overs endow the narration with an additional dimension; all the things that the characters cannot say to each other, they say directly to the audience, as if they are having imaginary conversations at the non-diegetic level. For instance, the woman with the wig tells us, 'I do not know when I became such a cautious person. Now whenever I wear my raincoat, I will also put on my sunglasses. You will never know when it will rain or shine.' However, when the young cop meets her in a bar – 57 hours after their collision in Chungking Mansions – he asks her about the sunglasses and she refuses to tell him. Furthermore, the cop is obsessed with pineapple cans because pineapple was his ex-girlfriend's favourite fruit and he wonders: 'Somewhere, somehow, things come with an expiry date. Sardine will expire, meat sauce will also expire, even Glad Wrap will expire. Is there anything on Earth that will not expire?' Later on, when the two protagonists are sitting at the bar, the woman says to us, 'Knowing a person doesn't mean having a person. A person changes. Someone who likes pineapples today may like something different tomorrow', as if she were trying to explain to him through the voice-over why his ex-girlfriend may no longer want him.

Lastly, as the first episode comes to an end, the young cop bumps into another woman mirroring his first encounter in the beginning of the film. In a highly knowledgeable and communicative narrative moment his voice-over says: 'At the high point of our intimacy, we were just 0.01 cm away from each other. I knew nothing about her. Six hours later, she fell in love with another man.' This phrase initiates the second episode and sets up the tone for a new love story, which is equally dominated by the voice-overs of the new characters.

As a whole, the narration in *Chungking Express* is unremittingly self-reflexive and obtrusive without relinquishing the desire to please and steer the viewers' emotions. The simple storylines and the informative voice-overs combined with the rich visuals reveal how the post-classical mode allows the amalgamation of experimentation and narrative pleasure in a way that had not been possible before. The secret lies once again in the careful orchestration of the qualities of self-consciousness, knowledgeability and communicativeness that collaborate and reinforce one another. In that respect, Wong Kar-wai's handling of story information shares many similarities with the previous case studies and attests to the consistency of the post-classical paradigm on the level of Sternberg's three narrative elements under scrutiny in this chapter.

City of God

The portrayal of life in the slums of Rio de Janeiro is just as hectic as its subject matter. The narration refuses to commit to a particular story or to a single point of view in the effort to do justice to the wild nature of the depicted events. Indeed, the copious acts of violence and the endless string of easily dispensable characters would make little sense, if it were not for the meticulous care of the homodiegetic narrator who struggles to forge a coherent storyline out of an otherwise absurd and chaotic reality.

The voice of Buscapé comes to our rescue right at the end of the explosive opening sequence with the chicken chase,[11] explaining the situation in the *favela* as follows: 'A photo might have changed my life … but in the City of God, if you run you're dead … if you stay, you're dead again. It has always been like that since I was a kid.' A graphic match takes us to the 1960s and the transition is indicated not only pictorially but also with the non-diegetic superimposition of the words 'IN THE 60s'. A few seconds later, the narrator is asked diegetically to identify himself and the frame freezes in order to allow him enough time to apologise in the voice-over, saying: 'I am sorry, I forgot to introduce myself.' Then the frame unfreezes and his name Buscapé is uttered diegetically. From these first few minutes, it becomes evident that this character is in full charge of narrating, openly addressing the audience and manipulating the images at will. The arduous task of drawing together the threads of the story of *City of God* forces him to openly acknowledge his role as the principal narrator who selects and organises information according to a carefully orchestrated plan. For that purpose, he explicitly declares the beginning of the story with the story of Trio Mortes and from then on he seeks to adopt an overarching chronological order that starts in the 1960s and ends in the 1980s. The conscious attempt to lay out the events as orderly as possible is often proclaimed as, for instance, when he picks out a character like Shorty (Gero Camilo) or Mané Galinha and says: 'I'll tell you later.'

The high self-consciousness of the narration deriving from the ubiquitous voice-over as well as the hypermediated stylistic options, as laid out in the chapter on cinematic space, is also accompanied by an increased omniscience and a strategic handling of the communicativeness. I have singled out two important moments that are fairly illustrative of this delicate balance. Firstly, there is the case of the hotel robbery that entails the mystery of the murders which remained unaccountable for years. The narration flaunts its omniscience through a non-diegetic composite image (figs 8.1–8.4), which reveals the bloody aftermath of the attack. At this point, the film knows the perpetrator but refuses to give him away. The bare truth will be disclosed later in a self-contained episode featuring the story of Lil' Ze. In the same episode we are also informed about the killing of Buscapé's brother Naïve, a fact deliberately suppressed earlier in the section of the Trio Mortes story. There, we had seen Naïve run into Lil' Ze on his way out of the *favela* but the outcome of their encounter was withheld. In both cases, Lil' Ze's brutal murders were apparently concealed in order to build suspense, on the one hand, and to facilitate the distribution of information, on the other.

Apart from the occasional fluctuations of the communicativeness, however, the overall narration escalates all three narrative qualities when it replays certain incidents two or three times from different angles. For instance, a meeting between Lil' Ze, Buscapé and other gangsters in the drug joint is replayed three times. Every time we change perspective, we are reminded of the omnipresent filmmaker who communicates his knowledge in separate instalments. Similarly, the repetitions that involve the life and death of Hane Galigna generate a startling effect not only due to the factual revelations but also due to the labyrinthine entanglement of the characters and their motives.

To sum up, the makers of *City of God*, having picked a convoluted story inhabited by hundreds of people and hundreds of murders, had no choice but to use the post-classical paradigm of narration and the rich palette of options that it offers. It would have been impossible to transmit the same amount of information using the classical model – or any other model for that matter – given the limitations that those contain. Instead, the post-classical narration indulges them with the freedom to acknowledge their narrative intentions, to manipulate the spatio-temporal co-ordinates in every conceivable way and to cram as much data as possible into two hours of screen time. There, of course, lurked the danger of losing control of the material and throwing the action into complete disarray. Yet, the masterful planning of the three narrative qualities through Buscapé's non-diegetic commentary ensured a truly engrossing result.

Oldboy

The complex narrational choices that I have examined so far in the systems of causality, space and time serve Park Chan-wook's avowed goal to present his viewers with a dense and demanding film that would require several viewings on a DVD in order to unravel all its dimensions.[12] And yet, there is an organising principle underlying the various levels of complexity and maintaining a high degree of intelligibility even for those who see it only once. The mechanism that holds the film together and attributes to it a considerable measure of coherence is related to the way the narration controls the transmission and the flow of story information.

Looking at the narration of *Oldboy* through the prism of Sternberg's three heuristic categories, one is immediately struck by the ubiquitous presence of self-consciousness that constantly reminds us of the fabricated quality of the film. Everything in the film – from the pervading use of the voice-over to the mannerist *mise-en-scène* and the regular manipulations of the chronology – brings forward the very act of narration, defying the directives of the classical model that dictate the suppression of any self-reflexive sign. What is intriguing, however, is how this constant foregrounding of the artificiality of the filmic signifiers not only strengthens our engagement with the action but also facilitates the intelligibility of a profusely tortuous story. Here, I would like to elaborate on Park's ability to handle the effects of self-consciousness in a way that mitigates the sources of complexity and amplifies the knowledge-ability and communicativeness of the narration.

First and foremost, the presence of an omniscient narrator who continually comments on the action bears a double function: it acknowledges in every instance the fabricated nature of the cinematic tale, while it simultaneously works as a navigational tool in a diegetic world that would otherwise seem chaotic. For instance, in the first scene where Oh Dae-Su appears locked in a room screaming at the guard and asking how long his captivity would last, his voice in the form of a non-diegetic narrator informs us right away that he would remain in the room for 15 years. This is a piece of crucial information that, on the one hand, helps us understand and position the entire phase of imprisonment within the story, while, on the other, it reassures us that the narration holds all the necessary information. Moreover, the long and fragmented episode of captivity, despite its complex temporality and, by extension, the high degree of self-consciousness, is held together by the regular intrusions of Oh Dae-Su's comments, offering detailed explanations regarding the methods and practices of his captors, such as the fact that he was drugged with the same gas that the Russians used on Chechen terrorists.

At the same time, the voice-over soundtrack becomes a parallel diegetic space where the protagonist's emotional and mental life can unfold. It is an ambiguous narrative realm where the most extreme levels of narration are welded together; on the one hand, Oh Dae-Su operates as a non-diegetic narrator who reveals his omniscience, while, on the other, a load of internally focalised sounds give us insight into the innermost workings of his mind. For example, as soon as Oh Dae-Su is liberated, he promptly shares with us the realisation that his enemy left him at the same spot from which he was abducted 15 years before: the rooftop of a building constructed where the telephone booth used to be. This information immediately explains the bizarre choice of location and reveals the meticulous planning of the villain's game. Moreover, the narration often grants us complete access to the character's inner dialogue and allows us to hear his thoughts as he encounters a new world, walking down the streets of Seoul. In one instance, he hears a new slang word and thinks to himself that television could not teach him such things, while later on he wonders if 15 years of imaginary physical training can be effective. After beating up a gang of young hustlers, he realises that it can indeed.

In addition to the presence of this omniscient narrator who not only possesses information but also shares it with the viewers, the film employs several other devices to transmit information. The selection of the television images in the secluded room indicate with precision the passage of the years, while the presence of clocks and calendars reminds us of the various deadlines that punctuate the action. Moreover, through the extensive use of cell phones, internet chat rooms, audiotapes and photographs the characters exchange information and communicate their plans and goals. There is one particularly decisive piece of the puzzle, for instance, which is added through the tapes that Oh Dae-Su violently extracts from his jailer. The recorded conversations reveal the instructions given to the jail manager, they describe the treatment that was prescribed by the villain and they give us a hint regarding the latter's motivation. This impersonal source of information, along with several others, increases the communicativeness of the narration and helps us slowly unravel the mystery of the story.

Finally, the resolution of this twisted narrative comes in a long chain of sequences where all the plot twists are revealed and the knowledge gaps are filled, fully satisfying the curiosity of the viewer. In fact, the final confrontation between the two male protagonists lasts for more than 25 minutes, in the course of which several earlier scenes are replayed in order for them – and for us – to reconsider our initial assumptions. This expository segment takes the aspect of self-consciousness to the highest level, while it strives to reassemble the chronological and causal chain of events. Apart from the diegetic exchange of information in the conversation between the two men, the narration employs extensive crosscutting as well as flashbacks in the form of split-screens, as previously mentioned, which communicate in a blatant manner the information regarding the characters' past actions. This point constitutes the peak of all three qualities of the narration and becomes an exemplary case of how extreme self-consciousness can be paralleled by an extreme knowledgeability and communicativeness.

With a lengthy denouement the film draws to a close after a series of very intense and dramatic revelations that can only lead to death and destruction; a physical death in the case of Lee Woo-Jin and a mental one for Oh Dae-Su. The increased omniscience and communicativeness of the narration, especially during the closing moments, succeeds in finally neutralising the complexity of the story and relieving the tension that the secrets and the reversals had created.

Trainspotting

This series of case studies will be concluded with Danny Boyle's *Trainspotting*, a film that incorporates the traits of the post-classical mode, as I have established them so far. The excessively self-conscious narration in this case, like in many of the others, derives from the fluctuations of narrative motivations, which include elements such as episodic storylines, multiple protagonists, parodic moments and a heavy dose of hypermediated and subjective realism. At the same time, the film brings forward the act of narration by relying extensively on the voice-over of the leading character, Mark Renton, who describes his and his friends' struggle with drugs, boredom and the meaning of their own existence. For the most part, Renton talks about his feelings, his thoughts and his personal experiences but he occasionally displays a non-diegetic omniscience, oscillating between a diegetic and an extra-fictional narrative authority.

The opening sequence is the most arresting moment of the film. With Iggy Pop's song 'Lust for Life' throbbing on the soundtrack and a stream of words pouring out from the voice-over, a series of non-diegetic scenes flash on the screen without any apparent causal links. More specifically, we have the following combination of visual and aural elements:

1. *Image*: A young man with a razor cut is running down the street, chased by two store detectives, and almost run over by a car. He stops and starts laughing at the camera. The frame freezes and the word Renton appears superimposed on the right.
   Voice-over: Choose life. Choose a job. Choose a career. Choose a family. Choose a fucking big television. Choose washing machines, cars, compact disc players and electrical tin openers.

2. *Image*: Cut to Renton standing in a room and smoking a cigarette with a lost look on his face.
   Voice-over: Choose good health, low cholesterol and dental insurance. Choose fixed interest mortgage repayments. Choose a starter home. Choose your friends.

3. *Image*: Cut to an indoor football court where Renton and his friends are playing football. The camera selects them one by one with freeze-frames and gives us their names. The ball hits Renton on the head and knocks him down.
   Voice-over: Choose leisurewear and matching luggage. Choose a three-piece suite on hire purchase in a range of fucking fabrics. Choose DIY and wondering who the fuck you are on a Sunday morning. Choose sitting on that couch watching mind-numbing, spirit-crushing game shows, stuffing junk food into your mouth. Choose rotting away at the end of it all, pissing your last in a miserable home, nothing more than an embarrassment to the selfish, fucked-up brats you spawned to replace yourself. Choose a future. Choose life...

4. *Image*: Match-cut to Renton falling down on the floor in the same room as in 2.

Voice-over: But why would I want to do a thing like that? I chose not to choose life. I chose somethin' else. And the reasons? There are no reasons. Who needs reasons when you've got heroin?

With a frantic pace and a distinctive freedom in switching time and place, the film manages in the opening sequence[13] to serve various narrative functions, such as introducing the narrator and his credo in life, presenting his friends and their group activities – football and petty crime – and acquainting us with the theme of drug addiction. All this information is provided in a knowledgeable and communicative segment that does not comprise a single diegetic scene.

The extreme self-consciousness is an unfailing characteristic of the film from start to finish and it comes in many shapes and forms. One of them is the direct address of the audience by the main characters on various occasions, which is certainly not limited to a glance at the camera, as was the case in early cinema. For instance, when Renton talks to us about the pleasures of heroin use, he admits that the principle drawback is that 'other losers' tell you that you are wasting your life. Then, he takes us to these other losers and lets them talk to the camera directly, giving advice such as 'It's a waste of your life, Mark, poisoning your body with that shit.'

This freedom to acknowledge the presence of the camera and ignore the rules and constraints of the diegetic world is a recurring feature that becomes even more tangible in the following scene that could be analysed in three parts:

1. All the friends are sitting in a bar and listening to Begbie talk about a pool game. Begbie brags about how he beat Tommy at that game and how he scared away an annoying onlooker. As soon as his recounting stops, the frame freezes and Renton says in the voice-over: 'And that was it. That was Begbie's story ... or at least that was Begbie's version of the story. Two days later I got the truth from Tommy.' The freeze-frame on Begbie's face changes to a freeze-frame on Tommy's.

2. A flashforward begins. Renton is at Tommy's place and hears the true version. Tommy initiates a flashback where we see the whole incident of Begbie losing the pool game and almost killing an innocent customer at the bar. The flashback ends and the two friends comment on Begbie's psychotic behaviour.

3. The flashforward ends and we are back at the freeze-frame on Begbie. Renton says, 'What a dick can one do? Just stand back and watch and try

not to get involved?' and as he utters the last words, the frame unfreezes and the scene continues diegetically.

The complex construction of these scenes not only demonstrates the narrator's non-diegetic authority but also exemplifies the exhibitionist tendency of the entire narration which resorts to freeze-frames, flashforwards and flashbacks in order to expose promptly and manifestly Begbie's violent and unreliable character.

Lastly, there is one interesting example of the flagrant self-reflexivity of *Trainspotting* that should not be overlooked. Although Renton uses the first person in his voice-over narration to convey his personal perspective on the events, there is a point where he parodies himself and the very act of narrating by switching to the third person and by replacing his slang expressions with a more formal and literary language. This voice-over begins as follows: 'The situation was becoming serious. Young Renton noticed the haste with which the successful in the sexual sphere, as in all others, segregated themselves from the failures', and then he continues to describe his strong sexual desire with elaborate, eloquent metaphors.

On the whole, Boyle's film exhibits most of the characteristics of the previous case studies and helps us understand the functions of self-consciousness, knowledgeability and communicativeness in the post-classical paradigm. In other words, it proves how a filmic narration can combine the extensive deployment of self-reflexive devices with flagrant omniscience and communicativeness, bombarding the viewer with information from constantly shifting narrative levels.

A concluding note

The scrutiny of the narration of the sample films according to the principles of self-consciousness, knowledgeability and communicativeness illuminates the distinction between the classical and the post-classical on a different plane from the one encountered in the discussion of causality, space and time. Here, we focused on the way the films transmitted the story information and we drew some invaluable conclusions, especially regarding the multifaceted nature of self-consciousness. We witnessed an exceptionally high degree of self-reflexivity that materialised with the help of a wide array of techniques, such as the bricolage aesthetics, the direct address of the audience and, above all, the powerful voice-over narrators who aimed at incessantly revealing the constructed nature of the narrating process and reminding viewers of the extra-fictional power of the filmmakers. Although my analyses often focused on the opening and closing scenes, it is important to stress that – unlike classical films – the self-consciousness in these cases is a constant and persistent element that permeates the narration completely and calls attention to the surface of the text from start to finish.[14]

Undoubtedly, the aspect of intense self-reflexivity in the post-classical cinema raises certain issues regarding its relation to other self-reflexive cinematic traditions, such as the avant-garde movements in the 1920s and 1930s as well as the European art cinema of the 1960s and 1970s. I have already hinted at this connection when I compared *Fight Club* with *Last Year in Marienbad* and tried to explain what differentiates them, despite the similarity of their stylistic artillery. The broader question that arises then is: what is it that distinguishes the post-classical self-reflexivity from the modernist? Instead of answering this question in Linda Hutcheon's manner, that is, through a discussion of ideology, history and gender issues (as noted in the introduction), I would like to draw a distinction between the classical and modernist self-consciousness in exclusively narrative terms.

Firstly, as already observed, the post-classical narratives respect compositional motivations and maintain an essential chain of causality, even if they loosen it or make it more episodic. They also sustain very strong generic motivations that provide the films with well-codified characteristics. The fact that hypermediated realism and parody become crucial narrative factors brings in important changes but it does not eliminate the workings of the other two types of motivation, which ensure a necessary level of narrative coherence and intelligibility in a way that was never present in the modernist films.

Secondly, the prominence of self-reflexivity in the post-classical films is also accompanied by a high degree of knowledgeability and communicativeness, which guarantees their accessibility to the audience. My analysis shows that the narration is extremely informative about the characters, plot and resolutions and refuses to leave any narrative gaps unfilled. In contrast, the modernist narratives used self-reflexivity in order to attack classical Hollywood realism and alienate viewers by refusing them the pleasure of identification with the characters. Thus, they accompanied the self-consciousness with a limited communicativeness that resulted in highly suppressive narratives that the viewers could not fully grasp.

Overall, the systematic study of the sample films demonstrates that the post-classical mode of narration exploits and reconfigures some of the options that have been available to other cinematic practices in the past and generates narratives that both challenge and reinstate narrative pleasure and coherence. Moreover, my analysis of the works of a wide range of contemporary international filmmakers has tried to prove how post-classical narration could be regarded by now as a well-established and fully developed paradigm that can sustain individual creation and accommodate very diverse personal visions and thematic concerns. From Lars von Trier's postwar Germany to Oliver Stone's media-saturated America and from Danny Boyle's drug-afflicted Edinburgh to Wong Kar-wai's lovelorn Hong Kong, the post-classical narration displayed an impressive consistency in renegotiating the functions of self-consciousness, knowledgeability and communicativeness and in differentiating itself from both the classical and other cinematic traditions.

CONCLUSION:
THE POST-CLASSICAL PARADIGM:
AN OVERVIEW

This chapter will bring the book to a conclusion after a long journey into the unmapped territory of a new paradigm of narration in contemporary international filmmaking. An overview and a relocation of the central methodological questions, theoretical concepts and research findings are essential before addressing the wider implications of the emergence of this paradigm and opening the discussion for other research issues.

First and foremost, the ambition of this work has been to follow the principles of 'historical poetics' as a model of research into cinema and pose a rather simple question: what are the principles according to which a number of films are constructed today? After a careful selection of 14 contemporary films, according to the criteria laid out in the introduction, I began a fastidious examination of their narrative form, remaining faithful to the tenets of historical poetics, which demands a data-driven approach, a bottom-up process of enquiry and open and falsifiable hypotheses.

The basic hypothesis that has been consistently explored, questioned and tested throughout this book is that there is a coherent post-classical mode of narration that sustains individual creation and consists of very specific constructional options. David Bordwell's work has been quite pivotal in helping me to formulate this hypothesis, as his ideas provided – paradoxically enough – the ground that I had to work both with and against simultaneously. On the one hand, he has undoubtedly enriched film scholarship with some of the most influential historical poetics projects and has created a coherent theory of narration adept at encompassing a wide range of cinematic traditions. Therefore, his two books – *The Classical Hollywood Cinema* and *Narration in the Fiction Film* – became an efficient model that provided me with a method and a vocabulary for analysing my own set of films in a consistent and reliable way. On the other hand, Bordwell's fixation on the persistence of the classical mode of narration up to this day and his negative response to the various claims about a new post-classical or postmodern phase in contemporary cinema was exactly what I had to refute if I were to confirm my own hypothesis. My personal feeling that something is indeed different in a section of current filmmaking practices, combined with my suspicion of Bordwell's perseverance in the opposite direction, was what encouraged me to begin this project.

At the same time, this book had to go between Scylla and Charybdis in order to identify 'what is different' in contemporary cinema without merely replicating the numerous other writers who proclaimed a radical break from the classical tradition and a totally new postmodern cinema that was mostly defined in tautological terms, as already demonstrated. Throughout the research process, I tried to concentrate on a close textual analysis that would allow the films to talk back to me, and proceeded to the deployment of concepts such as hypermediated realism, parody and self-consciousness only when the research data justified their use. This method helped me realise early on that the term postmodern was indeed too problematic to use for the simple reason that it has been copiously employed to describe entirely different phenomena in the arts and the humanities and, consequently, it would be unable to clarify the 'different kind of cinema' that I observed and sought to grasp. However, my decision to disconnect my work from the worn-out discourse of the postmodern did not signify that I opted for an ahistorical approach to contemporary cinema or disregarded the so-called ideological horizon of our epoch. It simply meant that the new paradigm of narration that I wanted to add to Bordwell's existing four could not profit – in the first instance at least – from the contradictory arguments about the postmodern phase of our culture. Now that my work is completed, different questions about the relation of this formal paradigm with the wider concerns and workings of postmodernity inevitably arise and require some consideration. These thoughts will be reserved for the second part of this chapter. For now, my priority is to look at the new narrative model that I constructed and summarise the fundamental characteristics that distinguish it from its predecessors.

The post-classical paradigm of narration consists of a set of constructional norms and provides contemporary filmmakers with various creative options that can be applied complementarily or alternatively. Although the films I have chosen contain the majority of these options – and could be considered as archetypes of the post-classical cinema – it is essential to stress once more that there is no film that embodies all the norms and rules of the post-classical system. In order to extract these rules from the sample and unlock their intricate configurations, I decided to scrutinise the narratives along the three main axes: narrative logic, space and time. Starting with the system of narrative logic, I was able to observe how the four types of motivation – compositional, realistic, generic and artistic – function in the new mode.

The compositional motivation in the post-classical narratives inherits from Hollywood cinema several constructional elements such as character-centred causality, recurring motifs and the double plot structure that combines the formation of the heterosexual couple with the undertaking of a mission. At the same time, it reinforces the centrality of the characters' actions with an exceptional emphasis on their personalities and a detailed description of their lives, which is usually conveyed in the ubiquitous voice-overs. The key novelty of the post-classical cinema, however, lies in the preference for multiple protagonists whose actions diverge and converge in a more episodic narrative structure that often takes the form of forking-paths or spliced plots, as in *Lola Rennt* and *Chungking Express* respectively.

The realistic motivation in the post-classical paradigm relinquishes the attachment to the classical realism defined in the terms of André Bazin, who regarded the screen as a 'window to the world' and argued for transparency, perspective and depth of field. Given that realism is a conventional concept that is 'infinitely corruptible' – to remember Thomas Elsaesser once more – the post-classical paradigm tries to capture the real in more contemporary terms by establishing a hypermediated realism, which favours the practice of remediation and the use of intermedia, layering and intensified continuity. This new 'windowed world' becomes hospitable to the most subjective experiences having as corollary a high dose of subjective realism that attempts to visualise inner mental and emotional states. Hence the long sequences of hallucinations and mental disorder in *Requiem for a Dream* and *Fight Club* or the manifold images of elation in *Amélie*. Unlike the compositional motivation that keeps the post-classical films fairly close to the classical tradition, the realistic motivation introduces an entirely new logic for justifying the realism of the story and transmitting the energy of the depicted events.

On the other hand, the third motivation, the generic type, brings the two models – classical and post-classical – closer again. The post-classical films are surely genre films that depend heavily on familiar and popular generic formulas, such as film noir, the musical or the western. As noted in the respective chapter, the close analysis of the films and a sober examination of the theory and history of genres does not allow us to make the common claim that contemporary films make a radical break from the past thanks to their generic hybridity. Hybrid films have always been around, as Steve Neale reminds us, and the mixture of diverse formulas has traditionally played a reinvigorating role in classical Hollywood (see Neale 1995: 171). However, the distinguishing feature of post-classical genericity is that it turns the hybrid and multi-generic identity into the norm, while it often attempts an archaeological dig into the classical generic codes to revive them triumphantly, as we saw in *Moulin Rouge!*'s celebration of the long tradition of musicals both in Hollywood and Europe.

Lastly, artistic motivation becomes another point of departure from the classical standards, as it allows the post-classical films to take full advantage of the workings of parody in order to engage in a dialogue with cinematic history. In contrast to classical films that had little space for disrupting techniques that could 'lay bare the device', the post-classical cinema has explored the formal strategy of parody with a broad logic that surpasses the limited scope of parody as a comic device. The post-classical filmmakers choose their materials, build their characters and motivate their stories by using the rich history of cinema and other arts as a source of inspiration but also as a possible source of critical irony. The settings, the characters, the genres and the auteurs of the past become words in a new cinematic vocabulary that endows the new works with a double meaning (see overview of motivations in Table 1).

The essential feature of the post-classical paradigm amounts to the collaboration of all the above motivations on equal terms. All four types are present in each film to varying degrees, but the overall narrative logic does not privilege *a priori* any single one of them. Whereas the classical film subordinated the realistic and generic motivations to tight cause-and-effect logic and the compositional parameters of the plot, the post-classical film invites an increased freedom that loosens the tight causal chain, without abolishing it, and allows other elements to come regularly into prominence, such as the heightened sense of realism in intense moments or the playful parodic references. This detailed schema and the numerous fluctuations that it accommodates put an end to the dilemma of narrative progression versus spectacle, an opposition that several theorists have nurtured in an effort to explicate the 'unclassical' elements of contemporary filmmaking.

The next issue on my agenda was the investigation of the system of cinematic space and the changes that it underwent, as we moved from the classical to the post-classical cinema. The filmic space in a classical film had a very clear goal: to become a vehicle for the narrative. This commitment was irrevocably altered – or rather made much wider and more profound – when the post-classical narrative logic established new motivations that called for different performative operations.

In technical terms, the key to the transformation of the post-classical space was the introduction of digital logic and computer technology that invited new approaches to spatial construction. According to Lev Manovich, the advent of digital techniques prioritised the graphic and painterly quali-

MOTIVATIONS				
	Compositional	Realistic	Generic	Artistic
Classical	Tight cause-and-effect logic, character-centred causality, recurring motifs, formation of the heterosexual couple, undertaking of a mission	Classical Bazinian realism (depth of field, perspective, verisimilitude, continuity editing), screen as a window to the world	Genres: both pure and hybrid	Limited
Post-classical	Character-centred causality, recurring motifs, formation of the heterosexual couple, undertaking of a mission but also loose, goal-oriented plot, episodic structures: spliced plots and multiple draft narratives	Hypermediated realism (remediation, layering, intensified continuity) and subjective realism (visualisation of mental/emotional states), screen as a windowed world	Genres: mostly hybrid and multi-generic, and an archaeological attitude towards classical genericity	Parody

Table 1

ties of the image over the photographic ones. The strategies that were once pushed to the margins of filmmaking practice because they were too artificial or self-reflexive, such as back projections, collages and optical tricks, are now coming back with a vengeance to express the mainstream logic of computer design (see Manovich 2001). All the films in the sample welcome the conceptual principles of Manovich's 'digital cinema', whether they use digital tools or not, allowing the post-classical paradigm to become the first type of narrative cinema that fully qualifies for this term.[1]

More specifically, the post-classical films, as Table 2 shows, adopt a different approach to cinematic space that emphasises its graphic qualities. While the classical system depended on a photographic realism that favoured staging in-depth, linear perspective and central positioning, the new system opts for layered images and special effects proud of their artificiality. Moreover, the classical strategy of continuity editing is ceaselessly challenged and reworked through the new strategies of intensified continuity, such as fast cutting rate, use of extreme lens lengths, close framings and free-ranging camera movements (see Bordwell 2002b). Lastly, the temporal montage, which reigned in the classical tradition, is now complemented by a spatial montage that allows different images to coexist in the same frame, blurring the distinction between the space 'in frame' and 'out of frame' and surpassing the logic of one image/one screen.

The System of Cinematic Space	
Classical	Photographic space: staging in depth, linear perspective, central positioning, continuity editing, temporal montage
Post-classical	Graphic space: clusters, special effects (back projections, split-screens, matte paintings, miniatures, optical tricks), intensified continuity, spatial montage

Table 2

Having traced all these differences, it is imperative to make two clarifications that will prevent misleading conclusions and theoretical overstatements. Firstly, the post-classical space does not eliminate the classical rules and conventions; it simply introduces new norms that become the technological and aesthetic dominant of this new narrative paradigm. For instance, there is no doubt that the films in the sample still contain 'classical' images that are carefully centred and staged in depth, as well as sequences that are constructed with the help of analytical editing. Besides, at no point does the post-classical paradigm abolish the classical rules altogether to replace them with some radically new ones. On the other hand, the novelties of this paradigm should not be downplayed nor should they be deemed as an evolution easily assimilated by the classical tradition. The important aspect of the post-classical space is that it establishes a new rationale for generating images, contradicting the 'invisibility' and 'seamlessness' of the classical film.

Secondly, there is a tricky issue regarding the technological novelties of digitality. Undeniably, the technical means for spatial montages and clustered images, such as miniatures and back projections, existed long before the coming of the digital era and were also used in mainstream classical films on several occasions. We should not forget that over eighty per cent of *Citizen Kane* consisted of special effects, like matte shots and double or multiple exposures (see Giannetti 1996: 472). The great distinction, however, is that the same means are now used for a completely different end; while the matte shots of Kane's Xanadu try to conceal their traces and convince the viewer of the mansion's grandiosity, the miniatures of Paris in *Moulin Rouge!* do not hide a single detail of their painted surface and artificiality. And the reverse is also true. The digital filmmaking techniques do not necessarily lead to a post-classical articulation of space. In fact, the vast majority of digital effects in Hollywood are still striving for a greater sense of classical realism. The dinosaurs in *Jurassic Park* (1993) or the feather in the opening scene of *Forrest Gump* are visualised with the help of the latest versions of digital compositing but, in this case, the direction is towards higher transparency and verisimilitude (see Manovich 2001: 309). The computer software has the capacity for

The System of Cinematic Time				
	Conception of time	Order	Duration	Frequency
Classical	Real time	Linear chronology, emphasis on successivity	Emphasis on (the illusion of) equivalence	Singulative
Post-classical	Mediated (manipulated) time	Complex chronology (flashbacks, flashforwards, loops), emphasis on simultaneity and non-seriality	Emphasis on reduction and expansion, use of the pause	Singulative and repeating forms

Table 3

emulating both photographic and graphic spaces but, compared to the analogue tools, it facilitates the mode of hypermediacy and invites experimentation with complex spatial effects and clusters.

The digital flair for testing and trialling various options in the phase of post-production has signalled significant changes in the system of post-classical time, the third major component of this new narrative paradigm (Table 3). Imbued with the logic of digitality that treats the analogue movement of time as merely one option among many, the post-classical works exhibit a complex and multifaceted system of time that problematises the natural progression of real time with numerous technical devices. As far as temporal order is concerned, the films of the sample tend to portray the events in the syuzhet in a non-linear manner by constantly making backward or forward movements in the story time with self-conscious and blatantly signalled flashbacks and flashforwards. Moreover, a popular choice seems to be the structure of the loop, as in *Lola Rennt*, which duplicates video-game logic and emphasises the reversibility of mediated time. In addition, the extensive use of spatial montage underscores the relation of simultaneity between the different images that coexist in the same frame, refuting the illusion of linearity and successivity embedded in the temporal montage of the classical tradition.

In the same vein, the quality of duration is manipulated extensively with an emphasis on the strategy of reduction and expansion, which render cinematic time more palpable than ever before. Apart from the ellipses that were also an indispensable element of classical films, the post-classical temporal system compresses the screen time with fast-motion cinematography to accentuate aspects of the action or to transmit the energy of the story. Furthermore, it regularly expands the duration of events both with slow-motion and with non-diegetic inserts. And since it can move back and forth or go quickly and slowly, the time in this system can also pause for a while. Freeze-frames have become a common device likely to appear at any point, either to indicate the closure of a story, as in *Chungking Express*, or to delay the action and allow the audience time to register certain information, as in *Magnolia* and *Trainspotting*. Lastly, the frequency is the temporal category that varies the least between the two paradigms, as the singulative form remains the dominant rule, dictating that each event should be represented only once. Nevertheless, a recurrent use of the repeating form is observed in more than half of the sample films, attesting to the renegotiation of a strong taboo of the classical tradition. All in all, post-classical time does not amount to a mere vehicle of causality, as in the classical tradition, but acquires a more complex and multifunctional role in the new narrative scheme, which is governed by multiple and competing motivations.

And this brings me to the broadest level of enquiry, that of the relations among the three principal systems. In the classical Hollywood cinema, according to Bordwell's study, the system of narrative logic subordinated the system of space and time in order to advance a narrow cause-and-effect chain of events. If we look at the post-classical cinema, it is evident that the new narrative logic, based on the readjustment of the motivations and the establishment of an equal status among them, demands new ways of articulating time and space on the screen. In this sense, the innovations described in the spatio-temporal axes could be attributed to the new agenda of the motivations. What we need to remember, nonetheless, is that the post-classical paradigm, being a much more elaborate construction than the classical, complicates these interactions among its different parts to an unprecedented degree. Therefore, the phrase that 'time and space are vehicles for causality' is no longer adequate to contain the intricate demands of the post-classical motivations and the different shapes that time and space are required to take in order to materialise them.

Finally, these significant changes in narrative logic, space and time in the post-classical system have caused other transformations in the way the narrative controls the transmission and flow of story information. In chapter four, I concentrated on three narrative qualities, self-consciousness, knowledgeability and communicativeness, in my endeavour to conceptualise, in yet another way, the similarities and differences between the new and the old paradigms. As Table 4 demonstrates, the reconfiguration of the three narrative axes resulted in a considerable reformulation of these three qualities.

The major difference in the post-classical narration depends on its high degree of self-consciousness accompanied by an equally explicit knowledgeability. In other words, the post-classical film reveals its constructed nature by exposing the means of its own making and flaunts its omniscience by conveying information through numerous channels beyond character subjectiv-

Narration			
	Self-consciousness	Knowledgeability	Communicativeness
Classical	Constantly low: the marks of narration become only moderately visible in the opening/closing	Potentially high: the narration knows it all due to its spatial omnipresence but tries to restrict it	Moderate: the narration progresses steadily towards complete disclosure
Post-classical	Constantly high: the narrating act comes forward from start to finish	Explicitly high: the narration is open about its temporal and spatial omnipresence	High: the narration is highly communicative, revealing crucial information even from the start

Table 4

ity. The novelty becomes clear when we compare it to a classical film, which may be moderately self-conscious during the opening and closing sequences but carefully hides all the traces of its construction throughout the rest of its duration. In addition, the classical tradition sought to reduce aspects of self-consciousness by controlling the knowledgeability of the narration and by transmitting most of the story information through the characters' dialogue. The common trait of both paradigms is the element of communicativeness that consistently enlightens the spectator on the progression of the story and the motives of the characters, without leaving any significant gaps unfilled in the end. The post-classical films often increase their communicativeness to an extreme level by disclosing essential story information and giving away important secrets from the very beginning, as in *Moulin Rouge!*, *Chungking Express* or *The Million Dollar Hotel*.

The intriguing aspect of the post-classical self-consciousness is that it does not work against the knowledgeability or the communicativeness of the narration, as was the case with self-consciousness in the art cinema paradigm. The use of self-reflexive devices in the latter favoured the obscurity of the plot by suppressing some key story information. Whereas art films aim to create a feeling of estrangement in the audience and oppose the accessibility and openness of the Hollywood style, the post-classical films share none of these concerns. Their self-consciousness derives from their need for a hyper-mediated realism that encourages a discontinuous and opaque visual space, as well as from a robust presence of parody that problematises the historicity of textuality. The post-classical cinema thus pursues its own agenda, while remaining widely accessible and pleasurable for its spectators.

On the whole, the close narrative analysis of a set of films enabled me to demarcate a new paradigm of narration that made its appearance in several places across the globe over the last twenty years. Although several of the elements of the post-classical narration had been observed and highlighted by theorists and critics, they have failed to organise these elements into a reasonably functional and organised narrative pattern that provides contemporary filmmakers with a range of specific creative options. But are these options the only ones available to them? To what extent can this new paradigm accommodate current world film production? What is the fate of the older paradigms? These are the questions that need to be addressed in the next stage.

The Boundaries of Difference

The model of narration that I have created, based on the textual analysis of a set of films, contains some specific principles of narrative construction that I consider to be typical of the post-classical cinema. My insistence on using the terms 'paradigm' or 'mode' throughout this book is aimed at indicating the relatively open concept of post-classical narration that cannot be defined by a series of necessary and sufficient conditions.[2] If we were to consider all the parameters of the post-classical narration as necessary and sufficient conditions in order to include a film in this tradition, then our approach would be too restrictive. Even among my sample films, which were carefully selected as archetypical of the new narrative mode, we can observe several fluctuations in the way they manifest the post-classical narration. For example, the element of parody is more extensive in *Arizona Dream* than in *Requiem for a Dream*, while the spatial montage is more frequent in *Europa* than in *The Million Dollar Hotel*. Similarly, *Arizona Dream* has the slowest editing pace in the sample, while *Trainspotting* has the most self-conscious and playful voice-over narrator. It would be futile to allow these minor disparities to overshadow the enormous similarities of these works and jeopardise the coherence of the paradigm that they epitomise.

At the same time, we have to be cautious about ascribing the label post-classical to any contemporary film because there lurks the danger of breaking down barriers among the different paradigms and thus invalidating them all. I cannot stress too much the fact that the presence of a *single* element of those found in the schematic tables above is not sufficient to classify a film as post-classical. Let us take the editing style of 'intensified continuity' as an example that is susceptible to several misconceptions. Bordwell initially coined the term to describe certain developments in contemporary Hollywood filmmaking that, nevertheless, do not attest to a paradigm shift. As he notes:

> Contrary to claims that Hollywood style has become post-classical, we are still dealing with a variant of classical filmmaking. An analysis of virtually any film from the period I've picked out will confirm a simple truth: nearly all scenes

in nearly all contemporary mass-market movies (and in most 'independent' films) are staged, shot, and cut according to principles which crystallised in the 1910s and 1920s. Intensified continuity constitutes a selection and elaboration of options already on the classical filmmaking menu. (2002b: 24)

This is a statement that actually finds me in complete agreement for the following reasons: the majority of the films that Bordwell discusses in this article, such as *Jaws* (1975), *L.A. Confidential* (1997) and *Jerry Maguire* are indeed fairly classical; intensified continuity is to a large extent a variation of the classical repertoire; and the sum of the stylistic devices under the umbrella term 'intensified continuity' are not enough to convince anyone that there is such a thing as post-classical cinema. On the other hand, these three concessions cannot negate the possibility of a post-classical cinema that arises from a different set of films, that depends on an intricate narrative construction and that also uses intensified continuity in its spatial system. My work so far has managed to substantiate such a paradigm shift by launching a wide-ranging enquiry into all the dimensions of the narrative – and not merely into some editing techniques – and by producing a model that cannot be reducible to any of its parts. Therefore, intensified continuity is undoubtedly an element of post-classical narration, as the textual analysis demonstrates, but it is not a necessary and sufficient condition for it. I believe that this clarification is vital if we want to evaluate the scope of the post-classical cinema with sobriety and to avoid the rhetoric of another 'grand paradigm' that would be so easy to refute.

Although it would be impractical or even undesirable to create an inventory of all the contemporary films that can be considered instances of the post-classical cinema, I would like to mention a few examples that clearly belong to this tradition and come from a variety of international filmmakers. One of the pioneers of the post-classical narration is undoubtedly Woody Allen, whose *Annie Hall* (1977) inaugurates this new mode. Of course, Allen's fascination with cinema could never confine him to a single narrative model; in an astounding career that spans more than five decades, he has tried out a variety of formulas – from early cinema to classical Hollywood and European art cinema – with *Deconstructing Harry* (1996) being his latest post-classical work. Similarly, Francis Ford Coppola and Martin Scorsese have also experimented with post-classical options; the former should be noted for his *Bram Stoker's Dracula*, whereas the latter for his *Goodfellas* (1990), *Casino* (1995) and *Gangs of New York* (2002). From the directors of the younger generation, Quentin Tarantino has created textbook post-classical works such as *Reservoir Dogs* (1992), *Pulp Fiction, Kill Bill Vol. I & Vol. II* (2003/2004) and *Death Proof* (2007). Moreover, Baz Luhrmann's *Romeo+Juliet* (1996) is analogous to

Moulin Rouge!, while his earlier *Strictly Ballroom* (1992) was much closer to the classical standards, despite its heavy doses of parody. From Tim Burton it is worth singling out *Big Fish* (2003), while a special mention should be made of Spike Lee's underappreciated *Bamboozled* (2000), which is a magnificent application of this new paradigm. Lastly, other films that follow the norms of the post-classical model include Todd Haynes' *Velvet Goldmine* (1998), Guy Ritchie's *Lock Stock and Two Smoking Barrels* (1998) and *Snatch* (2000), Pedro Almodóvar's *Todo sobre mi madre* (*All About My Mother*, 1999), Lee Myung-Se's *Nowhere to Hide* (1999), Kinji Fukasaku's *Battle Royale* (2000), Wes Anderson's *The Royal Tenenbaums* (2001), Spike Jonze's *Being John Malkovich* (2001), Christoffer Boe's *Reconstruction* (2001), Steven Soderbergh's *Full Frontal* (2002), Zhang Yimou's *Hero* (2002), George Clooney's *Confessions of a Dangerous Mind* (2003), Kazuaki Kiriya's *Casshern* (2004), Chen Kaige's *The Promise* (2005), Fernando Meirelles' *The Constant Gardener* (2005), Neil Jordan's *Breakfast on Pluto* (2005), Robert Rodriguez and Frank Miller's *Sin City* (2005), Park Chan-wook's *Lady Vengeance* (2005) and Johnny To's *Exiled* (2006).

Despite the emergence of the post-classical narration, however, what remains unquestionable is that the classical norms, which crystallised between 1917 and 1960, are still in full bloom. And this is where my theory converges with Bordwell's. Indeed, the bulk of Hollywood movies nowadays, as well as a large number of international productions, adhere to the conventions of classical filmmaking, despite some slight changes in the shooting techniques and the technologically advanced filming equipment. For instance, Steven Spielberg remains a remarkably classical filmmaker, while some of the most popular blockbusters of the last thirty years, such as *Raiders of the Lost Ark*, *The Silence of the Lambs* (1990), *Sleepless in Seattle* (1993) and *Titanic* (1997) to name just a few, comply with the basic tenets of the classical narration.

The practice of labelling various films as classical or postmodern/post-classical, though, relies entirely on the analyst's agenda, as Elsaesser and Buckland remind us (see 2002: 27). For that reason, perhaps, it would be interesting to see how my agenda relates to or contradicts some of the other theories that identified a break from the classical cinema and argued for the existence of a postmodern or post-classical phase.[3] Firstly, I would like to refer to Fredric Jameson's discussion of nostalgia films and *Body Heat* in particular. According to his criteria, Lawrence Kasdan's film is postmodern because it expresses nostalgia for the past, conspiring to blur any connections to contemporary social reality. Additionally, it performs the practice of pastiche – or what he calls the 'allusive and elusive plagiarism of older plots' – by reworking the story elements of *Double Indemnity* (1944) or *The Postman Always Rings Twice* (1946) (see Jameson 1983: 117). Yet, if we analyse the film from start to finish and categorise its constructive elements, we will have to go to great lengths to prove that it belongs to the post-classical paradigm. The only ingredient that differentiates it from the classical films of the 1950s and 1960s is indeed the strong presence of a parodic motivation that justifies the presence of the film noir plot, the duplicitous femme fatale and the echoing of some notable instances of the film noir tradition. However, the parodic motivation, as with the intensified continuity considered earlier, is not a necessary and sufficient condition for being post-classical. The fact that the overall narrative construction of *Body Heat* relies on a tight causality and a perfectly classical spatio-temporal system forces us to incorporate it into the classical tradition, despite the minor deviation that pertains to the parodic element.

Secondly, I would like to compare my views to Elsaesser and Buckland's approach, which uses *Die Hard* as a case study for arguing that Hollywood blockbusters can accommodate both a classical and post-classical reading. Their method of enquiry identifies the following post-classical elements: a layering of plot-lines that could be potentially transformed into a video game, a knowingness about its deep structure, an explicit address of issues of race and gender, the presence of a globalised world order and the use of 'sliding signifiers' such as visual and verbal puns. It is all too obvious that *Die Hard* does not qualify as a post-classical film in relation to its narrative construction, which is something that Elsaesser and Buckland do not contest. The issues of race, gender, globalisation and even 'sliding signifiers' are not included in the poetic research questions and thus cannot be registered as evidence for the film's post-classical nature. Even the aspects of 'layering of plot-lines' and 'knowingness' that sound similar to some of the terms I have deployed, such as 'multiple draft narratives' or 'self-consciousness', are handled in a broad manner that comprises non-narratological elements such as 'Oedipal logic' or 'deep/surface structure'. Hence, it becomes plain once more how different hypotheses and conceptual tools lead to dissimilar measurements and results, each time drawing a different line between the classical and the post-classical.

But these two traditions are not the only ones on the narrational map these days. Contrary to Torben Grodal's claims that art cinema has entered a period of decline and that 'it is not possible to predict when art-filmmaking will have a new renaissance' (2000: 53), a look at some of the tendencies in world cinema will prove otherwise. Undoubtedly, the forms of art cinema are themselves transformed as they adapt to new thematic concerns and acquire new functions in a social and cultural context that has hardly remained static since the late 1960s.[4] Yet, the socio-political changes have not diminished the impact of the art cinema norms on the form of contemporary films springing up in various corners of the earth.[5] For instance, Jeffrey Sconce (2002) identifies a new trend of art cinema that emerged in North America in the 1990s, which he calls 'the smart cinema' because it works in opposition to mainstream Hollywood. This new sensibility is exemplified by a young generation of independent filmmakers working in the United States and making films characterised by irony, black humour, fatalism and nihilism. Some typical examples include Todd Solondz's *Welcome to the Dollhouse* (1995) and *Happiness* (1998), Ang Lee's *The Ice Storm* (1997), Atom Egoyan's *The Sweet Hereafter* (1997), Neil LaBute's *Your Friends and Neighbors* (1998) and Hal Hartley's *Henry Fool* (1998), to mention only a few. In terms of style and narration, these films are distinguished by what Sconce calls 'blank' style, built with a static *mise-en-scène*, exceptionally long shots and 'de-emphasised' continuity.[6] The filming of the action strives to achieve a dampening effect and a clinical representation of the events, while the story depends almost entirely on coincidence and random synchronicity.[7] As to their relation to their art cinema predecessors, Sconce argues:

> American smart cinema has displaced the more activist emphasis on the 'social politics' of power, institutions, representation and subjectivity so central to 1960s and 1970s art cinema (especially in its 'political' wing), and replaced it by concentrating, often with ironic disdain, on the 'personal politics' of power, communication, emotional dysfunction and identity in white middle-class culture. (2002: 352)

A similar political agenda and an even stronger opposition to mainstream Hollywood practices are also expressed in the Dogme 95 movement that appeared across the Atlantic in the mid-1990s. A group of Danish filmmakers composed the ten commandments of a 'vow of chastity' for the Dogme 95 members in order to create a cinema of no illusions that would achieve what the various new waves failed to deliver in the 1960s. Whether their goal was accomplished or not is debatable but what is undeniable is that they steered around a lot of critical discussion and proposed an aesthetics that was embraced fully or partially by various European and international filmmakers. The ten Dogme rules aimed at shattering the cinematic illusion with the exclusive use of location shooting, hand-held camera movement and natural sounds and lighting, while they prohibited the use of optical work, superficial action, genres and the accreditation of the filmmaker. Two Danish films, Thomas Vinterberg's *Festen* (*The Celebration*, 1998) and Lars von Trier's *Idioterne* (*The Idiots*, 1998) were the pioneers of the movement and were soon followed by others, among which I should mention an American and an Argentinian, Harmony Korine's *Julien Donkey-boy* (1999) and Jose Luis Marques' *Fuckland* (2000).

The two trends that I presented – the new smart cinema and the Dogme movement – albeit quite different, do share an explicit opposition to the classical Hollywood model combined with the endorsement of several art cinema conventions. Perhaps it would be possible to create a new post-art cinema paradigm based on a close analysis of the numerous contemporary films that seem to be the successors of the art cinema of the 1960s and 1970s. Until that happens, however, I will assume that the art cinema paradigm still exists in various strands of world cinema, including filmmakers from Iran, Taiwan and Japan whose films mostly circulate in the international festival circuit.[8]

On the whole, a survey of film production around the world reveals that despite the emergence of a new and full-blown narrative model, such as the post-classical, the two long-standing narrative paradigms, classical and art cinema, still reign over the vast majority of films on a global scale. Moreover, it shows that contemporary filmmakers from around the world have abundant constructive options at their disposal and can choose different formulas every time they plan their films, depending on the institutional framework that supports them. Lars von Trier is the ultimate example of a filmmaker who shifts his cinematic language relentlessly, experimenting with different expressive means each time. After filming *Europa*, the definitive post-classical film, he made a drastic change with his Dogme 95 film *The Idiots*, then returned to more post-classical paths with *Dancer in the Dark* (2000) only to take an even more radical turn with *Dogville* (2003) and, more recently, *Antichrist* (2009). This creative promiscuity does not diminish in the least the importance of the post-classical paradigm and its heuristic value. The post-classical cinematic language took concrete shape within the last two decades and is probably here to stay. What remains to be examined are the motivating factors behind the paradigm shift in question as well as the bifurcating paths that cinema is invited to tread in a global, media-saturated and digitally-driven cultural environment.

Towards a post-classical mode of film practice

Now that this book has concluded the formal exploration of contemporary filmmaking, there is the second question of historical poetics that immediately follows: how and why have these forms arisen and changed in particular empirical circumstances? Although the remaining space will not allow me to sufficiently survey the reasons that led to the emergence of the post-classical paradigm of narration, I would like to pave the way for this research and introduce some of the key factors that appear to be related to the formation of this new narrative mode.

The historical poetics approach in general and David Bordwell's work in particular have often privileged a functionalist model of causation, whereby the institutional dynamics of filmmaking determine the options that are available to filmmakers and shape decisively their creative environment at any historical juncture. This means that the causes for the emergence, development and evolution of the various compositional and stylistic elements can frequently be traced in the institutional practices that govern the overall filmmaking process. For instance, in the case of the classical Hollywood cinema from 1917 to 1960, Bordwell, Staiger and Thompson argue that it was the mode of production in Hollywood and the consistency of the studio system that played the definitive role in crystallising and safeguarding the conventions of the classical style. The main argument of their book is presented in the preface as follows:

> A mode of film practice, then, consists of a set of widely held stylistic norms sustained by and sustaining an integral mode of film production ... Thus to see Hollywood filmmaking from 1917–60 as a unified mode of film practice is to argue for a coherent system whereby aesthetic norms and the mode of film production reinforced one another. (1985: xiv)

This overarching approach to classical Hollywood establishes a causal link between the classical narration that consists of narrative and stylistic norms, on the one hand, and the mode of production in the studio era, on the other, which comprises a very specific system of production policies and procedures. More specifically, Janet Staiger defines the mode of production as a complex and dynamic relationship between three elements: the labour force that includes all the people who work directly or indirectly in the production of the films; the means of production that include all physical capital employed in a film production such as building facilities, sets and costumes, as well as technological tools, materials and techniques; and the financing of production that includes the studios or other companies that invest in the filmmaking business (see Bordwell *et al.* 1985: 89–90). Staiger's thorough examination of the Hollywood mode of production and the close interactions among these three broad divisions in the span of four decades brought to the surface a number of insightful observations about the functions of the movie industry as a special case of capitalist enterprise that sustained the uniformity and consistency of the classical style, while it allowed a subtle product differentiation that distinguished films from other mass-manufactured goods.

On the contrary, European art cinema from the 1950s till the 1970s flourished in an alternative institutional framework that launched different filmmaking procedures and encouraged more openly individual creativity. In this context, the defining role of the European auteurs, albeit significant, should not be overstated; the entire mode exceeds the personal vision of any particular filmmaker and amounts, rather, to the product of a set of complex relations among various players. As Bordwell observes:

> But even if the director has played a privileged role, she or he cannot be seen as simply the prime mover of the film. For example, an analysis of the modernist cinema's or art-cinema's mode of production would have to trace the ideological notion of the *film d'art*, the national styles that grew up in opposition to Hollywood after World War One, the importance of the director's taking over the role of the scriptwriter, the functions of the small-scale and independent producer, the creation of an international audience of college-educated viewers, the scope of international co-production after World War Two, and the link of cinema to modernism in other arts... (Bordwell *et al.* 1985: 384)

All these different influences collaborated in the nurturing of the stylistic pattern of art cinema and, thus, the privileging of any single one of them would only impoverish the complexity and multiplicity of causes that are required for the evolution of style in general and the emergence of a new mode of narration in particular.

Along the same lines, the mapping of a potential post-classical mode of production that could be held responsible for the formal shift towards post-classical narration would call for a meticulous study of the new technological trends, the craft practices and the institutional forces that facilitated the development of the post-classical options. Such a study is evidently outside the scope of this book and, in all likelihood, it would require several volumes in order to provide evidence parallel to Staiger's work in *The Classical Hollywood Cinema*. However, I would like to venture some general observations regarding the post-classical mode of production, using my sample films once again as the precursors of this trend in world cinema. Although their production values are different in many respects, a careful look behind the scenes and a dig into the production environments that emerged in the United States, Europe, Hong Kong, South Korea and Brazil in the last twenty years could provide us at this stage with a broad idea about the institutional and technological changes that instigated this paradigm shift.

Production and distribution environments

Starting with the simple but fundamental observation that the average American blockbuster still relies on the classical narrative formulas and that the bulk of films coming out of the major Hollywood studios exemplify very little tendency towards experimentation and innovation, we realise that post-classical narration has so far not been the favourite option for high-concept film-making in the New Hollywood. Instead, the development of the new narra-tive mode appears to be related more to the rise of independent cinema over the last two decades and the different ambiguous paths that were opened in the course of this time.

The notable appearance of independent production companies in the US is usually positioned in the mid-1980s and attributed to the expanding video and cable television markets. These two new outlets demanded an increasing amount of film product that could not be catered for by the major studios, which were limiting their output and investing in few expensive blockbust-ers. Although this independent production boom was short-lived – due to the realisation that theatrical release was still a prerequisite for success in the ancillary markets – it drew a number of talented people into the world of independent production and distribution and consolidated a substantial institutional infrastructure (see Prince 2000). And despite the fact that inde-pendent companies to date go bankrupt at regular intervals, the same indi-viduals seem to resurface invariably as a type of 'permanent government' that confirms the solid presence of independent filmmaking in the contemporary American movie scene (see Pribram 2002: 33–5). In fact, more and more writers argue for 'the new American independent cinema' as a fully devel-oped film practice that works either as an alternative or, in increasingly more cases, hand-in-hand with the mainstream Hollywood industry.

The hot debates on the co-dependence and alliance between these two trends will be discussed shortly but, first, I would like to dwell upon Emanuel Levy's take on the independent film movement in his book *Cinema of Outsid-ers: The Rise of American Independent Film* (1999). Levy's work is intriguing not only for its wealth of information on numerous films and filmmakers but mainly for its systematic and scholarly attempt to map independent cinema as a concrete cinematic institution with specific roles and functions. The fol-lowing ten factors are the ones that he identifies as the driving forces shaping the new 'indie' cinema:

1. The need for self-expression.
2. Hollywood's move away from serious, middle-range films.
3. Increased opportunities and capital in financing indies.
4. Greater demand for visual media, driven by an increase in the number of theatres and the adoption of home video as a dominant form of entertain-ment in the United States.
5. Supportive audiences: the Baby-Boom generation.
6. The decline of foreign-language films in the American market.
7. The proliferation of film schools across the country.

8. The emergence of the Sundance Film Festival as the primary showcase for indies and the rise of regional festivals.
9. The development of new organisational networks.
10.Commercial success – the realisation that there's money to be made in indies. (1999: 20–1)

While the role of the filmmaker and his/her creative vision is still pivotal in the independent filmmaking process, the other factors on this list demonstrate that – as in the case of art cinema – the power of the individual should not be overestimated. Against the blockbusters and their soaring budgets, small or medium-scale independent films can cover the needs of an extensive audiovisual market – multiplexes,[9] video, DVD, cable and pay-TV – and satisfy the ever-more refined tastes of the thirty-something generation by taking the risk with formal and thematic experimentation, a prohibited venture for the big-budget studio movies that need to remain faithful to old formulas to secure profits.

Another interesting element of the independent film movement in the United States is its relation to Europe. With the decline of European art cinema in the late 1970s, foreign films began to occupy an ever-diminishing place in the American market, allowing the American independent filmmakers to take the place of François Truffaut, Jean-Luc Godard and Federico Fellini. Furthermore, the American independents began to reverse the flow and dominate the European and international art circuit, attracting not only a large segment of the audience but also of the investors. Nowadays, it is more common for American productions to depend heavily on foreign pre-sales, while they often receive funding from European conglomerates and pan-European broadcasters, such as Canal Plus, with equity co-productions. According to Toby Miller, treaty co-productions between American and European companies have been around for decades but the shift towards 'equity stakes' in the partnerships provide the parties involved not only with territorial rights but also with control over the creative output (see 2001: 98). The example he uses to illustrate the implications of equity co-productions is the film *Hard Rain* (1998), produced by a small American independent company called Mutual Film Company, which drew its finances from an international consortium giving equity positions to six giant distributors from Europe and Japan. Thus, by means of equity stakes, partners from across the globe can have a say in artistic decisions, each aiming at their own domestic audiences.

Nevertheless, geographical borders are not the only ones that are increasingly crossed in the contemporary cinematic universe. The last point on Levy's list, namely the commercial potential of this film practice, implies one of the thorniest issues regarding independent filmmaking: the crossing of the boundaries between mainstream and alternative film practices. At this point, the name that immediately comes to mind is Miramax. Miramax Films, run until 2005 by Bob and Harvey Weinstein,[10] and situated on the east coast, started in the mid-1980s as a small art/cult film distribution company that managed within two decades to change the landscape of film distribution across the globe. Its first major hit came in 1989 when the Weinstein brothers bought the rights for Steven Soderbergh's *sex, lies and videotape* before it won the Audience Award at the Sundance Film Festival and the Palme d'Or at Cannes. With an aggressive marketing campaign that capitalised both on the film's international critical acclaim and its theme of sexuality and romance, Miramax managed to attract a far wider audience than the art house circuit, grossing over $26 million domestically (see Wyatt 1998: 79). This initial success encouraged the Weinsteins to continue their fierce business practices, which included scouting the Sundance Film Festival every year, investing in huge marketing campaigns and considerably raising the production budgets for independent films. Quentin Tarantino, the notoriously independent but also avowedly post-classical filmmaker, began his career in close co-operation with Miramax, which distributed his first feature *Reservoir Dogs* and then turned his *Pulp Fiction* into one of the biggest box-office successes in the history of independent cinema, grossing more than $100 million and receiving seven Academy Award nominations. When Disney bought Miramax in 1993 in the context of a much wider wave of mergers and acquisitions in the global media scene, the paths of mainstream and independent filmmaking began to intertwine even more. With Disney financing the development, production and distribution of Miramax's features and providing them with safe ancillary markets, the Weinsteins maintained their creative control and turned their company into the largest employer of above-the line talent and below-the line crew in New York City (see Biskind 2004: 3). At the same time, Miramax developed a formidable presence around the world as a distributor of foreign-language films, promoting the works of many international filmmakers, four of which feature in my sample: Jean-Pierre Jeunet's *Amélie*, Danny Boyle's *Trainspotting*, Wong Kar-wai's *Chungking Express* and Fernando Meirelles and Kátia Lund's *City of God*. Whether distributing American, European, Hong Kong or Latin American films, however, the role of Miramax has been instrumental in bringing opposing traditions closer and bridging the gap between art and commerce. In Peter Biskind's words:

> Not only did the Weinsteins transform distribution, they brokered a marriage of indie and mainstream that resulted in a novel kind of picture that did more than just cross over; it exchanged DNA with commercial movies. An amalgam of difference and sameness, personal and commercial, genre and voice,

these films played like Hollywood movies while retaining the indie spirit, however vague and hard to define that may be. (2004: 470)

Although Miramax is emblematic of this current situation in American film-making, several other companies followed a similar trajectory; Time Warner bought New Line Cinema, Sony acquired Orion Classics, Universal purchased October Films, while Twentieth Century-Fox launched Fox Searchlight as a speciality division (see Levy 1999: 31). The major Hollywood studios, though still largely dedicated to producing blockbuster 'event' films and reaping the profits from synergies, have managed to build ties with the independent sector in order to secure access into more 'cutting-edge' material and talent that could sooner or later cross over to the other side of the industry. The key for this process, which also constitutes the major transformation of the movie business in the post-studio era, appears to be the shift of emphasis from production to distribution. Nowadays, the Hollywood studios, even when they do not directly own an independent production company, are capable of shaping the budget of a film by ensuring distribution and providing certain partial services, such as post-production facilities.

With this institutional setting in mind, the workings behind the production of the American films in the sample become significantly clearer. They were all affected in multiple ways by the hybrid situation laid out earlier, whether low-budget (the $4.5 million *Requiem for a Dream*) or mid-budget (the $63 million *Fight Club*). Darren Aronofsky's *Requiem for a Dream* is the most clear-cut case of an independent film that depended on numerous small-scale companies both for its production and distribution in the United States and abroad. Yet, one should not lose sight of Aronofsky's passage from the 16mm black-and-white *Pi* (1998) made for $60,000 to this second feature, which required a budget almost ten times higher to cover its digital effects as well as the high profile cast, including Ellen Burstyn who received an Academy Award nomination for her performance. Undoubtedly, the catalyst for this development was the Director's Award at Sundance for *Pi*, which turned Aronofsky into a hip name overnight offering him the possibility to acquire resources for a more expensive project that had both artistic and commercial potential. The opposite scenario applied to Oliver Stone's *Natural Born Killers*, which was produced and distributed by Warner Bros. In this case a famous filmmaker used his brand name to convince a major studio to spend $40 million, a very affordable sum by mainstream Hollywood standards, in order to experiment with a highly adventurous narrative and theme. Similarly, Twentieth Century-Fox gave the opportunity to David Fincher to make *Fight Club*, an equally daring and controversial film, hoping that the success of *Se7en* (1995) and *The Game* (1997) combined with Brad Pitt and

Edward Norton's star personas would allow the film to at least break even. Their calculations were soon vindicated, as the film managed to create a lot of critical discussion at the Cannes Film Festival and then slowly began to attract audiences around the world. Despite gaining considerably less than the mainstream blockbusters of that period, *Fight Club* acquired both a cult status in cinephile circles and became a video game five years later, illustrating the sheer paradox of post-classicism, namely the bizarre combination of cult status and substantial profits. On the other hand, Paul Thomas Anderson's *Magnolia* was made by New Line Cinema, another important independent company, which is often regarded as Miramax's sibling (see Wyatt 1998). The Janus face of the independent cinematic world is typified in the film's $37 million budget and the long list of stars who participated in it for a fraction of their regular salaries. *Magnolia* toured internationally, winning the Golden Bear at the Berlin International Film Festival, while, domestically, it earned three Academy Award nominations as well as respectable profits in the video and television markets. Lastly, *Moulin Rouge!* was a co-production between the Australian independent company, Bazmark Films, and Twentieth Century-Fox, with the latter buying the rights for worldwide distribution and offering its post-production facilities in Australia and Spain. The fate of Baz Luhrmann's film in the Academy Awards in 2002 is emblematic of the position of post-classical works in the mainstream American establishment: it was granted eight nominations but it was Ron Howard's *A Beautiful Mind* (2001) that went home with the Best Picture Award.[11]

On the European front, the film industry has been historically founded on an organisational model that consistently sought to resist Hollywood dominance and establish a common economic and cultural pattern among European countries. Ever since its inception, cinema had been regarded in Europe as an art institution that should be protected from market forces – and, by extension, Hollywood contamination – with the help of quotas, subsidies and co-production agreements. Although this policy fluctuated from country to country at various junctures, the 1970s marked a distinct era in European filmmaking. As Martin Dale observes:

> National centres were set up throughout Europe, and the State began actively influencing film commissioning through selective subsidies and investments by state television. Most leading film companies were taken over by new media groups who introduced 'technocratic' management styles that either cut back production entirely or shifted it into a 'cultural' plane. (1997: 132)

Ironically enough, this policy coincided with a time when national new waves began to lose their edge and the art cinema circuit in America slowly faltered, as previously noted. The institutional infrastructure described above ensured that the development of European popular cinema was no longer desirable or even feasible, whereas the bureaucracy in national centres favoured a small circle of filmmakers who, while concentrating exclusively on high art, managed to chase away European film viewers from the theatres. The severe financial crisis of European cinema in the 1970s and 1980s partly subsided in the 1990s, with the appearance of films such as *Lola Rennt*, *Trainspotting* and *Amélie* being a clear sign of significant changes under way.

First and foremost, the contemporary European filmmakers who aspire to address an international market begin to increasingly resemble the American independents in their effort to collect money from different sources. Apart from the various state subsidies, Anne Jäckel (2003) identifies two types of funding that have become important since the late 1980s: private financial sources, such as equity finance from television and media networks, co-production finance and pre-sales of distribution rights for various outlets (theatrical release, video and television); and European and pan-European programmes, such as Media and Eurimages. *Europa*, Von Trier's first major feature, is an illustrative case that combined almost all possible sources, from Eurimages to three different National Film Centres (French, Danish, German) and a European conglomerate. The fact that the leading French media group Havas, which owns Canal Plus and UGC, contributed half of the $4.7 million budget of *Europa* attests to a shift, albeit a faint one, in the investment strategies of the powerful European media groups, which in the past steered clear of the vast majority of subsidy-driven films. As Dale notes:

> Even Europe's media groups, who have a vested interest in securing software to drive their retail empires, are 'reactive' rather than 'proactive' when it comes to investing in domestic films. They are far more concerned with securing 'safe' local bets, and the best of American independent cinema. (1997: 226)

This reluctance abated in the 1990s, as a number of filmmakers decided to move past the art versus commerce dilemma and made films like *Arizona Dream* and *Amélie*, which could potentially penetrate the international market without relinquishing their artistic merits. Both these films were produced by UGC and were distributed in the United States by Warner Bros. and Miramax respectively. Miramax also bid for the distribution rights of Tykwer's *Lola Rennt* but reputedly lost due to Harvey Weinstein's aggressively arrogant behaviour during the negotiations (see Biskind 2004). The film was finally distributed in the US by Sony Pictures but Miramax soon retaliated with an enticing offer for X Filme Creative Pool, the production company that Tykwer ran with his partners. As Jäckel notes:

> The commercial potential of X Filme did not go unnoticed. In December 1998, the Berlin-based film collective signed an agreement with Miramax for X Filme to provide the speciality distributor with an exclusive first look at all properties owned, controlled or written by its members. In turn, Miramax submits projects to X Filme for its members to direct. (2003: 33)

However, Miramax has not only begun to interfere with European filmmaking but the wider Miramax impact on the American independent scene appears to be gradually migrating to Europe, as production budgets increase and marketing promotion becomes indispensable for a film's survival, let alone success. According to Jäckel:

> As more and more European distributors believe the success or failure of a movie at the box office depends on marketing strategy and spending, marketing departments are expanding, and advertising agencies specialising in film promotion are flourishing. Massive marketing campaigns ensure that, increasingly, positions are affirmed and opinions made before a film is released. (2003: 113–14)

Along with marketing, the domain of post-production is another flourishing area in the European film industry with the Max European Post-production Alliance offering a promising model for further developments. Taking advantage of Europe's shortcomings in the field of special effects and image processing, the Max project was launched in 1999, bringing together smaller post-production companies from Germany, France, Italy and Belgium in order to attract post-production work from ambitious projects from all over the world. Within two years of operation, the German partner in this alliance, the company Das Werk, had a breakthrough with the post-production of *Lola Rennt* and soon gained a strong foothold in the US market. The Max venture exemplifies a European attempt to become competitive in a fast-changing world and to overthrow some of the long-standing bureaucratic structures of the European film industry that are responsible for its decline.

As the old dichotomies between the US and Europe appear less pertinent in the contemporary globalised world, the other cinematic pole of post-classical cinema has undoubtedly arisen in Hong Kong, a cinematic city that always embraced a cosmopolitan spirit and nurtured a very vivid and successful film tradition. Hong Kong cinema is a remarkable case in film history, as it is one of the few national cinemas with a full-blown industry and a wide audience on a global scale. Although the production budgets are close to the European standards, Hong Kong never developed a state-subsidy system and grounded the viability of its cinema solely on public appeal. As Esther Yau underlines:

> Hong Kong has made its statements in the global screen culture with some of the most unbelievable and entertaining moments that have ever appeared on film. In the midst of billion-dollar media industries, Hong Kong movies are like speedboats breaking the waves alongside a daunting fleet of Hollywood titanics, charging ahead on the basis of their irreverent imagination, their unique mix of cultural references, and their reinvention of generic elements. (2001: 2)

From the rich and fascinating history of Hong Kong cinema I would like to point out four crucial elements that shaped the nature of contemporary Hong Kong films. Firstly, Hong Kong cinema developed out of an industry that remained politically neutral to the antagonisms between mainland China and Taiwan and was never burdened with the duty of national self-representation (ibid.). In terms of business ties, Hong Kong filmmakers were inclined to approach Taiwanese investors rather than the Chinese government for subsidies, thus maintaining a commercial profile and keeping a distance from art cinema practices. Secondly, in contrast to other national cinemas in the non-Western world, such as Iranian or Chinese cinema, Hong Kong cinema refrained from autoethnographic tendencies and openly incorporated elements from the Hollywood and European traditions. Thirdly, an attempt to break away from commercialism in the 1960s and 1970s never fully developed into a consistent new wave movement similar to the ones in Europe, due to the lack of support from the State and other critical communities. Most of the filmmakers who first related to that attempt soon re-entered the commercial enterprise, seeking to bring innovation from within (see Law Kar 2001). Lastly, the 1990s signalled an unprecedented Hong Kong craze in the cult scene in the United States that had its origins in kung fu films of the 1970s. After kung fu films began to falter both domestically and abroad, Hong Kong filmmakers struck back in the mid-1980s with films 'that could compete with Hollywood by offering familiar genres and stars in a dazzling modern package' (Bordwell 2000a: 35). These films slowly became popular with cult audiences in America thanks to video stores, screenings at university campuses and enthusiastic fans like Quentin Tarantino, whose fascination with Hong Kong films is well-documented (see Bordwell 2000a: 84).

All of the above factors have played a fundamental role in transforming a local cinema into the hippest strand of world cinema, capable of exerting creative influence on the American industry and exchanging ideas and talents. They were also instrumental in developing a national film tradition that could combine commercial orientation with the freedom to experiment with a mixture of classical and avant-garde formulas. In his attempt to answer the question 'how can mass-produced films be artful', Bordwell makes many insightful observations about the formal qualities of Hong Kong films in the 1990s and what he calls their 'avant-pop' potential, even though he refrains from terms like post-classical or postmodern. And, indeed, a number of contemporary Hong Kong films could qualify as post-classical – at least according to my line of reasoning – with Wong Kar-wai's works as the most successful examples in the international market.

The next stop on our journey across the globe is in South Korea, where we come across another film industry in pursuit of a balance between creativity and commerce (see Rist 2004). *Oldboy* is a representative product of the institutional changes in the national cinematic terrain since the late 1980s, which were spearheaded by an intensive liberalisation of the media sector. For several decades, Korean cinema had been regulated by the Motion Picture Law, a piece of legislation drafted in 1962 by Park Chung Hee, a military dictator whose principal aim was to retain strict governmental control over production and distribution practices. These protectionist measures, as in the case of European cinema, managed to keep the American threat at bay but did not prevent the local cinema from waning both domestically and internationally.

The first turning point came in 1985 with the sixth revision of the Motion Picture Law, which allowed the major Hollywood studios to distribute their films directly to local theatres and boosted the number of foreign films that were imported into Korea: from 27 in 1985 to 264 in 1989 (see Paquet 2005: 35). This sudden flood of imports threw the Korean film companies into a severe state of crisis and brought them face to face with the cruel demands of the globalised economy. But the awakening of Korean cinema did not take long; the Koreans were quick to realise that the only way to retaliate was through a strong local film industry that emulated the American system and followed the mantra 'learning from Hollywood' (Shim 2006: 32). The development of the national cinema as a full-blown industry that ensured the profitability and self-sufficiency of its films was a multi-staged process that entailed the collaboration of various factors. As Darcy Paquet argues:

> There was also a simultaneous push by the government and the film industry to build a stronger industrial base for filmmaking. This involved forming larger and more powerful film companies, building more technically advanced infrastructure, opening film schools to provide better training, and searching for new sources of finance for the making of the films. The new generation

of producers would make full use of Korea's *chaebŏl* [large conglomerates], venture-capital companies, and generous government funding to bring this about. (2005: 33)

The turn towards commercially viable films, which echoes the strategies we have encountered in the US, Europe and Hong Kong, led to the unprecedented rise of Korean cinema all over the world. By 2005 Korean films could claim up to fifty per cent of overall ticket sales in the domestic market, while the critical acclaim of Korean filmmakers abroad gradually left a distinct mark on the international festival circuit.[12] The sustainability of the current success is an issue of significant concern, given the unpredictable fluctuations of the globalisation process, but the local infrastructure that has been cemented in the last two decades combined with the artistic aspirations of the young Korean filmmakers seem to promise the world an even more impressive follow-up.

Finally, our closing destination is Latin America and, more precisely, Brazil. The making of a film like *City of God* with a budget of $3.3 million, stemming from a co-production between the Brazilian conglomerate Globo Filmes and a number of French companies including Wild Bunch and Studio Canal, is indicative of the shifting situation in Brazilian cinema in the 1990s and the new millennium. Charting the history of this national cinema has always been an uneasy task, given a permanent status of instability that gave rise to periodical births and rebirths as well as sudden deaths and long silences, to paraphrase Lucia Nagib (2003), an expert on this topic. In more recent years, the most decisive change came with the dismantling of Embrafilme – the State film enterprise – in 1990, which led to the sudden death of local film production: 74 films were made in 1989, 58 in 1990 and only nine in 1993 (see Rêgo 2005). Yet, there was no lasting silence this time. A series of new tax incentive laws were promptly introduced to encourage private investments in Brazilian films and to allow foreign distributors with local subsidiaries to invest part of their profits back into domestic productions. The entrance of private money into the game was not unrelated to the wider implications of the globalisation process, which ruled out any idea of national isolation or State protectionism. The burgeoning effect of international affiliations on the local film industry became crystal clear. As Cacilda Rêgo observes:

Another developing trend during this period was the internationalisation of the Brazilian film industry. This trend was in part generated by a growing awareness among industry professionals and government officials of both the necessity and the potential of international dealings such as treaty co-productions and co-ventures, and the importance of foreign investors and foreign markets for the industry's survival. (2005: 86)

The central pillars for the successful internationalisation of Brazilian cinema were once again the commercial orientation of the young filmmakers and their artistic potential. The former would be measured by their box-office performance, while the latter would be gauged by the critical merits reaped at the international festivals and other prize competitions. The commercial potential of Brazilian films was particularly pursued by the participation of Globo Filmes – the film branch of a giant conglomerate – in local productions, ensuring higher financial and technological resources and elevating the production standards in Brazilian filmmaking. On the other hand, the artistic ambitions of the so-called New Brazilian Cinema were flaunted through an aggressive promotional campaign that warranted the presence of Brazilian entries in the most prestigious film events worldwide. The results on both counts have been satisfactory, despite the fact that the chronic instability of the Brazilian film industry has not been fully treated. Both filmmakers and investors alike are required to keep on juggling numerous, often contradicting priorities in order to navigate their own creative vessels through the turbulent waters of world cinema.

The overview of the production and distribution environments that brought my sample films into being demonstrates how a number of forces in different parts of the planet converged and co-ordinated in order to create an institutional infrastructure that could promote the production of non-classical or artistic films with commercial potential. Even though there are still significant differences among the film industries in the United States, Europe, Hong Kong, South Korea and Brazil, it would be short-sighted to ignore an emerging pattern in these film worlds from the 1990s onwards, which allowed a category of films to bring art and commerce closer than ever before and to travel through the same circuits, whether that is the Cannes Film Festival, Harvey Weinstein's office or the nearby multiplex.

Technological developments and media convergence

In our attempt to understand and delineate the context in which post-classical films have developed in the last two decades, we should take into account the fact that this particular mode of production does not only entail creative filmmakers, medium-sized budgets, independent production companies, powerful global distributors and niche marketing but also an array of new technological tools and methods. The groundbreaking changes in the technological field in recent years did not leave the filmmaking business unstirred; the process of digitisation along with a panoply of new technology soon entered the movie industry and spawned numerous creative possibilities for directors and technical crew. It may be in vain to inventory these new technological products – they are likely to have been updated by the time this manuscript is published – but I would like to highlight the two main areas where the new technologies broke new ground.

Firstly, the production phase has been significantly helped by video-assist and motion control. The former allows the filmmaker and the crew to have simultaneous access to the composed image and make alterations on the spot instead of waiting for the dailies, thus saving precious time and money. The latter facilitates fluid camera movements and enables the representation of disembodied vision. In his description of motion control, John Thornton Caldwell includes:

> ...not just the computer-controlled units that automatically program cameras to perform and reduplicate complicated camera moves, but also the Steadi-cam, Camrail, robotic-controlled studio cameras, and much less cybernetic devices like jib arms and motorised cranes. All of these devices are alike in one important way: they physically take the camera away from the camera operator's eyes and move it through space in very fluid ways. (1999: 132)

All of these pieces of equipment and more generally the concept of 'motion control' have had a considerable impact on the formation of post-classical space and intensified continuity in particular.[13] At the same time, the new advances in digital cinematography offer the opportunity to simulate different film stocks on video, allowing even relatively low-budget films like *Lola Rennt* or *Requiem for a Dream* to experiment with different visual formats.

Secondly, the most radical transformation regards the post-production phase, which consists of the process of editing, animating or manipulating the live-action footage with the help of technology. While the practice of post-production has been executed by analogue means since the birth of cinema, the advent of digitality has opened new horizons for image construction by rendering optical effects highly accessible and comparatively effortless. The vast opportunities for manipulating moving images that are part and parcel of the new computer software and non-linear editing systems can be elicited from a professional editor: 'the Avid has 32 levels of undo and that completely frees up the editor to experiment' (quoted in Caldwell 1999: 135). This exceptional freedom to experiment was evidenced in the construction of the post-classical spatio-temporal system, where the resourceful capacities of digital technology infused the cinematic signifiers with a life of their own.

On the other hand, the same digital software can create a seamless classical space as easily as it can build a multilayered spatial montage. The post-classical preference for the latter could be attributed to the influence of several other contemporary media and the way they have incorporated the new technologies in their own repertory. In the modern media-saturated world, the powerful forces of digitisation and convergence are increasingly eroding older distinctions and boundaries among diverse media and facilitating the exchange of both labour and visual or expressive forms. For these reasons, the developments in the language of new media and television over the last two decades have affected decisively the moulding of the post-classical narrative model and have resulted in a growing similarity between various media formats. The formal connections between the products of computer technology, such as interface, CD-ROMs, video games and other types of software, and the post-classical narrational options have been hinted at throughout this book. For instance, the latter's tendency towards hypermediacy and spatial montage mirrors some of the inherent qualities of the computer screen, while the employment of multiple plot-lines and the non-serial distribution of information in the post-classical narratives owes a great debt to various forms of digital media.[14] At the same time, one should not underestimate the interaction between the post-classical cinema and television aesthetics, especially the trend that emerged in the 1980s towards extensive electronic post-production. Before the advent of new media, television had already begun to treat footage as raw material that would be composited, mixed and matched in post-production before going on air. As Caldwell notes:

> These *post*-dependent genres include the entire field of commercial television advertising, many studio-originated programmes, and a wide variety of non-programme materials that are broadcast, including promotionals, and pre- and post-title sequences. One cannot easily overlook the sheer semiotic density of visual signs in these programming categories. In fact, each year the semiotic density of the post-dependent genres and forms increases and threatens to encroach even more upon the diegetic world of feature programmes. (1995: 137–8; emphasis in original)

With CNN and MTV as the pioneers of this style, the mounting emphasis on post-production in television programmes created an acute hyperactivity, a visual density and an obsession with effects that have slowly permeated every strand of programming. Out of the gamut of programming categories, however, it is advertising and sports broadcasting that have left the most indelible marks on the post-classical films. Commercial spots have always been a site of experimentation in their attempt to exploit the discursive and emotive power of hyperactive and excessive visual styles within a very limited time slot. Many of their strategies, such as non-diegetic passages, powerful voice-overs and the direct address of the audience, are now a staple of the post-classical mode. Similarly, the repetitive use of replay, multiple camera angles and slow-motion in sports coverage has inspired many filmmakers to use these techniques for the same purpose, namely to offer the viewers the most spectacular but also the most informative view of the action (see Elsaesser 1998a). Thus, the opening scenes of *Magnolia* offer the most illustrative example of how a post-classical film often visualises a story event in the same way as a football game is broadcast on television.

With this last observation on the manifold interactions between cinema and television, I would like to conclude my brief overview of the various factors that *appear* to have played a role in the formation of the post-classical mode of narration. Without a doubt, what I have been describing is only the tip of the iceberg; the investigation into the causal forces that instigated this paradigm shift in contemporary world cinema requires further elaboration, before one is able to argue in concrete terms for the existence of a coherent post-classical mode of production, analogous to the classical mode of production that Janet Staiger substantiated in her study. The stakes in the case of the the post-classical cinema are also considerably higher on account of its international baseline that demands tremendously extensive research into all the parameters of world film production, including new divisions of labour, international contractual policies in the various professional guilds and inter-media collaborations at the production, distribution and exhibition levels, to name just a few.

In fact, the stakes are extremely high not only due to the practical difficulties, namely the bulk of data, but mostly due to the thorny issue regarding the origins of the post-classical forms. To explain: Bordwell, Thompson and Staiger's study on the classical norms was modelled upon the output of the Hollywood studios over a long period, from 1917 to 1960, which amounted to a fairly coherent and systematic sample. A significant implication of their account, however problematic, is that these norms were cultivated in American soil and were moulded by an American mode of production that was then exported all around the globe with unparalleled success.[15] Similarly, Bordwell's account of art cinema narration, which was predominantly exemplified by European films in the late 1950s and 1960s, disseminated the impression that these constructive options were mainly 'European'. But what about the post-classical? Could we ascribe to the post-classical choices in the axes of causality, space and time a specific geographical or even national origin? Is there something inherently American, European or Asian about forking-path plots or intensified continuity for instance? The answer is clearly no but the issue of transnational norms which is immediately triggered by this negative answer is markedly complex, not only as far as it concerns contemporary cinema but also as far as it concerns the cinematic medium from its inception.[16] For my purposes here, I would like to restrict myself to the observation that the post-classical mode of narration is the result of the convergence of several factors related to the institutional and technological developments in cinematic practice across the world. Despite their different geographical co-ordinates, the post-classical films began to emerge when a number of decisive changes in film industries and media environments permitted the creation of films that could be both artistically and commercially ambitious, breaking down a long-standing opposition between art and commerce. At the same time, these films profited from the state-of-the-art technology that both broadened the capacities of the moving image and promoted formal borrowings from television and new media, breaking down traditional barriers among different media. Wherever and whenever this institutional and technological pattern was formed, the post-classical model would be available for filmmakers to use. In places where these developments are still to come, like in Africa or Greece, the post-classical options are bound to remain dormant. Therefore, to look for a specific national origin or to seek a single creative source behind the formation of this new paradigm in an era of global cinematic flows and unprecedented media convergence would not only be a virtual impossibility, but a sign of misguided perception of the new phenomena in hand.

Inevitably, the very last question that awaits us now that this book is reaching its closure with an assertion about breaking barriers, hierarchies and distinctions and the lack of origins, regards the relation between the framework of postmodernism and post-classical narration. The common assertion that our world has entered the phase of postmodernity and our culture has been penetrated by the poetics and politics of postmodernism for more than four decades now, has led a substantial number of theorists to believe that the cinematic medium has joined the other arts in the same postmodern game. And on principle I have no reason to disagree. The problem, however, is that the concepts of 'postmodernity' and 'postmodernism' are so wide in scope and so multifaceted in their application that they could not be equated with any particular cinematic phenomenon or even an entire film movement. If we try to position the post-classical narrative paradigm within wider cultural production, we could trace numerous affinities with the so-called 'postmodern culture', especially if we adopt terms such as 'negotiated self-reflexivity', 'hybridity', 'blurred boundaries', 'transnationalism' and so on. Yet, gradually our vocabulary will become vague, slippery and finally vacant because everything can be labelled postmodern from a certain angle. Even if there is such a thing as a postmodern totality that manifests itself copiously and diversely in all contemporary cultural products, the analysts' task is to disengage themselves from tautological exercises and to engage in research that flaunts theoretical and historical rigour. The choice of historical poetics was quite successful for that matter; it led to the demarcation of a new mode of narration that characterises a large segment of films from various corners of the world today. Whether this mode is also postmodern is not pertinent. Similarly, I suggested a meticulous delve into the institutional and technological developments at a global level in order to discover the driving forces behind this new narrative mode. Whether these developments could be labelled postmodern is also not pertinent. At this stage the term 'postmodern' can have blinding effects both for those who prefer to use it and those who have sworn against it, with Bordwell the most typical victim. His obsessive resistance to the postmodern discussions described in the introduction to this book have prevented him from observing the development of a new paradigm and from adding a new chapter to his *Narration in the Fiction Film*. But for this last part I, personally, should be most grateful.

NOTES

introduction

1   Some of Bordwell's major books include *French Impressionist Cinema: Film Culture, Film Theory and Film Style* (1980), *The Films of Carl-Theodor Dreyer* (1981), *Making Meaning: Inference and Rhetoric in the Interpretation of Cinema* (1989), *On the History of Film Style* (1997), *Ozu and the Poetics of Cinema* (1998) and *Planet Hong Kong: Popular Cinema and the Art of Entertainment* (2000).

2   The authors of the book have made an unprecedented step selecting an unbiased sample of 100 films from the period 1915–60 with the help of a rather scientific sampling method. Their data was complemented with an extended sample that comprised about 200 films from the same period, which were considered to be important for more subjective reasons.

3   In *Narration in the Fiction Film* Bordwell also begins to touch upon the films' reception and particularly the issue of comprehension. In a nutshell, he claims that the spectator comprehends the film by following 'cues' in the narrative and by applying schemata and hypotheses that derive partly from experience with the various narrational modes. This is a research area that has been further explored by cognitive theorists like Branigan (1992), Smith (1995), Grodal (1997) and Buckland (2000), but does not constitute part of my personal research interests.

4   The detailed findings of his previous research in *The Classical Hollywood Cinema* are presented in this edition in a more condensed manner, accompanied by some close textual readings.

5   For a strong criticism of the use of the term 'classical' to describe Hollywood cinema, see Hansen (2000).

6   Along the same lines, Kristin Thompson, co-author of *The Classical Hollywood Cinema*, argues that storytelling in the New Hollywood remains predominantly and largely classical because the classical system is so stable that it can selectively assimilate avant-garde devices such as fast cutting, jump-cuts and discontinuous editing style. A significant difference, however, is that Thompson acknowledges that films like *Blue Velvet* (1986) or *Pulp Fiction* (1994) are clearly non-classical, instead of stretching the classical rules to include everything in the group. Her argument regarding classical storytelling thus becomes rather quantitative inasmuch as she considers these movies as 'blips on the radar screen when seen within the history of Hollywood' (1999: 340–1).

7   The issue of 'intensified continuity' will be discussed at length in chapter two and the conclusion.

8   It is important to note that various strands of Asian cinema are increasingly characterised as postmodern and particularly the contemporary Hong Kong cinema; see Teo (1997).

9   The term 'world cinema' is rather problematic, as it was traditionally used to encompass all non-Western cinemas. Its use is beginning to change, since increasingly more theorists try to remap world film production by avoiding binary distinctions between the Western world and the rest of the world (see Andrew 2004). My study will argue that the post-classical mode of narration has arisen in different corners of the world over the last two decades and it has important global implications. Hopefully, this book will be seen as a contribution to the wider debate on world cinema by emphasising the formal parameters on this new agenda in film studies.

10   A detailed filmography is provided as a separate section at the end of the book. I would also like to note that in most cases I will be referring to the films with their original titles, with three exceptions: *Chongking Senlin* will be called by its international title *Chungking Express*, *Le Fabuleux Destin d' Amélie Poulain* will be called *Amélie* and *Cidade de Deus* will be called *City of God*.

11   On several occasions I choose to analyse the same scenes more than once in different chapters in order to illustrate how they operate at different levels of generality and to prove how intricately interwoven the motivations and the spatio-temporal elements are in the narration of a film.

chapter one

1   The phenomenon of narrative has been explored from many different perspectives (existential, psychological, cognitive or technical) and with respect to very different media (literature, film, music, painting and computer games). Narratology, the formal study of narrative, has shed light on the various levels and

qualities of the narrative process and remains to date a work in progress. My book will not go into diverse deep-seated narratological problems because the issue here is not to create a new narrative theory; rather, it is to use a specific cinematic theory of narration, that of David Bordwell, and to try to delineate a new historical mode of narration. However, there will be times when his theory will be inadequate to ask some questions about the films' construction, as in the case of the narrative voice that I will discuss in chapter four. Whenever an occasion arises, I will engage in a critical evaluation of his theory and turn to other theorists whose work is better equipped for my analytical purposes.

2   The various functions of the narrative devices and the levels of narration that they initiate will be discussed in detail in chapter four.

3   For the cognitive issues that the Möbius strip narrative structure raises, see Buckland's analysis of *Lost Highway* (1997) in Elsaesser and Buckland (2002).

4   We could consider the immediacy/hypermediacy dichotomy in the mode of representation as part of a wider discussion about the contrast between the classical and the baroque sensibility. Omar Calabrese has argued that many important cultural phenomena of our times are characterised by a neo-baroque aesthetic that resembles the baroque (see 1992: 15). Similarly, Angela Ndalianis observes: 'The seventeenth and late twentieth/twenty-first-century nurtured cultural climates that permitted the baroque to become "formula and canon": both epochs reflect wide-scale baroque sensibilities that, while being the product of specific socio-historical and temporal conditions, reflect similar patterns and concerns on formal and aesthetic levels' (2003: 358).

5   Here Bolter and Grusin support their argument by paraphrasing Jacques Derrida's account of mimesis and it would be pertinent to quote it: 'mimesis is defined not ontologically or objectively in terms of their resemblance of a representation to its object but rather intersubjectively in terms of the reproduction of the feeling of imitation or resemblance in the perceiving subject' (1999: 53).

6   The characteristics of post-classical space and time will be thoroughly analysed in chapters two and three respectively.

7   A detailed analysis of *Europa*'s spatial system is presented in chapter two.

8   One of the arguments regularly raised about postmodern cinema is that it favours generic hybridity in contrast to the classical Hollywood years when genres were pure and distinct. The most noteworthy attempt to describe the preference for hybridity in contemporary American cinema is found in Jim Collins' (1993) writings on what he calls 'eclectic irony'.

9   I would like to note that the generic motivation in this paradigm is highly influenced by the other two types of motivation, namely the hypermediated realism that I described in the previous section and the parodic motivation that I will present in the next. The interaction between these three principal construc-

tive elements – hypermediacy, parody and genres – seems to reinforce the tendency towards both hybridity and the attempt to revive and quote elements from the cinematic past.

10 The combination of dramatic elements with humorous incidents or, more generally, an entertaining mood is found even in the films whose themes are extremely tragic and violent as in *City of God*, *Oldboy*, *Magnolia* and *Trainspotting*.

11 Although Carroll does not employ the term 'parody', his description of allusionism becomes pertinent to my account of parodic motivation, if we take into consideration the fact that the parodic process is textualised through a set of references and allusions.

12 For the effect of parody on character construction, see Baron (1998).

chapter two

1 For a detailed description of continuity editing techniques and a comparison with other editing styles, see Bordwell and Thompson (1993: 261–1).

2 The article appeared in *Film Quarterly* in 2002 and then Bordwell transformed it into a chapter in the book *The Way Hollywood Tells It* (2006) where he added a few more examples but kept his arguments intact.

3 I will discuss the significance of Bordwell's argument on intensified continuity and the persistence of the classical in more detail in the conclusion in the section on the boundaries of difference between the classical and the post-classical.

4 For the concept of Average Shot Length (ASL) and the way to calculate it, see Salt (1992).

5 Bordwell's observation about shorter ASL in contemporary films is also verified by an empirical research paper called 'Traditional Film Editing vs. Electronic Nonlinear Film Editing: A Comparison of Feature Films' by Michael Brandt. The paper also argues that digital editing has led to the more extensive use of optical effects and a more complex staging of dialogue scenes. See http://www.nonlinear4.com/brandt.htm; accessed 3 January 2005.

6 Here I am combining Manovich's terminology with the terms from Bolter and Grusin's work that I introduced in chapter one. Even if the former does not use the term 'hypermediacy' per se, his observations about the use of digital tools and their double ability to create both classical realist images and composited ones mirrors the latter's argument about the ability of all media to create transparency and hypermediacy. The reason I am using Manovich in this chapter on space is because his work offers more specific observations about various cinematic devices as well as useful definitions about spatial constructions, such

as spatial montage. Whether there are deep-seated discrepancies between the overall works of these theorists is not relevant for this research, as they seem to be in complete agreement as far as the issues I am interested in are concerned.

7   From a similar perspective, another new media theorist, Yvonne Spielmann, describes these types of digital images as 'clusters'. Spielmann seeks to capture the aspect of density by borrowing the term 'cluster' from music theory to characterise the images that are produced from processing. She notes: 'Transferred to media, in particular visual media, the term cluster means the simultaneity of different images or elements effected through multiple layers. The cluster results in spatial density or fusion' (1999b: 139).

8   This is another significant point of convergence between Manovich's theory with Bolter and Grusin's.

9   I will discuss the impact of digital technology on television aesthetics in the conclusion where I will examine the interactions between cinema and other media.

10 Rybczynski's *Tango* is not even digitally made but exemplifies all the elements of digital cinema with the use of traditional technical tools like optical printers. This is similar to *Europa*, which will be one of the case studies in this chapter.

11 I have already mentioned briefly an example of Von Trier's unconventional 'staging in depth' in the section on hypermediated realism in chapter one.

12 I quoted Durgnat's definition of 'energy realism' in the section on realistic motivation in chapter one.

13 My observations are based mostly on the non-musical parts of the film, although the musical numbers are highly narrativised and cannot be separated easily from the story.

14 He explains how he maintained his discipline in his DVD commentary to the film. *Moulin Rouge!*, dir. Baz Luhrmann, Twentieth Century Fox, 2001.

15 Step-printing is the technique used to show fast action moving slowly via duplicated frames. It is created in post-production using an optical printer.

16 I discussed the argument on 'bricolage aesthetics' in the introduction.

17 Although the ASL of the entire film may be shorter than the ASL of this particular scene, it can still be included in the average editing rate (three to six seconds) of films in the 1990s, as calculated by David Bordwell in his article on intensified continuity.

18 The issue of self-consciousness will be the main focus of chapter four on post-classical narration.

19 See his interview in http://millimeter.com/ar/video_practical_virtues_four/; accessed 3 January 2005.

chapter three

1   Noël Carroll explains that the medium-specificity thesis consists of two axes of thinking: the internal component considers what a medium does best of all the things it does, and the comparative component considers what a medium does best compared to other media (see 1999b: 322–8).

2   Joan Dagle argues against this thesis, exploring ways to discern the possible temporal qualities of the single shot (see 1980: 47–59).

3   In broad terms there are very few discrepancies between the way Bordwell and Chatman apply Genette to categorise time-relations in cinema. The main theoretical difference is that Chatman maintains Genette's *histoire/recit* (story/ discourse) distinction, while Bordwell replaces it with the fabula/syuzhet pair. This delicate theoretical difference renders Bordwell's account of cinematic time slightly more elaborate and better adjusted to the specificities of the cinematic medium.

4   For definitions of the fabula and syuzhet, see my outline of Bordwell's narrative theory in chapter one.

5   For the original account of this distinction, see Chatman (1978: 32).

6   I would like to stress that I am, like most theorists, focusing on the events that are enacted and not on those that are recounted. The syuzhet recounts significantly more freely the events of the fabula whereas the order of the presentation of an event is strictly coded.

7   The issue of self-consciousness along with the other two principal aspects of narration, i.e. communicativeness and omniscience, will be analysed in detail in chapter four.

8   Burch distinguishes between measurable and indefinite ellipses and offers a detailed analysis of their functions (see 1997: 135–48).

9   For a detailed analysis of the entire scene and the complex mixture of flashbacks, flashforwards and freeze-frames, see chapter four.

10   The levels of narration according to Edward Branigan's theory will be presented in detail in chapter four.

11   For a description of focalisation, see the levels of narration in chapter four.

12   I do not dwell on the aspects of equivalence nor ellipsis because they are manifested in the post-classical in broadly the same manner as in the classical tradition, if more accentuated. My lack of emphasis on these two temporal qualities by no means implies that they have a limited role in the post-classical narratives.

13   This scene will be thoroughly analysed in the next chapter.

14   Oliver Stone discusses his technique of 'vertical cutting' in his DVD commentary. *Natural Born Killers*, dir. Oliver Stone, Warner Bros., 1994.

15 The type of repetition in *Fight Club* is also found in *Oldboy* where the replayed images serve the compositional need for revealing the key plot twists, while the repetitions in *Magnolia* are on a par with those in *City of God* where a number of scenes are repeated two or three times from different perspectives to highlight the complexity of the situations in hand.

16 The practice of rewinding and replaying is also a function of video technology and a characteristic of sports broadcasting on television. For a discussion about the origins of post-classical cinematic language, see the conclusion.

chapter four

1 In chapter three of *Classical Hollywood Cinema*, Bordwell examines the classical narration according to the principles of self-consciousness, knowledgeability and communicativeness.

2 I choose not to discuss this part of Bordwell's account in detail because it focuses on the spectators' activity and on how they generate meaning following certain cues in the film. Bordwell's observations hint at a cognitive approach in film theory but this theoretical realm is outside my scope, as I explained in the introduction.

3 At this point, I would like to emphasise that the different chapters of this book are intricately interwoven and affect one another. They all explore the post-classical narration at various levels of generality and they depend on one another. For instance, the narrative motivations shape the degrees of self-consciousness, which is often translated into the manipulations of time and space that I discussed in chapters two and three. I have put particular effort into organising the material in a clear and distinctive way that illuminates the relations between the various observations but a certain overlapping and repetition is inevitable.

4 The mode of art cinema narration is also characterised by a high degree of self-consciousness but in that case the narration relinquishes its knowledgeability and communicativeness in order to create ambiguity and uncertainty concerning the story.

5 The fact that I discuss another theorist about this issue is due to Bordwell's lack of emphasis on and interest in reflexivity in his account of the classical Hollywood cinema, since Hollywood films largely excluded this element from their expressive repertory. On the other hand, Bordwell does indeed refer more to self-consciousness with respect to other historical modes of narration, such as art cinema, historical-materialist and parametric. Yet, his piecemeal references and the lack of a clear theoretical approach to this concept have only resulted in some significant inconsistencies regarding the act of narration, and especially the narrative voice, as I will shortly demonstrate.

6   See the section 'Artistic motivation' in chapter one.

7   All these elements of spatial and temporal articulation in the post-classical paradigm were thoroughly analysed in chapters two and three respectively. At this level of generality, I am simply interested in inventorying the various self-reflexive devices that contribute to the high degree of self-consciousness and omniscience that distinguishes very clearly the post-classical from the classical paradigm of narration.

8   For a brief but thorough overview on this topic, see Burgoyne (1990).

9   Although Branigan's main focus is narrative comprehension, as the title of his book clearly denotes, he develops a narrative theory that takes into consideration all the elements of the narrative system (sender, message and receiver) and can be particularly illuminating in the case of the post-classical cinema, which employs complex narrative devices.

10   In the introduction I referred to Bordwell's analysis of *Lola Rennt* and the term 'bricolage aesthetics' that he used to describe its visual style.

11   For a detailed description of the scene, see the chapter on space.

12   At the news conference following the award presentations at the Cannes Film Festival, Park admitted that he made the film with the DVD viewers in mind so that they could watch it several times and discover new elements each time. See http://www.festival-cannes.fr/films/fiche_film.php?langue=6002&id_film=4182985; accessed 20 July 2007.

13   It is difficult to identify the boundaries of what we would call an 'opening sequence' in the film. There are two main options: the short version is to consider as an opening sequence the part described; the long version is to consider as an opening sequence all the scenes before the appearance of the title 'Trainspotting' since there is no credit sequence.

14   One of the issues that I have not included in this chapter is the analysis of the function of music in the post-classical paradigm. Bordwell's work always privileges the image over the sound and the narrative function of music in the classical Hollywood cinema has yet to be fully explored. As a provisional observation, however, I would like to note that the role of sound in general, and music in particular, become significantly more prominent in the post-classical films. The motivation of hypermediated realism and parody create many more opportunities for sound to come forward and contribute dynamically to the narration. Although I would have to write an entirely new book if I were to do justice to the workings of music in the sample films, one of my preliminary observations at this point is that use of musical elements adheres completely to the rules that govern the overall post-classical narration. This means that the music in all case studies is highly self-conscious, knowledgeable and communicative and works as a supplement to the images for the satisfaction of the four main motivations of the post-classical narrative logic.

conclusion

1   In chapter two I underlined the fact that Manovich describes elaborately the characteristics and the potential of 'digital cinema' but his cinematic examples are limited to a handful of fugitive films, while the non-cinematic ones include CD-ROMs and music videos.

2   For the method of necessary and sufficient conditions, see Carroll (1999a: 7–11).

3   For an overview of these theories, see the introduction.

4   Robert Burgoyne discusses the new uses of art cinema conventions in his article on Milcho Manchevski's *Before the Rain*. He paraphrases Mikhail Mikhailovich Bakhtin thus: 'Through the process Bakhtin calls "genre memory", aesthetic forms both "remember the past, and make their resources and potentials available to the present ... redefining present experience in an additional way"' (Burgoyne 2000: 129).

5   It is essential to note that the paradigm of art cinema was constructed by Bordwell from a relatively different set of criteria from the classical. Hence the stylistic diversity of this paradigm that can accommodate films as dissimilar as Vittorio di Sica's neorealist *Ladri di biciclette* (*Bicycle Thieves*, 1948), Ingmar Bergman's Smultronstället (*Wild Strawberries*, 1957) and Resnais' *Last Year in Marienbad*.

6   This 'de-emphasised' continuity is defined as opposed to the intensified continuity that the majority of contemporary films privilege, whether they are classical or post-classical.

7   Sconce's account of the new smart cinema is very convincing but in order to maintain the coherence of his argument, he should exclude some of the films on his list. In particular, *The Royal Tenenbaums*, *Magnolia* and *Fight Club* are distinctively different from the rest of the films on the list and would fit more comfortably in the post-classical paradigm.

8   It is worth quoting Bordwell's view on this issue, expressed in an interview in *Otrocampo*. He says: 'With other countries it's more complicated. If we take Taiwanese cinema, for example. Taiwan started making ... popular films as a sort of classical martial arts drama but then the market collapsed because of Hong Kong films coming in and then the American films coming in. So there wasn't ... an audience for the popular, classical-style story ... in Taiwan. So they realised that they could make films for kind of a festival market. They didn't need to make films for the Taiwanese audience necessarily, now they'd rather make films that would bring international attention to them. So Hou Hsiao-hsien, Edward Yang, made films which were very much more influenced by art cinema ... I mean, if you see Edward Yang's early films, like *That Day, On*

the Beach [1983], it's basically Antonioni in Taiwan. And Hou Hsiao-hsien – I would argue it's more complicated, but it's basically, in some of his later films particularly, well, he's really making films for European critics more than for Taiwanese audiences ... And this is true also for Japan, and a few other countries where they decided that the way they would make their cinema noteworthy, was by making films that carry on this kind of experimentation that you find in art cinema' (in Rival 2001).

9   The increase in the numbers of screens with the proliferation of multiplexes worldwide now allows the screening of more alternative and non-conventional films.

10   On 30 September 2005, the Weinstein brothers left Miramax after twelve years to launch a new production/distribution company called The Weinstein Company.

11   During the final stages of production of this book, the position of post-classical films has been significantly elevated confirming the momentum of the new poetic scheme: Danny Boyle's *Slumdog Millionaire* (2008), which is another textbook case of post-classical narration, caused worldwide sensation and earned the lion's share at the 2009 Academy Awards.

12   In 2002 Korea had its breakthrough year when Im Kwon-taek's *Chihwaseon* won the Best Director award at Cannes and Lee Chang-dong's *Oasis* won no fewer than three awards at Venice. In 2004 *Oldboy* won the Grand Prix du Jury at Cannes and became one of the biggest box-office successes in Korea.

13   For an elaborate account of the technological tools that facilitated the development of intensified continuity, see Bordwell (2002b: 16–28).

14   A thorough investigation into the two-way relation between new media and cinema can be found in Lev Manovich's *The Language of New Media*.

15   For the multi-ethnic identity of Hollywood cinema, see Sassoon (2002).

16   Bordwell begins to tackle this problem in his book on cinematic staging and I would like to quote him at length. He writes: 'Thus a craft tradition binds film-makers across cultures. Common problems emerge and analogous solutions develop. Sometimes two filmmakers converge on similar solutions without mutual influence, as we've seen with Hou Hsiao-hsien and Mizoguchi Kenji. In addition, because cinema has been a global medium from its inception, it has been easier for filmmakers to learn from each other than, say, writers in different languages could. In their home markets Feuillade and Mizoguchi could view films from the United States and Europe. Today massive theatrical distribution, television and cable, home video, archival screenings, and film festivals allow filmmakers unprecedented access to artistic strategies and tactics from many points in film history' (2005: 260).

FILMOGRAPHY

Arizona Dream (produced by Claudie Ossard and Yves Marmion, directed by Emir Kusturica, screenplay by David Atkins, 1993, starring Johnny Depp, Jerry Lewis and Faye Dunaway).

Chongking Senlin (*Chungking Express*, produced by Chan Yi-Kan, directed and written by Wong Kar-wai, 1994, starring Tony Leung and Faye Wong).

Cidade de Deus (*City of God*, produced by Andrea Barata Ribeiro, directed by Fernando Meirelles and Kátia Lund, screenplay by Bráulio Mantovani, 2002, starring Alexandre Rodrigues and Leandro Firmino).

Europa (produced by Peter Aalbaek Jensen and Bo Christensen, directed by Lars von Trier, screenplay by Lars von Trier and Niels Vörsel, 1991, starring Jean-Marc Barr, Barbara Sukowa and Udo Kier).

Fight Club (produced by Ross Grayson Bell, Cean Chaffin and Art Linson, directed by David Fincher, screenplay by Jim Uhls, 1999, starring Edward Norton and Brad Pitt).

Le Fabuleux Destin d'Amélie Poulain (*Amélie*, produced by Claudie Ossard and Jean-Marc Deschamps, directed by Jean-Pierre Jeunet, screenplay by Guillame Laurant, 2001, starring Audrey Tautou and Matthieu Kassovitz).

Lola Rennt (*Run Lola Run*, produced by Stefan Arndt, directed and written by Tom Tykwer, 1998, starring Franka Potente and Moritz Bleibtreu).

Magnolia (produced by Joanne Sellar, directed and written by Paul Thomas Anderson, 1999, starring Tom Cruise, Philip Seymour Hoffman and Julianne Moore).

The Million Dollar Hotel (produced by Bono, Nicholas Klein, Bruce Davey, Deepak Nayar and Wim Wenders, directed by Wim Wenders, screenplay by Bono and Nicholas Klein, 2000, starring Mel Gibson, Jeremy Davies and Milla Jovovich).

Moulin Rouge! (produced by Martin Brown, Baz Luhrmann and Fred Baron, directed by Baz Luhrmann, screenplay by Baz Luhrmann and Craig Pearce, 2001, starring Nicole Kidman and Ewan McGregor).

Natural Born Killers (produced by Jane Hamster, Don Murphy and Clayton Townsend, directed by Oliver Stone, screenplay by David Veloz, Richard Rutowski and Oliver Stone, 1994, starring Woody Harrelson, Juliette Lewis and Robert Downey Jr.).

Oldboy (produced by Seung-yong Lim, directed by Park Chan-wook, screenplay by Park Chan-wook, Hwang Jo-yun, Lim Chun-hyeong and Lim Joon-hyung, 2004, starring Choi Min-sik and Yu Ji-tae).

Requiem for a Dream (produced by Eric Watson and Palmer West, directed by Darren Aronofsky, screenplay by Hubert Selby Jr. and Darren Aronofsky, 2000, starring Jared Leto, Ellen Burstyn and Jennifer Connelly).

Trainspotting (produced by Andrew Macdonald, directed by Danny Boyle, screenplay by John Hodge, 1996, starring Ewan McGregor and Robert Carlyle).

BIBLIOGRAPHY

Altman, Rick (1999 [1984]) 'A Semantic/Syntactic Approach to Film Genre', in Leo Braudy and Marshall Cohen (eds) *Film Theory and Criticism: Introductory Readings*. New York: Oxford University Press, 630–41.

Andrew, Dudley (1993) 'The Unauthorized Auteur Today', in Jim Collins, Hilary Radner and Ava Preacher Collins (eds) *Film Theory goes to the Movies*. London: Routledge, 77–85.

_____ (2004) 'An Atlas of World Cinema', *Framework*, 2, 9–23.

Balio, Tino (1996) 'Adjusting to the New Global Economy: Hollywood in the 90s', in Albert Moran (ed.) *Film Policy: International, National and Regional Perspectives*. London and New York: Routledge, 23–38.

Baron, Cynthia (1998) '*The Player*'s Parody of Hollywood', in Christina Degli-Esposti (ed.) *Postmodernism in the Cinema*. New York: Berghahn Books, 21–43.

Barton Palmer, Robert (1988) '*Blood Simple*: Defining the Commercial/Independent Text', *Persistence of Vision*, 6, 3–19.

Bazin, André (1967) *What is Cinema?* Vol. I. Berkeley: University of California Press.

_____ (1971) *What is Cinema?* Vol. II. Berkeley: University of California Press.

bell hooks (1998) 'Postmodern blackness', in James Storey (ed.) *Cultural Theory and Popular Culture: A Reader*. London: Prentice Hall, 417–24.

Bhaskar, Ira (1999) '"Historical Poetics": Narrative and Interpretation', in Toby Miller and Robert Stam (eds) *A Companion to Film Theory*. Oxford: Blackwell, 387–412.

Biskind, Peter (2004) *Down and Dirty Pictures: Miramax, Sundance and the Rise of Independent Film*. New York: Simon and Schuster.

Black, David Alan (1986) 'Genette and Film: Narrative Level in the Fiction Cinema', *Wide Angle*, 8, 19–26.

Bolter, Jay David and Richard Grusin (1999) *Remediation: Understanding New Media*. Cambridge, MA: MIT Press.

Bordwell, David (1980) *French Impressionist Cinema: Film Culture, Film Theory and Film Style*. New York: Arno Press.

_____ (1981) *The Films of Carl-Theodor Dreyer*. Berkeley: University of California Press.

_____ (1983) 'Textual analysis revisited', *Enclitic*, 7, 1, 92–5.

_____ (1985) *Narration in the Fiction Film*. London: Routledge.

_____ (1989a) *Making Meaning: Inference and Rhetoric in the Interpretation of Cinema*. Cambridge, MA: Harvard University Press.

_____ (1989b) 'Historical Poetics of Cinema', in Robert Barton Palmer (ed.) *The Cinematic Text: Methods and Approaches*. New York: AMS Press, 369–98.

_____ (1994a) 'The Power of a Research Tradition: Prospects for Progress in the Study of Film Style', *Film History*, 6, 59–79.

_____ (1994b) 'Toto le moderne: la narration dans le cinéma européen d' après 1970', *Revue Belge du Cinéma*, 36–7, 33–9.

_____ (1997) *On the History of Film Style*. Cambridge, MA: Harvard University Press.

_____ (1998) *Ozu and the Poetics of Cinema*. London: British Film Institute.

_____ (2000a) *Planet Hong Kong: Popular Cinema and the Art of Entertainment*. Cambridge, MA: Harvard University Press.

_____ (2000b) *Visual Style in the Cinema*. Munich: Verlag des Autoren.

_____ (2002a) 'Film Futures', *SubStance*, 31, 1, 88–104.

_____ (2002b) 'Intensified Continuity: Visual Style in Contemporary American Film', *Film Quarterly*, 55, 3, 16–28.

_____ (2005) *Figures Traced in Light: On Cinematic Staging*. Berkeley: University of California Press.

_____ (2006) *The Way Hollywood Tells It: Story and Style in Modern Movies*. Berkeley: University of California Press.

Bordwell, David, Janet Staiger and Kristin Thompson (1985) *The Classical Hollywood Cinema: Film Style and Mode of Production to 1960*. New York: Routledge.

Bordwell, David and Kristin Thompson (1993) *Film Art: An Introduction*. New York: McGraw-Hill.

Brandt, Michael (1994) 'Traditional film editing vs. electronic nonlinear film editing: a comparison of feature films', http://www.nonlinear4.com/brandt.htm (accessed 3 January 2005).

Branigan, Edward (1992) *Narrative Comprehension and Film*. London and New York: Routledge.

_____ (2002) 'Nearly true: forking plots, forking interpretations: a response to David Bordwell's Film Futures', *SubStance*, 31, 1, 105–14.

Brooker, Peter (ed.) (1997) *Postmodern After-Images: A Reader in Film, Television and Video*. London: Arnold.

Brown, Royal S. (1994) *Overtones and Undertones: Reading Film Music*. Berkeley: University of California Press.

Buckland, Warren (1998) 'A Close Encounter with the Raiders of the Lost Ark', in Steve Neale and Murray Smith (eds) *Contemporary Hollywood Cinema*. London: Routledge, 166–77.

____ (2000) *The Cognitive Semiotics of Film*. Cambridge: Cambridge University Press.

Buhler, James, Caryl Flinn and David Neumeyer (eds) (2000) *Music and Cinema*. Hanover and London: Wesleyan University Press.

Burch, Noël (1997) 'Spatial and Temporal Articulations', in Peter Lehman (ed.) *Defining Cinema*. London: Athlone Press, 135–48.

Burgoyne, Robert (1990) 'The Cinematic Narrator: The Logic and Pragmatics of Impersonal Narration', *Journal of Film and Television*, 17, 1, 3–16.

____ (2000) '*Before The Rain*: ethnic nationalism and globalization', *Rethinking History*, 4, 2, 129–34.

Byars, Jackie (1991) *All that Hollywood Allows: Re-reading Gender in 1950s Melodrama*. London: Routledge.

Cahoone, Lawrence (ed.) (1996) *From Modernism to Postmodernism: An Anthology*. London: Blackwell.

Calabrese, Omar (1992) *Neo-baroque: A Sign of the Times*. Princeton: Princeton University Press.

Caldwell, John Thornton (1995) *Televisuality: Style, Crisis, and Authority in American Television*. New Brunswick, NJ: Rutgers University Press.

____ (1999) 'Modes of Production: The TV Apparatus', in Robert Stam and Toby Miller (eds) *A Companion to Film Theory*. Malden, MA: Blackwell, 125–43.

Cardwell, Sarah (2003) 'About Time: Theorizing Adaptation, Temporality, and Tense', *Literature/Film Quarterly*, 31, 2, 82–92.

Carroll, Noël (1991) 'The Moral Ecology of Melodrama: The Family Plot and *Magnificent Obsession*', in Marcia Landy (ed.) *Imitations of Life: A Reader on Film & Television Melodrama*. Detroit: Wayne State University Press, 183–91.

____ (1996) *Theorizing the Moving Image*. New York: Cambridge University Press.

____ (1998) 'The Future of Allusion: Hollywood in the Seventies (and beyond)', in *Interpreting the Moving Image*. Cambridge: Cambridge University Press, 240–64.

____ (1999a) *Philosophy of Art: A Contemporary Introduction*. London and New York: Routledge.

____ (1999b) 'The Specificity Thesis', in Leo Braudy and Marshall Cohen (eds) *Film Theory and Criticism: Introductory Readings*. New York: Oxford University Press, 322–8.

Chatman, Seymour (1978) *Story and Discourse: Narrative Structure in Fiction and Film*. Ithaca, NY: Cornell University Press.

_____ (1990) *Coming to Terms: The Rhetoric of Narrative in Fiction and Film*. Ithaca, NY: Cornell University Press.

Chaudhuri, Shohini (2005) *Contemporary World Cinema*. Edinburgh: Edinburgh University Press.

Collins, James M. (1998) 'The Musical', in Wes D. Gehring (ed.) *Handbook of American Film Genres*. New York: Greenwood Press, 269–85.

Collins, Jim (1989) *Uncommon Cultures: Popular Culture and Post-Modernism*. London: Routledge.

_____ (1993) 'Genericity in the Nineties: Eclectic Irony and the New Sincerity', in Jim Collins, Hilary Radner and Ava Preacher Collins (eds) *Film Theory goes to the Movies*. London: Routledge, 242–63.

Conley, Tom (2000) 'Noir in the Red and the Nineties in the Black', in Wheeler Winston Dixon (ed.) *Film Genre 2000: New Critical Essays*. New York: State University of New York Press, 193–210.

Corbin, Carol and Robert A. Campbell (1999) 'Postmodern Iconography and Perspective in Coppola's *Bram Stoker's Dracula*', *Journal of Popular Film and Television*, 27, 2, 41–8.

Corrigan, Timothy (1991) *A Cinema Without Walls: Movies and Culture after Vietnam*. New Jersey: Rutgers University Press.

Creed, Barbara (1977) 'The Position of Women in Hollywood Melodramas', *Australian Journal of Screen Theory*, 4, 27–31.

Crofts, Stephen (1998) 'Authorship and Hollywood', in John Hill and Pamela Church Gibson (eds) *The Oxford Guide to Film Studies*. Oxford: Oxford University Press, 310–24.

Cubitt, Sean (1998) *Digital Aesthetics*. London: Sage Press.

_____ (1999) 'Phalke, Méliès, and Special Effects Today', *Wide Angle*, 21, 1, 115–29.

Currie, Gregory (1995) *Image and Mind: Film, Philosophy and Cognitive Science*. Cambridge: Cambridge University Press.

Dagle, Joan (1980) 'Narrative Discourse in Film and Fiction: The Question of the Present Tense', in Syndy Conger and Janice R. Welsch (eds) *Narrative Strategies. Original Essays in Film and Prose Fiction*. Mancomb: Western Illinois University Press, 47–59.

Dale, Martin (1997) *The Movie Game: The Film Business in Britain, Europe and America*. London: Cassell.

Dancyger, Ken (2002) *The Technique of Film and Video Editing: History, Theory, and Practice*. New York: Focal Press.

Darley, Andrew (2000) *Visual Digital Culture: Surface Play and Spectacle in New Media Genre*. New York: Routledge.

Degli-Esposti, Christina (1998) 'Postmodernism(s)', in Christina Degli-Esposti (ed.) *Postmodernism in the Cinema*. New York: Berghahn Books, 3–18.

Denzin, Norman (1991) *Images of Postmodern Society: Social Theory and Contemporary Cinema*. London: Sage.

Dissanayake, Wimal (1998) 'Issues in World Cinema', in John Hill and Pamela Church Gibson (eds) *The Oxford Guide to Film Studies*. Oxford: Oxford University Press, 527–34.

Dixon, Wheeler Winston (ed.) (2000) *Film Genre 2000: New Critical Essays*. New York: State University of New York Press.

____ (2001) 'Twenty-five Reasons Why It's All Over', in Jon Lewis (ed.) *The End of Cinema As We Know It: American Film in the Nineties*. London: Pluto Press, 356–66.

Doane, Mary Anne (1991) *Femmes Fatales: Feminism, Film Theory, Psychoanalysis*. New York: Routledge.

Durgnat, Raymond (1976) *Durgnat on Film*. London: Faber.

Eco, Umberto (1984) 'Postmodernism, Irony and the Enjoyable', in *Postscript to The Name of the Rose*. New York: Harcourt Brace Jovanovich, 65–7.

Eichenbaum, Boris (1965) 'The Theory of the "Formal Method"', in Lee T. Lemon and Marion Reis (eds) *Russian Formalist Criticism*. Lincoln: Nebraska University Press, 99–139.

Eidsvik, Charles (1999) 'Machines of the Invisible: Changes in Film Technology in the Age of Video', in Brian Henderson and Ann Martin (eds) *Film Quarterly: Forty Years – A Selection*. Berkeley: University of California Press, 341–50.

Elsaesser, Thomas (1975) 'The Pathos of Failure. American Films in the 70s: Notes on the Unmotivated Hero', *Monogram*, 6, 13–19.

____ (1991 [1972]) 'Tales of Sound and Fury: Observations on the Family Melodrama', in Marcia Landy (ed.) *Imitations of Life: A Reader on Film & Television Melodrama*. Detroit: Wayne State University Press, 68–91.

____ (1993) 'Hyper-, Retro- or Counter-cinema: European Cinema and Third Cinema Between Hollywood and Art cinema', in John King, Ana Lopez and Manuel Alvarado (eds) *Mediating Two Worlds: Cinematic Encounters in the Americas*. London: British Film Institute, 119–35.

____ (1998a) 'Digital Cinema: Delivery, Event, Time', in Thomas Elsaesser and Kay Hoffman (eds) *Cinema Futures: Cain, Abel or Cable?* Amsterdam: University of Amsterdam Press, 201–22.

____ (1998b) 'Specularity and Engulfment: Coppola and *Bram Stoker's Dracula*', in Steve Neale and Murray Smith (eds) *Contemporary Hollywood Cinema*. London: Routledge, 191–207.

Elsaesser, Thomas and Warren Buckland (2002) *Studying Contemporary American Film*. London: Arnold.

Fiske, John (1997) 'Global, National, Local? Some Problems of Culture in a Postmodern World', *Velvet Light Trap*, 40, 56–66.

Fredericksen, Don (1979) 'Modes of Reflexive Film', *Quarterly Review of Film Studies*, 4, 3, 299–320.

Friedberg, Anne (1993) *Window Shopping: Cinema and the Postmodern*. Berkeley and Los Angeles: University of California Press.

_____ (2000) 'The End of Cinema: Multi-media and Technological Change', in Christine Gledhill and Linda Williams (eds) *Reinventing Film Studies*. London: Arnold, 438–52.

Gaudreault, André (1987) 'Narration and Monstration in the Cinema', *Journal of Film and Video*, 39, 29–36.

Gehring, Wes D. (1999) *Parody as Film Genre: Never Give a Saga an Even Break*. Westport: Greenwood Press.

Genette, Gérard (1980) *Narrative Discourse: An Essay in Method*. Ithaca, NY: Cornell University Press.

Giannetti, Luis (1996) *Understanding Movies*. New Jersey: Prentice Hall.

Grodal, Torben (1997) *Moving Pictures – A New Theory of Film Genres, Feelings, and Cognition*. New York: Oxford University Press.

_____ (2000) 'Art Film, the Transient Body and the Permanent Soul', *Aura*, 6, 3, 33–53.

Gunning, Tom (1990 [1986]) 'The Cinema of Attractions: Early Film, Its Spectator and the Avant-Garde', in Thomas Elsaesser (ed.) *Early Cinema: Space, Frame, Narrative*. London: British Film Institute, 56–62.

Hal, Foster (1983) *The Anti-Aesthetic: Essays on Postmodern Culture*. Seattle: Bay Press.

Hallam, Julia and Margaret Marshment (2000) *Realism and Popular Cinema*. Manchester: Manchester University Press.

Hansen, Miriam (2000) 'The Mass Production of the Senses: Classical Cinema as Vernacular Modernism', in Christine Gledhill and Linda Williams (eds) *Reinventing Film Studies*. London: Arnold, 332–50.

Harries, Dan (2000) *Film Parody*. London: British Film Institute.

Heath, Stephen (1986) 'Narrative Space', in Philip Rosen (ed.) *Narrative, Apparatus, Ideology: A Film Theory Reader*. New York: Columbia University Press, 379–420.

Henderson, Brian (1983) 'Tense, Mood, and Voice in Film', *Film Quarterly*, 36, 3, 4–17.

Hill, John (1986) *Sex, Class and Realism: British Cinema, 1956–63*. London: British Film Institute.

Hoesterey, Ingeborg (2001) *Pastiche: Cultural Memory in Art, Film, Literature*. Bloomington: Indiana University Press.

Horton, Andrew and Stuart McDougal (eds) (1998) *Play it Again, Sam: Retakes on Remakes*. Berkeley: University of California Press.

Huhtamo, Erkki (1995) 'Encapsulated Bodies in Motion: Simulators and the Quest for Total Immersion', in Simon Penny (ed.) *Critical Issues in Electronic Media*. Albany, NY: State University of New York Press, 159–86.

Hutcheon, Linda (1988) *A Poetics of Postmodernism: History, Theory, Fiction*. London: Routledge.

_____ (1990) 'An Epilogue: Postmodern Parody: History, Subjectivity and Ideology', *Quarterly Review of Film and Video*, 12, 125–33.

_____ (2000) *A Theory of Parody: The Teachings of Twentieth-Century Art Forms*. Urbana and Chicago: University of Illinois Press.

Huyssen, Andreas (1986) *After the Great Divide: Modernism, Mass Culture, Postmodernism*. Bloomington: Indiana University Press.

Jäckel, Anne (2003) *European Film Industries*. London: British Film Institute.

Jackson, Timothy Allen (2001) 'Towards a New Media Aesthetic', in David Trend (ed.) *Reading Digital Culture*. Malden, MA: Blackwell, 347–53.

Jameson, Fredric (1983) 'Postmodernism and Consumer Society', in Hal Foster (ed.) *The Anti-Aesthetic: Essays on Postmodern Culture*. Seattle: Bay Press, 111–25.

_____ (1991) *Postmodernism, or the Cultural Logic of Late Capitalism*. London: Verso.

Jenkins, Henry (1995) 'Historical Poetics', in Joanne Hollows and Marc Jancovich (eds) *Approaches to Popular Film*. Manchester: Manchester University Press, 100–22.

Jullier, Laurent (1997) *L'Écran Postmoderne*. Paris: L'Harmattan.

King, Geoff (2000) *Spectacular Narratives: Hollywood in the Age of the Blockbuster*. London and New York: I.B. Tauris.

Kipnis, Laura (1998) 'Film and Changing Technologies', in John Hill and Pamela Church Gibson (eds) *The Oxford Guide to Film Studies*. Oxford: Oxford University Press, 595–604.

Klinger, Barbara (1994) *Melodrama and Meaning: History, Culture, and the Films of Douglas Sirk*. Bloomington and Indianapolis: Indiana University Press.

Kozloff, Sarah (1988) *Invisible Storytellers: Voice-Over Narration in American Fiction Film*. Berkeley: University of California Press.

Kramer, Peter (1998) 'Post-classical Hollywood Film: Concepts and Debates', in John Hill and Pamela Church Gibson (eds) *The Oxford Guide to Film Studies*. Oxford: Oxford University Press, 289–309.

Landy, Marcia and Lucy Fischer (1994) 'Dead Again or Alive Again: Postmodern or Post-mortem?', *Cinema Journal*, 33, 4, 3–22.

Lastra, James (1997) 'From the Captured Moment to the Cinematic Image: A Transformation in Pictorial Order', in Dudley Andrew (ed.) *The Image in Dispute: Art and Cinema in the Age of Photography*. Austin: University of Texas Press, 263–91.

Law Kar (2001) 'An Overview of Hong Kong's New Wave Cinema', in Esther C. M. Yau (ed.) *At Full Speed: Hong Kong Cinema in a Borderless World*. Minneapolis: University of Minnesota Press, 31–52.

Lefebvre, Martin and Marc Furstenau (2002) 'Digital Editing and Montage: The Vanishing Celluloid and Beyond', *CiNéMAS*, 13, 1–2, 69–107.

LeGrice, Malcolm (2001) *Experimental Cinema in the Digital Age*. London: British Film Institute.

Lev, Peter (1993) *The Euro-American Cinema*. Austin: University of Texas Press.

Levy, Emanuel (1999) *Cinema of Outsiders: The Rise of American Independent Film*. New York: New York University Press.

Lewis, Jon (ed.) (2001) *The End of Cinema As We Know It*. London: Pluto Press.

MacCabe, Colin (1985 [1974]) 'Realism and the Cinema: Notes on Some Brechtian Theses', in *Theoretical Essays: Film, Linguistic, Literature*. Manchester: Manchester University Press, 33–57.

Mamber, Stephen (1990) 'Parody, Intertextuality, Signature: Kubrick, De Palma, and Scorsese', *Quarterly Review of Film and Video*, 12, 1–2, 29–35.

Manovich, Lev (2001) *The Language of New Media*. Cambridge, MA: MIT Press.

Martin, Adrian (1992) '*Mise en scène* is Dead, or the Expressive, the Excessive, the Technical and the Stylish', *Continuum*, 5, 2, 87–140.

Miller, Toby, Nitin Govil, John McMurria and Richard Maxwell (2001) *Global Hollywood*. London: British Film Institute.

Mitchell, William J. (1992) *The Reconfigured Eye. Visual Truth in the Post-Photographic Era*. Cambridge, MA: MIT Press.

Moran, Albert (1996) *Film Policy: International, National and Regional Perspectives*. London and New York: Routledge.

Morson, Gary Saul (1989) 'Parody, History, and Metaparody', in Gary Saul Morson and Caryl Emerson (eds) *Rethinking Bakhtin: Extensions and Challenges*. Evanston, IL: Northwestern University Press, 63–86.

Mukařovský, Jan (1978) 'The Aesthetic Norm' in *Structure, Sign and Form*. New Haven and London: Yale University Press, 49–56.

Murray, Timothy (1999) 'By Way of Introduction: Digitality and the Memory of Cinema, or, Bearing the Losses of the Digital Code', *Wide Angle*, 21, 1, 3–24.

Nagib, Lúcia (2000) 'The New Cinema Meets Cinema Novo: New Trends in Brazilian Cinema', *Framework: The Journal of Cinema and Media*, 42, http://www.frameworkonline.com/42ln.htm (accessed 3 August 2007).

____ (ed.) (2003) *The New Brazilian Cinema*. New York: I.B. Tauris.

Ndalianis, Angela (2003) 'Architectures of the Senses: Neo-baroque Entertainment Spectacles', in David Thorburn and Henry Jenkins (eds) *Rethinking Media Change: The Aesthetics of Transition*. Cambridge, MA: MIT Press, 355–73.

____ (2004) *Neo-Baroque Aesthetics and Contemporary Entertainment*. Cambridge, MA: MIT Press.

Neale, Steve (1976) 'New Hollywood Cinema', *Screen*, 17, 2, 117–22.

____ (1986) 'Melodrama and Tears', *Screen*, 27, 6, 6–22.

____ (1995) 'Questions of Genre', in Barry Keith Grant (ed.) *Film Genre Reader II*. Austin: University of Texas Press, 157–83.

____ (2000) *Genre and Hollywood*. London and New York: Routledge.

Neale, Steve and Murray Smith (eds) (1998) *Contemporary Hollywood Cinema*. London: Routledge.

Nelson, Thomas Allen (1987) 'Through a Shifting Lens: Realist Film Aesthetics', *Film Criticism*, 11, 1–2, 133–43.

Ngai, Jimmy (1997) 'A Dialogue with Wong Kar-Wai: Cutting Between Time and Two Cities', in Jean-Marc Lalanne, David Martinez, Ackbar Abbas and Jimmy Ngai (eds) *Wong Kar-Wai*. Paris: Dis Vois, 83–117.

Nichols, Bill (1989) 'Form Wars: The Political Unconscious of Formalist Film Theory', *South Atlantic Quarterly*, 88, 2, 487–515.

____ (1994) *Blurred Boundaries: Questions of Meaning in Contemporary Culture*. Bloomington and Indianapolis: Indiana University Press.

Nowell-Smith, Geoffrey and Steven Ricci (eds) (1998) *Hollywood and Europe: Economics, Culture, National Identity 1945–95*. London: British Film Institute.

Olson, Scott Robert (1999) *Hollywood Planet: Global Media and the Competitive Advantage of Narrative Transparency*. Mahwah, NJ: Erlbaum.

Paquet, Darcy (2005) 'The Korean Film Industry: 1992 to the Present', in Chi-Yun Shin and Julian Stringer (eds) *New Korean Cinema*. New York: New York University Press, 32–50.

Payne, Robert M. (2001) 'Ways of Seeing Wild: The Cinema of Wong Kar-Wai', *Jump Cut – A review of Contemporary Media*, Online Journal, 44, http://www.ejumpcut.org/archive/jc44.2001/payne%20for%20site/wongkarwai1.html (accessed 3 February 2005).

Pierson, Michelle (1999) 'No Longer State-of-the-Art: Crafting a Future for CGI', *Wide Angle*, 21, 1, 28–47.

Pribram, Deidre E. (2002) *Cinema and Culture: Independent Film in the United States, 1980–2001*. New York: Peter Lang.

Prince, Stephen (1996) 'True Lies: Perceptual Realism, Digital Images, and Film Theory', *Film Quarterly*, 49, 3, 27–37.

____ (2000) *A New Pot of Gold: Hollywood Under the Electronic Rainbow 1980–1989*. New York: Scribner's Sons.

Ray, Robert (1985) *A Certain Tendency of the Hollywood Cinema*. Princeton: Princeton University Press.

____ (1995) 'The Bordwell Regime and the Stakes of Knowledge', in *The Avant-Garde Finds Andy Hardy*. Cambridge, MA: Harvard University Press.

Rêgo, Cacilda (2005) 'Brazilian Cinema: Its Fall, Rise, and Renewal (1990–2003)', *New Cinemas: Journal of Contemporary Film*, 3, 2, 85–100.

Reisz, Karel and Gavin Millar (1968) *The Technique of Film Editing*. London: Focal Press.

Rist, Peter Harry (2004) 'Korean Cinema Now: Balancing Creativity and Commerce in an Emergent National Industry', *CineAction*, 64, 37–45.

Ryall, Tom (1998) 'Genre and Hollywood', in John Hill and Pamela Church Gibson (eds) *The Oxford Guide to Film Studies*. Oxford: Oxford University Press, 327–42.

Ryan, Marie-Laure (ed.) (2004) *Narrative Across Media: The Languages of Storytelling*. Lincoln: University of Nebraska Press.

Salewicz, Chris (1998) *Oliver Stone*. New York: Thunder's Mouth Press.

Salt, Barry (1992) *Film Style and Technology: History and Analysis*. London: Starword.

Sassoon, Donald (2002) 'On Cultural Markets', *New Left Review*, 17, 113–26.

Schatz, Thomas (1981) *Hollywood Genres: Formulas, Filmmaking and the Studio System*. New York: McGraw-Hill.

____ (1991) 'The Family Melodrama', in Marcia Landy (ed.) *Imitations of Life: A Reader on Film and Television Melodrama*. Detroit: Wayne State University Press, 148–67.

Schrader, Paul (1995 [1971]) 'Notes on Film Noir', in Barry Keith Grant (ed.) *Film Genre Reader II*. Austin: University of Texas Press, 218–23.

Sconce, Jeffrey (2002) 'Irony, Nihilism and the New American "Smart" Film', *Screen*, 43, 4, 349–69.

Sesonske, Alexander (1980) 'Time and Tense in Cinema', *Journal of Aesthetics and Art*, 38, 2, 419–26.

Sharrett, Christopher (1990) 'No More Going Back and Forth as in the Past: Notes on the Fate of History in Recent European films', *Persistence of Vision*, 8, 29–44.

Shim, Doobo (2006) 'Hybridity and the Rise of Korean Popular Culture in Asia', *Media, Culture & Society*, 28, 1, 25–44.

Shin, Chi-Yun and Julian Stringer (eds) *New Korean Cinema*. New York: New York University Press.

Smith, Evan (2000) 'Thread Structure: Rewriting the Hollywood Formula', *Journal of Film and Television*, 51, 3–4, 88–96.

Smith, Jeff (2001) 'Popular Songs and Comic Allusion in Contemporary Cinema', in Pamela Robertson Wojcik and Arthur Knight (eds) *Soundtrack Available: Essays on Film and Popular Music*. Durham, NC: Duke University Press, 407–30.

Smith, Murray (1995) *Engaging Characters: Fiction, Emotion and The Cinema*. Oxford: Clarendon Press.

Solomon, Stanley J. (1976) *Beyond Formula: American Film Genres*. New York: Harcourt Brace Jovanovich.

Spielmann, Yvonne (1999a) 'Aesthetic Features in Digital Imaging: Collage and Morph', *Wide Angle*, 21, 1, 131–48.

____ (1999b) 'Expanding Film into Digital Media', *Screen*, 40, 2, 131–45.

Stam, Robert (1992) *Reflexivity in Film and Literature: From Don Quixote to Jean-Luc Godard*. New York: Columbia University Press.

Stam, Robert, Robert Burgoyne and Sandy Flitterman-Lewis (1992) *New Vocabularies in Film Semiotics: Structuralism, Post-structuralism and Beyond*. London: Routledge.

Stam, Robert and Toby Miller (eds) (1999) *A Companion to Film Theory*. Malden, MA: Blackwell.

Tasker, Yvonne (1996) 'Approaches to the New Hollywood', in James Curran, David Morley and Vivien Walkerdine (eds) *Cultural Studies and Communications*. London: Arnold, 213–28.

Telotte, Jay Paul (1992) 'The Fantastic Realism of Film Noir: Kiss Me Deadly', *Wide Angle*, 14, 1, 4–18.

Teo, Stephen (1997) *Hong Kong Cinema: The Extra Dimensions*. London: British Film Institute.

Thompson, Kristin (1999) *Storytelling in the New Hollywood: Understanding Classical Narrative Technique*. Cambridge, MA: Harvard University Press.

Tomasulo, Frank (1999) 'Raging Bully: Postmodern Violence and Masculinity in *Raging Bull*', in Christopher Sharrett (ed.) *Mythologies of Violence in Postmodern Media*. Detroit: Wayne State University Press, 175–99.

Turim, Maureen (1989) *Flashbacks in Film: Memory and History*. New York and London: Routledge.

____ (1999) 'Artisanal Prefigurations of the Digital: Animating Realities, Collage Effects, and Theories of Image Manipulation', *Wide Angle*, 21, 1, 49–62.

Uricchio, William (2003) 'Historicizing Media in Transition', in David Thorburn and Henry Jenkins (eds) *Rethinking Media Change: The Aesthetics of Transition*. Cambridge, MA: MIT Press, 23–38.

Vachon, Christine (1998) *Shooting to Kill*. London: Bloomsbury.

Walsh, Michael (1996) 'Jameson and "Global Aesthetics"', in David Bordwell and Noël Carroll (eds) *Post-Theory: Reconstructing Film Studies*. Madison: Wisconsin University Press, 481–500.

Wasko, Janet (1994) *Hollywood in the Information Age*. Austin: University of Texas Press.

Wasser, Frederick (2001) *Veni, Vidi, Video: The Hollywood Empire and the VCR*. Austin: University of Texas Press.

Williams, Linda (1998) 'Melodrama Revised', in Nick Browne (ed.) *Refiguring American Film Genres: History and Films*. Berkeley: University of California Press, 42–88.

Wong, Cindy Hing-Yuk (1999) 'Cities, Cultures and Cassettes: Hong Kong Cinema and Transnational Audiences', *Post Script*, 19, 1, 87–106.

Wyatt, Justin (1998) 'The Formation of the "Major Independent": Miramax, New Line and the New Hollywood', in Steve Neale and Murray Smith (eds) *Contemporary Hollywood Cinema*. London: Routledge, 74–90.

Yau, Esther C. M. (ed.) (2001) *At Full Speed: Hong Kong Cinema in a Borderless World*. Minneapolis: University of Minnesota Press.

reviews and interviews

Audé, Françoise (1991) 'Le point de vue du noyé', *Positif*, 369, 39–40.

Bonnaud, Frédéric (2001) 'The *Amélie* Effect', *Film Comment*, 37, 6, 36–8.

Bosley, Rachael (2001) 'Bohemian Rhapsody', *American Cinematographer*, 82, 6, 38–51.

Bourguignon, Thomas (1993) '*Arizona Dream*: L'étoffe des rêves', *Positif*, 383, 18–19.

Chappell, Crissa-Jean (1999) 'Movie Maid', *Film Comment*, 39, 5, 4.

Coursodon, Jean-Pierre and Michael Henry (2000) 'Paul Thomas Anderson', *Positif*, 468, 12–19.

Danton, Amina, Thierry Jousse and Fredéric Strauss (1991) 'Europa-Express/Entretien avec Lars von Trier', *Cahiers du cinéma*, 449, 32–9.

Dubeau, Alain (1992) '*Europa* ou à la manière des plus grands', *Séquences*, 158, 21–3.

Falcon, Richard (1999) '*Run Lola Run*', *Sight & Sound*, 9, 11, 52.

____ (2000) '*The Million Dollar Hotel*', *Sight & Sound*, 10, 5, 53–4.

Fuller, Graham (2001) 'Stricly Red', *Sight & Sound*, 11, 6, 14–16.

Gombeaud, Adrien (2004) '*Old Boy*. La cloche de verre', *Positif*, 524, 29–30.

Gross, Larry and Nick James (1995) 'Exploding Hollywood', *Sight & Sound*, 5, 3, 8–9; 44–5.

Jones, Kent (2001) 'Real Artifice', *Film Comment*, 37, 3, 22–5.

Jousse, Thierry (1991) '*Europa*', *Cahiers du cinéma*, 445, 35–6.

____ (1994) 'Les tueurs de l'image', *Cahiers du cinéma*, 484, 50–3.

Kennedy, Harlan (1991) 'Go Deeper', *Film Comment*, 27, 4, 68–71.

Kinder, Marsha (2002) '*Moulin Rouge!*', *Film Quarterly*, 55, 3, 52–9.

Macnab, Geoffrey (1995) '*Arizona Dream*', *Sight & Sound*, 5, 7, 39–40.

Macnab, Geoffrey and Andrew O' Hagan (1996) 'The Boys Are Back in Town', *Sight & Sound*, 6, 2, 6–11.

Martin, Kevin (2001) 'Love Among the Ruins: Phedon Papamichael, ASC dives onto skid row in *The Million Dollar Hotel*', http://www.cameraguild.com/index.html?magazine/stoo201.htm~top.main_hp (accessed 4 January 2005).

Olsen, Mark (2000) 'Singing in the Rain', *Sight & Sound*, 10, 3, 26–8.

Oppenheimer, Jean (2003) 'Boys From Brazil', *American Cinematographer*, 84, 2, 82–90.

Pellerin, Dominique (1999) 'Cours, Lola, Cours', *Séquences*, 204, 45–6.

Pizzello, Stephen (1994) '*Natural Born Killers* Blasts Big Screen with Both Barrels', *American Cinematographer*, 75, 11, 36–54.

____ (2000) 'The Downward Spiral', *American Cinematographer*, 81, 10, 50–61.

Probst, Christopher (1999) 'Anarchy in the USA', *American Cinematographer*, 80, 11, 42–53.

Rival Silvina (2001) 'Interview: David Bordwell', *Otrocampo*, Online Journal, http://www.otrocampo.com/5/bordwell_ing.html (accessed 3 February 2005).

Rouyer, Phillippe, Julien Carbon and Michel Ciment (1995) 'Wong Kar-wai', *Positif*, 410, 33–45.

Sauvaget, Daniel, Danièle Parra and François Chevassu (1991) 'Lars von Trier ou les délices de l' ambiguïté', *Revue du cinéma*, 476, 66–76.

Smith, Gavin (1994) 'Oliver Stone. Why do I have to provoke?', *Sight & Sound*, 4, 12, 10–12.

_____ (1999) 'Inside Out', *Film Comment*, 35, 5, 58–68.

Spencer, Liese (2004) 'Revenger's Tragedy', *Sight & Sound*, 14, 10, 18–20.

Thompson, Andrew (1996) 'Trains, Veins and Heroin Deals', *American Cinematographer*, 77, 8, 80–6.

Vincendeau, Ginette (2001) 'Café Society', *Sight & Sound*, 11, 8, 22–5.

Whalen, Tom (2000) '*Run Lola Run*', *Film Quarterly*, 3, 33–40.

Wisehart, Cynthia, Jennifer Vacchio, Matt Cheplic and Michael Speier (1997) 'Practical Virtues: Four Directors Discuss the Limits of Digital Production', *Millimeter*, http://millimeter.com/ar/video_practical_vir¬tues_four/ (accessed 3 January 2005).

INDEX